EXECUTIVE ROCK

A Fan's Perspective on the Evolution of Popular Music Since 1950

By Willie G. Moseley

Executive Rock
A Fan's Perspective on the Evolution of Popular Music Since 1950
By Willie G. Moseley

Vintage Guitar® Books
An imprint of Vintage Guitar, Inc., P.O. Box 7301, Bismarck, ND 58507, (701) 255-1197, Fax (701) 255-0250, publishers of *Vintage Guitar*® and *Vintage Guitar*® *Classics* magazines, and of Vintage Guitar® on the World Wide Web at http://www.vguitar.com.

©1996 by Willie G. Moseley, all rights reserved. No part of this book may be reproduced or transmitted in any form or by any means, electronic or mechanical, including but not limited to photocopying, recording, or by any information storage and retrieval system, except in the case of short quotations embodied in articles or reviews, without permission in writing from the author and publisher.

ISBN 1-884883-04-4

The opinions contained in this book are those of the author, and not necessarily those of the publisher, writer of this book's Foreword, or writers of back cover comments. Don't like some of the opinions contained in this book? Read the First Amendment, Bubba.

Cover Photography: Bill Ingalls Photography

Cover Concept: William G. Moseley, Jr.

Cover Design: Vintage Guitar

Printed in the United States of America

Stratocaster® is a registered trademark of Fender Musical Instruments, Inc. and is used by permission.

For My Sports Heroes (and Heroine):
Pop, Bart Starr, Evelyn Ashford, Eric Liddell, and Roy Jones, Jr.

LEFT TO RIGHT: Julian Driver, Bill Moseley, Charles Driver, Max Moseley. Photo taken circa 1935.

FOREWORD

Photo by Matt Sherlock

THE PEN BE MIGHTIER THAN THE GUITAR—*LIKE HELL!*

Being the venomous healer by word and sound myself, I can connect with one Willie G. Moseley. Not only do we share the reverence for the vintage sonic bombast and American craftsmanship of the almighty stimulating electric guitar and its music, but we also pummel communications in the night for our respective publications, his being *Vintage Guitar* magazine; mine, the bold and ever-dynamic *Ted Nugent Adventure Outdoors*.

Here we have a Bloodbrother of Twang, Willie, whippin' out

his good looking, resonating goodword book, projecting his unique feel for the ramifications of socially-engineered rock & roll history, as seen through the eyes of a true craver. I, too, crave the uninhibited mating call, drive, emotion, clamor, swing and rhythm of this non-stop pulse that moves us all, and Willie's environmentally sound verbiage overview is a bullseye. I like bullseyes.

This boy is so organic, I'm gonna have to take him on a moose hunt and use his Southern ass for bear bait. There is nothing sacred about the inner mechanizms of our beloved music, and here Sir Will does a fine job in his never-ending pursuit of detail, giving an enlightening, streetwise and honest tilt to what it all means to him, and to many of us.

No Xcess baggage here, my friends; just a gut-level, knee-jerk, spontaneous combustion flex from the heart and soul of a man genuinely inspired by all things rock. A Nugent Bloodbrother Salute to you, Willie, and may all your dancin' be heterophiliac and challenging, spurred on by visions of huge, spruce Gibson Byrdland guitars, circa 1961.

Ted Nugent

TABLE OF CONTENTS

FOREWORD *by Ted Nugent* iv
INTRO 1
LISTS
   THE FIRST CUT IS THE DEEPEST 7
   TIME WARP TO THE TONE AGE: Great Guitarists You Should Hear ... 10
   EVERYMAN'S DREAM BAND 14
   ORIGINAL "LONGHAIR" MUSIC: Classical Works for Rockers 18
   THE LOST ART OF AUDIENCE PARTICIPATION 21
   DIAMONDS IN A DUNG HEAP 25
   ROBINSON CRUSOE AND HIS WALKMAN 30
   THE COVER STORY 33
   SOLE SURVIVORS OR TIME WARP BANDITS? 38
   BATTLE OF THE ULTRA-BOOGIES 41
   THERE ARE NO WORDS 45
   WHO'DA THUNK IT? 49
   IN SEARCH OF... 54
OCCURRENCES
   TWO 1968 "FAREWELL" CONCERTS: A Study in Contrasts 57
   LIVE AID AND FARM AID RE-EXAMINED — HALF A
      DECADE LATER 62
   MTV'S DECADE OF DECADENCE 66
   RATING THE MTV CONCERTS 69
   MOSH DIVE INTO ETERNITY 72
   BULLFROG BLUES/IN TERMS OF TWO 75
   A FEW MOMENTS WITH THE MASTER 78
   IN MEMORY OF RORY GALLAGHER 82
GENRE-MANIA!
   DO THE COLLECTIVE GUILT BOOGIE! 85
   ERNEST TUBB IS TURNING OVER IN HIS GRAVE 88
   SHRAPNEL 91
   THE GODFATHER: PARTS 1, 2, 5, 7, 19 & 23 94
   THIS AIN'T "THE OLD RUGGED CROSS" 98
   "RAP MUSIC": An Oxymoron? 101
   AS FUZZY AS FLANNEL 103
THE ROCK & ROLL CURMUDGEON
   BRING BACK THE MELLOTRON! 111

LET'S GET SANCTIMONIOUS 113
FAMOUS MUSICIANS AND SINGERS I THOUGHT WOULD BE
    DEAD BY NOW 117
CURSE OF THE TWILIGHT CLONES 118
MATCH THAT MALEFACTION/ROLE MODEL ROULETTE! 119
OUTTAKES AND THROWAWAY CUTS: An Average
    Consumer Gets P.O.'ed 121
DON'T QUIT YOUR DAY JOB 124
A COMPLETE LIST OF ADMIRABLE THINGS ABOUT
    MADONNA, GANGSTA RAP, AND THE LATE SEVENTIES
    DISCO PHENOMENON 125

MISCELLANEOUS COLUMNS AND ESSAYS
"RICKY NELSON WAS RIGHT" 127
IN MEMORY OF PETER GREEN 131
IN PRAISE OF SNOOZE-AGE GUITARISTS AND INSTRUMENTS ... 135
LEMMY OUTTA HERE! Seventeen reasons
    (in No Particular Order) Why Kilmister is Cool 140
THIS MONTH'S CONTEST: Name That Gobber! 142
THIS MONTH'S CONTEST:
    Name the World's Ugliest Rock & Roll Trio 143
RANDOM RUMINATIONS, UPDATES, VERITIES
    AND BALDERDASH 144

SLOG ON, YOU TARNISHED AND/OR OUT-OF-HOCK DIAMOND
DARK SIDE OF THE SUN/PUNK FREUD 153
"...THE SHOW THAT NEVER ENDS" 161
THE ULTIMATE "FACELESS" BAND 165
GOD RE-EXAMINED 169
"OLDFIELD IN THE OZONE"/"BOY WONDER BOUNCES BACK" ... 173
WISHBONE ASTERISK 176
THE HOWARD COSELL OF HARD ROCK 180
THE DEVIL GOES ICE SKATING 183
2/3 OF A DREAM... OKAY, MAKE IT 90% OF A DREAM 187
YES: A Definite Maybe 189
"THE LIL' OL' CONGLOMERATE FROM TEXAS" 195
STARS AND BARS FOREVER 203
"PHASE THREE" BANDS (AND BEYOND) 205
SHORT VERSIONS 211
STILL IN THE GAME (IF NOT STILL THE SAME) 213

OUTRO
BLACK BIRDS, SILVER LINING 217

vii

INTRO

During the summer of *Star Wars*, Elvis died, and a couple of weeks later the-first-woman-I-was-married-to decided she wanted a divorce. It might be interesting to speculate as to what effect the King's bathroom croak had (at least subliminally) in hastening the dissolution of the relationship, but neither she or I were Elvis fans. I did, however, always find it interesting to monitor .the Elvis "phenomenon", as very few (if any) entertainers got near to the icon status of this baby-faced singer from Tupelo, Mississippi.

I'm not going into the gory details of my divorce or the reasons for it, but it seems to me that for all of the angst one has to experience, a lot of the machinations and clichés that come into play would be familiar to almost anyone who has had to go such a terribly personal trauma.

Yet one of the facets for which I'll take responsibility was an outright *obsession* with music. Back in those days I had a gargantuan record collection (and even a retail store-type display rack, complete with alphabetical tabs, in the den), and I used to go into the Peaches record store in Atlanta and drop sixty or seventy bucks per visit on new albums (and keep in mind this was in Seventies dollars). That a lot of nights were spent rehearsing or playing with a bar band wasn't exactly nurturing to a marriage, either.

Once I was a "recycled single" I sold or gave away hundreds of albums in an effort to get my act together (clichéd, but true). Yet I still hung on to favorites, and gradually-but-carefully added a few new records here and there. When the time came to make the transition to Compact Disc (detailed in the "Who'da Thunk It?" essay), old favorites were the largest segment of my CD collection.

The Beatles' appearance on the Ed Sullivan TV show in February of 1964 represented not only a defining moment in popular music history, it was also a clarion call to any "un-jock" who might have been watching. Here was a way to meet girls that was non-athletic, and who knows how many budget

Executive Rock

electric guitars from Sears were sold due to the British Invasion phenomenon ("Hundreds of thousands, I would think", says veteran rock guitarist Jon Butcher. "I had one of those; who *didn't?*")?

And a lot of aging Boomers who were of that ilk in those days are still frustrated musicians, and they still play in a weekend bar band, and/or they still have a humongous music collection. "It gets in your blood", says my friend F.N., a former bandmate who's already a grandfather.

For my money, the most creative half-decade in the history of popular music may have been from approximately 1967 to 1972, beginning with the release of *Sgt. Pepper's Lonely Hearts Club Band* through the release of *Tubular Bells* (the first so-called New Age album?). The Beatles had alluded to going beyond cutesy pop songs with *Revolver* and *Rubber Soul,* but it's doubtful that even longtime Beatles fans were expecting the milestone that *Sgt. Pepper* was (and still is).

But think about all of the other musical genres and phenomena that blossomed and flourished during the late Sixties and early Seventies. What was being created and heard was an incredibly diverse mix:

THE MOTOWN AND MEMPHIS STAX/VOLT SOUL GENRES WERE STILL VIABLE: Even though Otis Redding was killed in a 1967 plane crash. And this facet even included a monumental "conceptual" work, Marvin Gaye's remarkable *What's Goin' On.*

THE ADVENT OF THE FRISCO ACID ROCK GENRE (which didn't last too long).

THE ADVENT OF THE BRITISH PROGRESSIVE ROCK/ART ROCK GENRE.

THE EMERGENCE OF SO-CALLED "HARD ROCK": Which supposedly evolved (some would say "de-evolved") into so-called "Heavy Metal", which supposedly evolved (or "de-evolved") into all sorts of sub-genres.

THE EMERGENCE OF ROCK AS AN ART FORM: There was *Sgt. Pepper,* the Who's *Tommy,* and other works. And who the hell knows about whether or not Frank Zappa and the Mothers of Invention should be cited in this category...

ART-AS-ROCK: Big difference between this and "art rock" and "rock as an art form", as far as I'm concerned. Handy examples for this oddball piece of the popular music pie include Yoko Ono and the Hello People (mimes), and the "tradition" is being kept alive these days by folks like Laurie Anderson. For the most part, "musicians" of this ilk will be avoided like the plague in this tome. I mean, if Yoko Ono can rock and roll, then I'm Yo Yo Ma.

THE EMERGENCE OF ROCK AS POLITICS: The most brutal example being the MC5, of course. Nowadays, the liner notes on the first few Chicago (nee Chicago Transit Authority) albums seem incredibly silly.

THE ADVENT OF COUNTRY ROCK: There was the transition of the Byrds, plus the Buffalo Springfield, which beget the likes of the Flying Burrito Brothers and Poco. The Eagles' first album was released in 1972. And look what's happened to the so-called Country Music genre itself these days!

THE ADVENT OF SOUTHERN ROCK: Which was of course dominated by the Allman Brothers band and other artists on the Capricorn label.

This book had been in the planning stages for some time, but several events in 1994 (cited elsewhere) acted as sort of a catalyst to give a lot of the random thoughts that were going to be in here a lot more cohesiveness, and there were also three books I read that year which were a bit, um, "motivating". The three authors would probably be surprised to see their literary efforts lumped together; in fact, Greil Marcus would probably be outraged.

Yet Marcus's *DEAD ELVIS: A Chronicle of a Cultural Obsession* showed that the veteran writer does indeed care about his subject matter; the book is about exactly what its subtitle says, and it's written in a meaningful manner. Unfortunately, it's also written in a style that's about one intellectual level above mine, so every page or so I found myself reaching for a dictionary to look up the meaning of words like "scabrous" and "evanescent".

Then there's Michael Medved's *HOLLYWOOD VS. AMERICA: Popular Culture and the War on Traditional Values*. Medved is one of the hosts of PBS's "Sneak Previews", and this detailed look at how the entertainment business is causing the fabric of American society to unravel was hailed by conservatives and viciously excoriated by liberals. The book is simply a "just-the-facts" look at the way, in the author's opinion, the fare offered by so many of the major show business personalities and companies in U.S. is contributing to the decline in social values, ethics, and morality in this country, and Medved presents his case in an eloquent, easy-to-read manner, without affecting the appearance of pulpit-pounding. Medved reported that some of the invective flung in his direction from the left when *HOLLYWOOD VS. AMERICA* was published included accusations of his being a right-wing Christian radical (or words to that effect), when in fact he is a practicing Jew.

And Martha Bayles's *HOLE IN OUR SOUL: The Loss of Beauty and Meaning in American Popular Music* seems to borrow a bit from the other two books. On the one hand, Bayles *is* an academic (a Harvard grad, no less), so some of her pronouncements are beyond the grasp of an average music fan. I

Executive Rock

for one don't give a **** how the likes of Rimbaud or Nietzsche affected the development of music and culture, so I skipped over to the essays discussing the more current and controversial trends in music. Bayles's effort is a bit more of an intellectual dissection, of course; considering her credentials and the book's subtitle, such an approach ought to be expected by a reader. Nevertheless, she makes a lot of sensible points in her dissertation, deftly puncturing the pomposity and posturing of certain rap artists, and (bless her heart) she even disses Yoko Ono. Even the aforementioned Greil Marcus gets labeled as a "New Leftist". Accordingly, it shouldn't come as any surprise that *HOLE IN OUR SOUL* also received its share of disrespect; in the "Books" section of the 1994 year-in-review issue of *Rolling Stone*, writer Mark Coleman observed that "Bayles comes off like an unholy cross between Tipper Gore and Camille Paglia."

A FEW WORDS ABOUT THE WAY THIS BOOK IS PRESENTED: Most of the essays that originally appeared as "Executive Rock" columns in *Vintage Guitar* have been revised and updated. Among those that *haven't* been revised is every essay in the "OCCURRENCES" section, since they're chronology-oriented (updates to some of 'em will be found in the "Random Ruminations, Updates, Verities and Balderdash" essay).

While most of the commentaries are about the type of music that is the second word in this book's title, other popular musical styles get token essays in the "GENRE-MANIA!" section. A column with the same title as the essay about rap music herein has already been published in *Vintage Guitar* and the *Stellas & Stratocasters* anthology, but I couldn't think of a cooler title for this essay on the rap phenomenon.

Some of the commentaries that are technically lists are better-suited for other sections besides the one designated for "LISTS" The sections called "THE ROCK AND ROLL CURMUDGEON" and "SLOG ON, YOU TARNISHED AND/OR OUT-OF-HOCK DIAMOND" need (and get) their own introductory essays.

Among the persons and companies that need to be acknowledged for their help are Ted Nugent, Jeff Carlisi, Jim Roberts, Greg Martin, Mick Ralphs, Hartley Peavey, Richard Young (Colonial Bank), Cherry Orchard Studios, and Bill Ingalls Photography.

It goes without saying that I need to express my thanks and love to Gail and Elizabeth once again. Likewise, I need to note the help, cooperation, and opportunity I've been afforded by Cleo, Alan, and the *Vintage Guitar* staff.

Intro

So this book is for *fans* of rock music; i.e., stereotypical consumers. There's more of us than there are "rock stars", "music critics", and "rock journalists" combined.

And this ain't no "history of rock music". Things may get a tad irreverent at times, and I've my best to avoid what may be construed by certain sanctimonious types as "slurs", but hopefully I haven't glossed over the facts about certain facets of popular music, either. Just remember that what's contained herein are simply the observations, recollections and opinions of a singular peckerwood/cracker/hick/unabashed Peter Green fan/redneck/good ol' boy who loves his rock and roll.

Howard Beale and Larry Kroger are still alive and well.

W.G.M.
February 1996

LISTS

THE FIRST CUT IS THE DEEPEST

There have been some bands or performers that have made such an impression on me that I can remember exactly what the first song of theirs was that I heard. Sometimes, the songs weren't particularly hits, nor did the artists particularly go on to mega-star status, but I'm sure at one time or another everyone's had his/her head turned by a certain riff, voice or style to the point that the listener says something along the lines of "What the hell was *that*?", and subsequently, he/she makes an earnest effort to purchase the album or single.

What's more, in some cases the songs that hooked me *weren't even the first singles released by the artists*. It's just that such tunes would cause me to tilt my head to one side like Nipper, the RCA mascot, and say to myself: "Hmmm. This merits checking out." Examples include—

"GOOD TIMES BAD TIMES" (LED ZEPPELIN): This was indeed the Zeps' first single, and I had already made a mental note to watch out for them, as I'd seen Jimmy Page in June of 1968 on the last Yardbirds tour, and had subsequently been reading about his upcoming new band which had the working moniker of "Jimmy Page's New Yardbirds", according to *Circus* magazine (or was it still *Hullabaloo* then?). However, the sheer force of this song surprised even a dyed-in-the-wool Yardbirds fan like me. The stop-and-start intro, the punch of John Bonham's drums, Page's murky but frantic leads, and of course Plant's wail all combined to kick my head into a ditch. Sometimes I think it *still* may be my all time favorite Led Zeppelin tune.

"KICK OUT THE JAMS" (MC5): Speaking of sheer force, this live number from the Detroit quintet of would-be revolutionaries is rivaled only by Blue Cheer's "Summertime Blues" as the most brutal song ever

7

Executive Rock

played on late Sixties AM radio; tunes like these were I suppose responsible for "underground radio" (Gawd, what a cliché!) coming into being since there's barely any melody in either of them, and I bet AM programmers went berserk. The situation concerning the first time I heard "Kick Out the Jams" was *hilarious:* Seems that a local DJ who wasn't particularly fond of rock and roll anyway (he was a big Hank Williams fan) had to play Top 40 over his station's 50,000 watt AM signal, and he pulled out the MC5's Elektra single after someone had referred to them as the "Motor City Five" by request; the DJ thought they were a new *Motown*-type group! After the song crashed to an end in a cacophony of noise, the DJ fumed: "I've just been instructed by my station manager to play that song between the hours of midnight and dawn..." Live and learn.

"HAPPY JACK" (THE WHO): *The Who Sing My Generation* was already out as an LP but I'd never heard any of it; all I'd read was that this was some new English band with a lunatic drummer and a guitarist who liked to smash his instruments. When I first heard "Happy Jack" on the radio, its initial loping beat tweaked my curiosity, but as the band was building to the first chorus and Moon's tom-toms came blasting into the forefront along with everything else I went: "Huh?" I'd never heard drums that were that much of an integral part of a song, with the exception of course of "Wipeout" and a few odd Sandy Nelson tunes, but here was a plethora of percussion that was actually part of the mix rather than serving to merely keep the beat and/or do an unaccompanied solo. Small wonder I used to listen to the Who back then much more often than the Beatles, Stones, or Kinks. Not only did they write great stuff, they also played the bejeezus out of it.

"TOCCATA" (MANNHEIM STEAMROLLER): This is the first cut on the *Fresh Aire III* album; the *Fresh Aire* series has been state-of-the-art, hi-tech recordings of instrumentals that not only use lutes, recorders, and oboes, but drum kits and synthesizers as well; "Seventeenth Century Rock & Roll" is a line I once heard when this combo was being discussed. I first heard "Toccata" being used as a demo in a high-end stereo shop; time was those were the only places such recordings were sold. It has a slippery synthesizer riff as an intro, which pans out all over both speakers, so the fidelity hooks the listener as well as the music. Another cut on the same album, "Mere Image", would make my "desert-island-Top-Ten" list. Later albums by Mannheim Steamroller have also featured the London Symphony Orchestra, and they also recorded a nifty collaboration with Mason "Classical Gas" Williams.

"I WANT CANDY" (BOW WOW WOW): OK, so I'm old enough to recall that the original version of this ditty was recorded by the Strangeloves in the Sixties, but once again the percussion snagged me, albeit this time

Lists

from the intro, since the rollicking Burundi drums are heard for several bars before the guitar cuts in. Bow Wow Wow was yet another of the insufferably egotistical Malcolm McLaren's ventures; McLaren also claims to have invented punk rock. The Bowzers featured a jailbait female singer (who posed semi-nude for one of their album covers), Mohawk haircuts, and the aforementioned Burundi drum-based sound, but "I Want Candy" was about the best thing they ever offered; the original stuff *stunk*.

"PURPLE HAZE" (JIMI HENDRIX EXPERIENCE): Not only do I remember the first time I heard this tune, I also remember the first time I ever saw a publicity photo of Hendrix; it was a small black and white photo affixed to a wall in a local radio station. Hendrix was standing in a field, wearing nothing but a loin cloth, and brandishing a spear. One could have easily mistaken this for something ripped out of a *National Geographic* if it hadn't been for the two white guys (Redding and Mitchell, also sporting beach-ball Afros) squatting next to him. Ironically, the first time I ever heard "Purple Haze" it wasn't the Jimi Hendrix Experience playing it; a local trio at a YMCA dance stomped into the atonal, unmelodic intro (THAT SOMEHOW MADE SENSE!), and of course I ran out and purchased *Are You Experienced?* the very next day. The guitarist/vocalist for that trio, by the way, was a diminutive blond kid from the other side of town named Tommy Shaw, who hit the big time a decade later with an arena rock band called Styx.

"SATISFACTION" (DEVO): In the late Seventies, when no one knew where the hell contemporary music was going to end up next, this extremely oddball quintet sprang out of Akron, Ohio, which is the same town that beget televangelist Ernest Angley (seems appropriate). I'd read a bit about them in a few music publications, and I can't remember if the term "new wave" was being applied to them yet or not; at any rate, this example also included *visuals,* on accounta they showed up on an episode of "Saturday Night Live" (hosted by Fred Willard) in the Fall of 1978, and the tune they selected for their national television debut was their quirky reworking of the Stones' classic, complete with an odd tempo and staccato singing. Devo was hip enough to know that appearance counted in the coming synthesis of music and video, so they were sporting yellow rubber jumpsuits and sunglasses; they looked like refugees from a nuclear waste disposal site. Two guitarists were playing Gibson L6-Ss, the bass player had a chopped-up, left-handed Gibson (I think it was something like a Ripper), and the singer/guitarist toted a garbage-trimmed solidbody which I think was an old Hagstrom. I still have that song on video, and whenever I pull it out to watch, the Missus rolls her eyes skyward. That's one of the reasons I'm glad we got hitched; she has the patience of Job with me when it comes to harmless weirdness like this.... Another visual example of a

Executive Rock

"first encounter" was the appearance of the Stray Cats in a pre-MTV video by Dave Edmunds (a rollicking cover of Buck Owens' "The Race Is On"). I betcha umpteen viewers saw this on HBO's filler program called "Video Jukebox" and did a double take upon spying the trio's tattoos, earrings and gargantuan pompadours.

It doesn't really surprise me that occasions such as the ones just described seem to be occurring far less frequently these days. For me personally, it's another reason why the "Classic Hits" (in either pop *or* rock formats) have come back so strongly in recent times. Ain't too many classic riffs or lyrics among the new stuff, in my opinion. How 'bout you?

TIME WARP TO THE TONE AGE: Great Guitarists You Should Hear

Ain't it a curiosity that even though vinyl twelve-inch discs are for all intents and purposes extinct as an audio format, the retail emporiums in which they used to be retailed (which now only market Compact Discs and cassettes) are still called "record stores" by most folks? I know there are still some exceptions (Pearl Jam's *Vitalogy* LP, f'ristance), but these days most of the albums bought in such establishments don't require a needle and turntable in order to be played.

Given the ongoing interest in so-called "classic rock" over the last few years, more and more older albums are finally turning up on Compact Disc, *if not on cassette* (the implication being that someone will pay a higher price for a practically indestructible copy of an album that he/she considers to be a classic). It boggles the mind to note that an all-time favorite album might finally be available in a format other than a record, even if the record itself was rare some years ago (see "Who'da Thunk It?" for some examples). As might be expected, *imported* CDs may be the only source for such rare-but-personal favorites, but the premium price is probably justifiable to most listeners who've purchased such CDs.

Lists

A sidebar of this phenomenon is that it's an opportunity for more than a few semi-obscure players to finally be heard by a whole new generation of listeners. What with a lot of players sounding a lot alike these days, it seems refreshing to finally hear a classic riff or tone on CD; it seems to give that particular player a bit of vindication after all those years. Some prime examples include:

RANDY CALIFORNIA: Spirit's lead guitarist had a signature guitar tone on their first few albums that was oozing and siren-like (similar examples include Ted Nugent in the Amboy Dukes, and the Guess Who's Randy Bachman on "American Woman"). One of the most intriguing songs from Spirit's debut album was "Mechanical World", which was a mysterious, plodding tune with overdubbed harmony guitar leads accompanied by a string section. This first album from Spirit was arguably their best, even if they did go on to get some airplay with "I Got A Line On You" from their second release. Their fourth album, *Twelve Dreams of Dr. Sardonicus*, found on occasion as a "Nice Price"/"Sound Value"-type release. Two great rumors I heard about California back when Spirit was in their heyday were (1) He got his sound from a cheap Danelectro/ Silvertone electric guitar (TRUE), and (2) Spirit's bald, bizarro drummer Ed Cassidy was California's *father* (HALF-TRUE; he's the guitarist's stepfather). California's still around with an incarnation of Spirit that includes Cassidy on drums, but it seems like some of his more recent playing has an Eighties techno-edge, and it barely resembles the brooding, murky riffing that distinguished California in the late Sixties.

RORY GALLAGHER: It's confounding why this Emerald Isle player didn't get the amount of recognition that he deserved. Gallagher first came into public view fronting Taste, a psychedelic blues band; their first album (self-titled) is a killer (the drums are as raucous-sounding as what's heard on Blue Cheer's *Vincebus Eruptum*!). Usually seen playing what may have been the most worn-looking Fender Stratocaster in existence, this guy was sort of an Irish John Fogerty; i.e., he favored flannel shirts and his singing and playing were respected among his peers. However, Gallagher stuck closer to the blues than many guitarists (even when interest in the genre was in one of its cyclical downward trends, so maybe that's part of keepin' the faith). The live albums from his post-Taste solo career (particularly *Irish Tour '74*) are chock fulla nifty slide work and worthwhile licks. Last I heard from Gallagher was an album called *Fresh Evidence* on IRS in the early Nineties. He died in mid-1995, as these essays were being revised.

BILL NELSON: To some people, Be-Bop Deluxe sounded like a more pop-oriented version of the Yes (that is, the Yes of the mid-Seventies, when Be-Bop Deluxe was around), and one prime reason for the comparison

Executive Rock

was singer/guitarist Bill Nelson. His fast, melodic playing reminds a listener of Steve Howe with an edge; unfortunately, the band's main drawback was that Nelson sounded like a sissy when he sang, although most listeners would probably have opined that Jon Anderson's vocals were more effeminate. Be-Bop Deluxe's *Live in the Air Age* is exemplary, but if you're into studio albums as 'yardsticks', try *Modern Music.* Regrettably, Nelson opted to shift gears and get into a sort of New Age mode that is far too weird to be accessible for most folks. His more recent stuff has shown up in cutout racks quickly, and a definitive example of this later "music" is *Chance Encounters in the Garden of Light,* a two-disc set from 1988. A collection of short instrumental passages that is supposed to assist in meditation (even the liner notes allude to such), this is boring beyond belief; Lou Reed's *Metal Machine Music* is probably the only worse offender. If *Chance Encounters in the Garden of Light* is supposed to help me get in touch with my inner self, that's all well and good, but I'll take anything by the Mahavishnu Orchestra instead; at least their presentations have some sort of musical structure.

PETER GREEN: See "In Memory of Peter Green".

FRANK MARINO: Some time ago, when the first special edition of a guitar magazine dedicated exclusively to Jimi Hendrix came out, one rock star who was interviewed referred to erstwhile Procol Harum guitarist Robin Trower as Hendrix's "spiritual double". *Nonsense.* Trower's earliest albums (*Twice Removed From Yesterday, Bridge of Sighs*) were obviously Hendrix-inspired and quite listenable, but Mahogany Rush's Frank Marino managed to play like Hendrix, sing like Hendrix, and write like Hendrix, yet he never did come across as a Hendrix clone act a la Randy Hanson's Machine Gun. Check out *Maxoom, Child of the Novelty, Strange Universe,* or the first live album by this Canadian trio; such offerings would probably delight any newer Hendrix fan who might not have heard Mahogany Rush in the Seventies.

TERRY SMITH: I heard two albums by some semi-jazz combo called If, and can't really recall any song titles except the leadoff cut on the first ("What Can A Friend Say"). Another distinguishing feature of the first album was that it was "chrome-plated", a la original copies of Cream's *Wheels of Fire.* The band had a couple of horns, but Smith's superfast, jazzy-but-bluesy playing sounded almost "bubbly", for lack of a better term. A definitive example of a player and his tone being more memorable than the band in which he played....

LESLIE WEST: Somewhat of a soul-mate to Randy California, in that he's still around, and both of 'em participated in the first IRS *Guitarspeak* album as well as the "Night of the Guitar" tour (from which a live album was marketed). Also like California, West's guitar tones as Mountain's

Lists

guitarist were much more notable than his more recent offerings. Mountain released a disproportionate amount of live material, which seemed to show that Leslie West was at his best in a concert environment. In particular, the live side of *Flowers of Evil* is outstanding. It consists of three songs; "Roll Over Beethoven" begins with West teasing the audience with an unaccompanied guitar solo. First he coaxes violin-like sounds out of his Les Paul Jr. by working the volume control. That's followed by roaring power chords, then West's trademark squealing harmonic runs, followed by yet more soft Stradivarius mimicry. After a few minutes of this melange, West charges into the Chuck Berry classic, doing the first verse solo before the rest of the band kicks in on the second. "Dreams of Milk and Honey" is an extended jam, and "Mississippi Queen" finishes out the live side, which clocks in at about twenty-seven minutes. Whew!

"FAST" EDDIE CLARKE: For all of the durability of Phil Campbell and Wurzel as Motorhead's guitarists, it seems like some of the most memorable songs and riffs are attributable to the days when the band was a trio consisting of Clarke, Lemmy, and Phil Taylor (and that wasn't the first incarnation of the band, for that matter). Clarke was equally at home using a Gibson Les Paul or Fender Stratocaster, and an anthology called *Welcome to the Bear Trap* or the live *No Sleep 'Til Hammersmith* are worth getting. Clarke's "plaintive-but-in-your-face" tone on "Stone Deaf Forever" is awesome, and it's interesting to speculate how such a tune would sound nowadays, since Lemmy's bass playing has, uh, "matured", so to speak.

NICK SEMPER: Token bass player. While many of the arrangements and psychedelic effects offered by the earliest incarnation of Deep Purple sound a mite dated these days, one commendable and still-listenable facet is Nick Semper's bass plunking, which sounds like he's playing a Fender Precision with a very thick pick. While Jon Lord's organ and Ritchie Blackmore's fretwork seem to have maintained signature sounds over the decades, Semper's bright-but-beefy tone seems to have been *way* ahead of its time, and from where I stand it blows Roger Glover's lumbering Rickenbacker off the planet.

PETER KAUKONEN: Jorma's younger brother once had an album (and band?) called *Black Kangaroo*, and while he sounds a bit Hendrixish (albeit not as blatant as Marino), Kaukonen's singing and playing could stand on their own merits. Peter Kaukonen once appeared in a group photo of one incarnation of Jefferson Starship (his moniker was listed as "Peter Kangaroo").

JOHN FOGERTY: Thass right, Ol' Flannel Shirt hisself. While Fogerty is every bit as viable these days as he was in the late Sixties, his guitar tone on Creedence Clearwater Revival's first album was utterly unique, even

Executive Rock

when compared to CCR's subsequent recordings. The cover story from the October 1985 issue of *Guitar Player* (written by Dan Forte with Steve Soest) describes the lead guitar work on CCR's re-working of Dale Hawkins's "Susie Q" as "howling", and a more applicable adjective probably doesn't exist. The same paragraph nails the song as "one of the rare instances of a cover becoming as definitive a version as the original." I dare say Boomers who were in bar bands (and may still be today) would opt to perform Creedence's version of "Susie Q" as opposed to attempting a cover of the Hawkins original; the CCR version is that awesome (By the way, the lead guitar work on Dale Hawkins' original "Susie Q" was done by James Burton; Fogerty and Burton are big fans of each other). The thing is, the guitar tone on "Susie Q" is *all over* that first album, which is why it should be a must-hear for any aspiring electric guitarist.

Can't say that all of the albums cited herein are available in the Compact Disc format (yet); I've never seen any If CDs or *Black Kangaroo*, for example. What's more, while most of these players are probably still around and still playing, it might be debatable as to whether their more recent efforts are legitimate new ventures, bona fide comeback attempts, or nostalgia exploitation. That's why in some cases such players' *signature sound(s)* may be "missing in action" as opposed to the players themselves.

Yet if more classic rock is heard by younger players and music fans (whether on a newly-released CD or a parent's LP), some players from such earlier times may get a bit more recognition, which most of 'em probably deserved then and probably deserve now.

EVERY MAN'S DREAM BAND

If any halfway-serious fan of rock music (or for that matter, *any* genre of popular music) hasn't fantasized at one time or another about a "dream band" composed of his/her favorite players, said fan might not be as much of a fan of a particular genre as he/she might think. I mean, who among us hasn't conjured up an imaginary all-star aggregation in our minds? I betcha

Lists

the choices by, uh, "participants" in such daydreaming would be as varied as their personalities, and thank goodness for that.

Fact is, *Creem* magazine used to do a monthly feature on "dream bands" back in the Seventies, asking certain famous musicians who they'd choose as lead guitarist, lead vocalist, etc. if they could form their own outfit. Among the noted players who listed their ideal lineups were Rick Wakeman and Leslie West.

So apparently this harmless bit of self-indulgence is common to the famous and not-so-famous, and when I broached the subject to Malcolm, I knew full well he'd want to know who I'd pick for which slot, and why. I also knew he'd affect the part of a sardonic devil's advocate at various times, even though he declined to come up with his own list. Malc, like me, is a pretty good "fan", but he doesn't feel like he'd have a complete handle on selections. While I respect such an attitude, it invariably led to him asking "Who?" immediately after I announced some of my own selections (Guess which ones). We got some, er, "ground rules" out of the way first:

"Does it matter if a musician is alive or dead?" I asked.

"Nope."

"How 'famous' should they be?"

"Ummm..... I would think that the general public might should have heard of 'em, but I realize that might not be possible in some cases, 'specially if you're gonna cite studio musicians or guys in some star's backing band. Howzabout they have to be talented enough to where they actually have some recorded product out?"

"Fair enough. Speaking of talent, you're not asking who I think is the 'best' or 'fastest', right?"

"Right. Anything else?"

"Lessee .... What about the personality factor?"

"Whaddaya mean?"

"I may be a bit idealistic, but in some cases I'd be leery of certain players' egos; I'd want someone who'd hopefully be a 'team player', y'know?"

"Jeezus, Mose, really...."

LEAD GUITAR: I might've picked Peter Green, but Malc would've bellowed "Now *that's* idealistic!" immediately, for reasons that are obvious to longtime Green fans. Since there are so many different styles of contemporary players out there (the "pigeonholing" of guitarists these days makes the popular music landscape look like a honeycomb), it might be difficult to find a guitarist who could present a style that would be different enough to attract attention, but for my money SCOTTY ANDERSON would be more than appropriate. This Cincinnati-area fingerpicker has a blazing-yet-lyrical style that seems to cross back and forth between genres

Executive Rock

with ease *inside a single song.* Anderson is still somewhat of a "Great Unknown"; however, his album featured liner notes by Chet Atkins, James Burton, and the late Thumbs Carlisle. If I had to go with someone who's more famous, I'd probably gravitate towards a lyrical player like DAVE MASON; a more recent example is ROLAND ORZABAL of Tears for Fears.

PIANO: COREY LERIOS, who was the keyboard player/vocalist for Pablo Cruse (I think he's doing studio work in the L.A. area these days). Lerios has a bouncy, exuberant style that's a bit like Billy Joel's.

ELECTRONIC KEYBOARDS: Gawd, I dunno. The thing is, I agree with Malc's opinion about synthesizers *sounding* like synthesizers (see "Bring Back the Mellotron!") so I'd probably end up with RICK WAKEMAN.

BASS: Most likely BAGHITI KHUMALO or ARMAND SABAL-LECCO, both of whom have backed Paul Simon in his multi-cultural ventures, or LOUIS JOHNSON of the Brothers Johnson. All three have monster chops, but methinks they're also professional enough to know when to stay *right in the pocket* if need be, and what amount of "flash" is appropriate.

MALE VOCALS: Plaintive and British. Candidates would include the likes of GREG LAKE and JOHN WETTON (who are also fine bass players) but I'd probably opt for Procol Harum's GARY BROOKER, whose voice is still remarkable after all these years. Malc and I tussled a bit at this juncture, on accounta I wanted a subcategory for blues singers (in which case I'd pick CHRIS YOULDEN).

FEMALE VOCALS: TRACY NELSON. No, not the star of *The Father Dowling Mysteries* on TV (she's the daughter of the late Ricky Nelson). The Tracy Nelson I'm referring to was the vocalist for Mother Earth, and she's still around. Nelson has one of the most passionate, earthiest voices (no pun intended) ever recorded; her singing could make you cry even if she was in an acapella mode. Did I see her onstage as a backing vocalist for Neil Young at some benefit a few years ago?

At this point, Malc interceded. "Whaddabout Patsy Cline? I know how much you've jabbered about her in times past."

"Oops."

DRUMS: Another tempest in a teapot, because I've always been a fan of double drummers in a rock band. The interplay found in bands like the Allman Brothers and the Grateful Dead is an integral and irreplacable part of those groups' sounds, therefore their longevity, in my opinion. Therefore, if I could select two drummers, I'd want one of 'em to be a 'rock steady'-type and the other to be more of an 'experimental'-type; the latter could do all of the odd tempo stuff on weird percussion instruments and/or

Lists

electronic drums. In that scenario, whoever that original semi-lefty drummer for the Romantics was could handle the 'rock steady' part (he sang "That's What I Like About You", and the last time I saw him on an MTV concert he had his hair styled like a fright wig and both of his ears pierced); the 'experimental' drummer should be someone like BILL BRUFORD.

However, if only one drummer was allowed, sign up JIM FOX from the James Gang, or maybe DANIEL SERAPHINE (Chicago) or maybe NEIL PEART (Rush). I don't think Seraphine's with Chicago anymore.

RHYTHM GUITAR: Curiously, this slot should be filled by a player who is perfectly capable of handling lead guitarist duties as well (in case the designated lead guitarist broke a string or whatever). I've seen lead guitarists from famous bands filling in as rhythm players with other aggregations, and using that criterion, I'd choose MICK RALPHS of Mott the Hoople and Bad Company fame. He handled his rhythm chore on David Gilmour's *About Face* tour in an easygoing and confident manner, and he's polite and businesslike concerning his craft. An alternate choice might be GARY DUNCAN, based on his performance on Quicksilver Messenger Service's *Happy Trails* album.

HORN SECTION: Tower of Power Horns; no question about it.

BACKING VOCALS: MERRY CLAYTON, OLETA ADAMS, and whoever the black female is that's heard on the Eurythmics' "Missionary Man". All three of these women are/were integral in their respective roles in (primarily white) rock bands, as would be the case here. Clayton's passionate vocals on the Rolling Stones' "Gimme Shelter" is as much a part of that song as is that ratchet-like percussion instrument (a guiro?). Ditto Adams on Tears for Fears' *The Seeds of Love* album.

EXTRANEOUS INSTRUMENTATION: PAUL BUTTERFIELD (harmonica). Has anyone ever really played this instrument any better? Unfortunately Butterfield was apparently another example of someone who took the phrase "living the blues" all too seriously. Last time I saw him was on television, sitting in at some all-star jam session. He had bags the size of baseballs under his eyes, and his paunch protruded from underneath his olive drab t-shirt. He looked doomed, which was ultimately the case.

OTHER EXTRANEOUS INSTRUMENTATION/OPENING ACT: Those Russian street musicians seen in a Kit Kat candy bar commercial.

SONGWRITER: MARSHALL CRENSHAW. Snappy lyrics, dynamic chord structures that go off at a right angle from what you'd expect, low-end guitar licks that would do Duane Eddy proud, and a singalong sensibility. Crenshaw can even write a song with a stoopid title like "Fantasic Planet of Love" and make it fun. Why isn't this guy more famous?

CHOREOGRAPHY: THE NICHOLAS BROTHERS. There were times

Executive Rock

when it appeared that the upper and lower halves of the bodies of Harold and Fayard were being controlled by different entities.

ARRANGER: Either SPIKE JONES or FRANK ZAPPA. 'Nuff said.

All in all, Malc didn't have as much to question or lampoon as I might have expected, and ultimately he agreed with my observation at the outset of this essay about folks' choices for their own dream band lineup being as varied as the persons who do the dreaming. I'm sure I'll mull over this list for a while, then realize that I should have put So-and-So somewhere on it. For the time being, however, this is what my own idealistic lineup would look like, and if and when anybody with his/her own idealistic lineup goes back and "touches up" the list, it's an indication that the music matters to that particular individual.

And that's encouraging.

ORIGINAL "LONGHAIR MUSIC": Classical Works for Rockers

Time was, the term "longhair music" wasn't a reference to the Beatles or some other British invasion group; instead, it was a cynic's definition of classical music. Every now and then I'll read about some rock guitarist listing his classical influences, or maybe an article will compare a rocker's musical chops to classical works (Paganini's name pops up a good bit, f'rinstance).

That's all well and good, but for the average or armchair guitarist (or for that matter, any average or armchair *musician)* an appreciation of symphonic works is way down on the list of priorities if you were raised on Top 40 radio, or even progressive FM radio from the Seventies, although naturally many British progressive bands of that era (Yes, King Crimson, ELP, etc.) might have made a listener more aware of classical works in an off-the-wall way.

If I'm going to listen to symphonic works, the main things that will

Lists

grab my attention and hold it are (1) melody and (2) arrangement (the more orchestrated the better). None of this weird, abstract stuff for me, thankyouverymuch. Not surprisingly, Frank Zappa cited Varese as an influence, but I'll take works by the Old Masters, even if I did hear such music for the first time as performed by a rock group or in a movie soundtrack.

What follows is a short list of albums that the average rock musician should consider owning as a token collection; they fit into the aforementioned "melody" and "arrangement" guidelines for yours truly, and if they might have been heard in another format such as rock bands or movie soundtracks I've noted such. I know some classical purists might turn up their noses due to my using these type of references, but so what? Anytime a rocker might happen to hear a snippet of original longhair music and says to himself/herself: "Hey, man, I've heard that riff, it's on So-and-So's album", that's an accomplishment of sorts.

"PICTURES AT AN EXHIBITION" (MUSSORGSKY): Yeah, yeah, yeah, I'll admit the first version of this I heard was the live Emerson, Lake & Palmer album, and I'll even confess that the *second* version of this I heard was by the Japanese synth artist Tomita. Until I bought the symphonic version I didn't know that the original work was a piano suite completed by Mussorgsky in 1874, and that it wasn't until 1922 that the orchestrated version was done by Maurice ("Bolero") Ravel. This work is readily accessible for a classical music simpleton, because each section is the title of a picture, and several times they're bridged by a "Promenade" (walking from one picture to the next). Usually this can be found on same LP/cassette/CD with the redoubtable "Night on Bald Mountain" (from the movie *Fantasia* ; more about that later).

"THE PLANETS" (HOLST): OK, so I'll also admit that ELP (this time it was Emerson, Lake and *Powell)* did a version of "Mars, the Bringer of War", and Tomita also did a version of the entire symphony as well (but it's far too weird to be accessible to most folks). First performed in 1918, this is a collection of seven, uh, "songs" about the known planets of the solar system besides Earth; Pluto had yet to be discovered. There's no "Promenade"-like piece to bridge the movements, but each one is strong enough to stand on its own: "Mars, the Bringer of War" is a creepy, mechanical march, for example. In the movie *The Right Stuff*, the sequence where John Glenn is launched into orbit features music that is a melange of "Mars, the Bringer of War", "Jupiter, the Bringer of Jollity", and "Neptune, the Mystic". Music from "The Planets" also showed up in *Alien* .

ALMOST ANYTHING BY RUSSIAN COMPOSERS: Seems like Russian classical works have got more "Oooomph" to them, which would naturally be more attractive to rock & rollers. Tchaikovsky, Rimsky-

Executive Rock

Korsakov, and the aforementioned Mussorgsky are all quite listenable, and Glinka's Overture to "Russian & Ludmilla", and Borodin's "In the Steppes of Central Asia" might be found on Russian classical anthologies as well.

"LES PRELUDES" (LISZT). Theme music from the old "Flash Gordon" serials, starring Buster Crabbe. I'm old enough to remember those as well.....

ALMOST ANYTHING FROM THE MOVIE *FANTASIA*: On accounta there's a lot of visuals to go with the music, which might mean that technically, *Fantasia* was the world's first anthology of music videos. I'd heard Dukas' "The Sorcerer's Apprentice" when I was nine years old; my fourth grade teacher was a classical music fanatic who insisted that her students learn an appreciation of the "fine arts" (I still can't figure out how a group of nine-year-olds could relate to such a policy). Too bad she put subjects like English on the back burner, on accounta my grammar could be gooder.... yet the Mickey Mouse sequence in *Fantasia* (which I saw for the first time when I was twenty-one) did a commendable job of bringing my childhood fantasy imagery to animation on the screen. The music itself is sort of like an early Grateful Dead tune, in that it starts off slow and mysterious, picking up steam as it goes along. Beethoven's Sixth Symphony ("Pastorale") is another good choice (it's the mythology sequence), but there's no telling how many brain fries or acid flashbacks were generated when that batwinged demon revealed himself during the "Night on Bald Mountain" segment. And while the dinosaur animation is great, Stravinsky's "Rites of Spring" isn't very melodic.

ALMOST ANY BEETHOVEN SYMPHONY: Beethoven's works all tend to be very melodic and fairly different from each other. If you could only purchase one of 'em, make it either the aforementioned Sixth, or the Seventh.

"THE PINES AND FOUNTAINS OF ROME" (RESPIGHI): Somewhat akin to "The Planets" and "Pictures at an Exhibition" in that are eight different "songs" (four pines, four fountains).

"ORGAN" SYMPHONY IN C MINOR (SAINT-SAENS): A bit unusual in that here's a symphony orchestra with an organ working its way into the proceedings about halfway through Side One. Unique, and it works.

Many times one can find a plethora of classical cassettes at great prices in music stores; Columbia's "Great Performances" series and London's "Treasury" series are excellent examples of budget-priced albums that make for fine listening. All in all, they're an inexpensive way to introduce yourself to some music that you may have heard previously, albeit in a radically altered version. Enjoy!

Lists

THE LOST ART OF AUDIENCE PARTICIPATION

In the late Sixties and early Seventies, one "come-on" designed to indicate to consumers that So-and-So might be worth a listen was for the record company to release a *Live at the Fillmore* album. Naturally, the first such live records were by Frisco acid-rock bands, but ultimately a plethora of musicians from Aretha Franklin to Virgil Fox came out with live recordings from either of Bill Graham's two venues; by the way, Aretha's album is a *killer*, with electrifying versions of "Eleanor Rigby" and "Doctor Feelgood", plus a duet with Ray Charles on a reprise of "Spirit in the Dark." Even groups I'd never heard of came out with *Live at the Fillmore* albums; one band called Black Pearl (with a lead singer named Bernie) marketed such a product, complete with photos on the album jacket of their group's name on the Fillmore marquee, *third-billed* under two better known groups.

A legitimate criticism of today's "arena rock" performances is that they're as soulless as a floppy disk; slickly produced, professionally executed, with very little stretching out done by the musicians, and in most cases the same can be said about the live albums that we get from the artists. 1989 releases by Pink Floyd and Rush are excellent examples; it's almost like listening to the original studio cuts with canned applause added. When one can listen to a double length cassette and pick out only a couple of beefed-up riffs compared to studio versions, something's wrong.

Yet another thing about today's live recordings is an apparent lack of intimacy between performer and audience that was prevalent in the days of the Fillmore and other smaller concert halls. In the case of today's recordings all one hears is the mighty roar of applause plus an occasional clap-along, whereas many of the older live albums had conversations between the musicians and members of the audience, unsolicited comments or yells from the concert-goers, etc. One writer wrote an extended essay some time ago about the "Whipping Post!" yelp heard on The Allman Brothers' Fillmore double set, admitting that he too would yell "Whipping Post!" at concerts he attended, no matter who was performing, just to see what the musicians' reactions would be.

Admittedly the "Whipping Post!" request would be one of the better-known audience participation episodes, since the album was an success, but there are other sometimes comical, sometimes weird occasions on older live albums that merit your listening. Sometimes one has to search them out (like backwards masking in some songs, or better yet, "Paul is dead" clues on Beatles albums), but if nothing else they serve to remind the listener of a time when the bond between musician and concert-goer was apparently genuine. I don't know how many of the following incidents

21

Executive Rock

were recorded at a Fillmore, but I'd bet dialogue like this happened all the time at the Fillmores and other concert halls:

QUICKSILVER MESSENGER SERVICE - *HAPPY TRAILS*: One of the aforementioned Frisco acid rock bands, Quicksilver's best albums were the first three, before whiny-voiced songwriter Dino Valenti became a permanent member. This second album weaves in and out of live and studio cuts on side Two, but the first side is an extended jam of "Who Do You Love", featuring John Cippolina's blistering finger-picked SG leads. At one point during the proceedings the band begins simply grunting and chanting, with the audience following suit; the noise grows to a crescendo like some pagan ritual accompanied by a drum kit (women in the audience are screaming!) before Cippolina cuts back in with his guitar and the song takes off again. Jeezus.

LOU REED - *ROCK & ROLL ANIMAL*: Cited by many as one of the better guitar albums of the early Seventies (the players were Dick Wagner and Steve Hunter), there's a disturbing little incident in the middle of "Heroin", the stop-and-start Velvet Underground chestnut. There's one section where just the organ is playing; it's a classic Hammond B-3 type of solo, growling and murky. As the volume drops to a slight drone, one geek in the crowd apparently thinks the song is over, 'cause he whoops and begins clapping, like what used to be heard at the end of every "Rowan & Martin's Laugh-In."

LOU REED - *LOU REED LIVE*: Other songs culled from the same sessions that beget *Rock & Roll Animal*. The problem here is that a yell from the audience occurs right as the applause is fading out after the last song ("Sad Song") so the listener might overlook it, and in some cases a turntable might reject before the comment is heard (put it on Manual); at any rate, just as the crowd noise is subsiding some would-be critic is heard roaring "Lou Reed sucks!!!"

JOHN MAYALL - *THE TURNING POINT*: Perhaps the most innovative album ever released by the grand old man of British blues, this post-Bluesbreakers incarnation was a *drummerless* quartet featuring Johnny Almond on sax and flute, Jon Mark on acoustic guitar, Steve Thompson on bass, and Mayall on electric guitar and harmonica. Quite refreshing for 1970, this live album was the group's first release. Listen for an America vs. Great Britain cultural clash; as Mayall tries to introduce the final song ("Room to Move") he gets distracted by some offstage banter and asks what's going on, only to be further confused by the proceedings, to which he responds "Chicky-Chicky wot?"

KING CRIMSON - *U.S.A.*: Not one, but *two* occurrences on the same album, made all the more hilarious by the fact that the Crimsons were considered by most people back then to have been the definitive British

Lists

progressive art-rock band: Lots of lush Mellotron, and Robert Fripp's oozing, mysterious guitar leads in the first generation of this group beget even more out-in-the-Twilight-Zone music from the second edition, which included former Yes drummer Bill Bruford and the redoubtable John Wetton on bass and vocals, to say *nothing* about the so-called *third* edition of K.C., which came along in the early Eighties and was originally slated to be named Discipline. The live *U.S.A.* album was from the second edition, but they *did* play "21st Century Schzoid Man". The first incident is an inquiry from a female member of the audience to violinist Eddie Jobson, who also played on the live album. He'd previously been with Roxy Music (post-Crimson ventures have included UK and Jethro Tull, circa the *A* album). Jobson played a bizarre-looking violin that was almost skeletal in appearance; it looked like it was made of tubular stainless steel or maybe some kind of plastic. After the opening cut ("Larks' Tongues in Aspic Part II") a bleary, stoned-out feminine voice is heard amidst the applause, asking "Who made yer violin??." The other (and funnier) comment comes between two songs as someone hollers "Boogie!" then yells in approval as the band drones into yet another melange of abstract noodling. Yet another K.C. edition appeared in the mid-Nineties.

JIM MORRISON - *AN AMERICAN PRAYER*: Actually, there is a solitary live cut by the Doors that appears on the quirky album that consists mostly of spoken word poetry recited by Morrison, accompanied (about a decade after Morrison's death) by the remaining Doors. Bizarre concept, but at least it's not as ghoulish or calculating as some Hendrix albums such as *Crash Landing*. The Doors' "Roadhouse Blues" is followed by a wacko live commentary by Morrison that turns into a conversation with a female member of the audience:

Morrison: "Alright, alright, alright... hey lissen, lissen, lissen man... lissen, man ... I don't know many of you people believe in astrology...."

Female: "Are you a Sagittarius?"

M: "Yeah, thass right, thass right baby.... I *am* a Sagittarius..... the *most philosophical* of *all* the signs...."

F: "I know, so am I..."

M: "But anyway I don't believe in it..."

F: "I don't either!"

M: "I think it's a buncha bull****, myself ... but I tell you this, man... I tell you this.... I don't know what's gonna happen, man, but I wanna have my kicks before the whole ****house goes up in flames, alright.... *ALRIGHT!*"

As the audience roars in approval, an explosion, most likely a cherry bomb, is heard. Seems somewhat prophetic.

MOTHERS OF INVENTION - *BURNT WEENIE SANDWICH*: One

Executive Rock

exchange between Zappa and a member of the audience that is found on this album appears to have been bordering on anarchy. Apparently the dialogue was recorded in Great Britain, because the heckler has a *monster* Limey accent. I can't understand the first part of his raving, but the latter part sounds something like "Take off yore bloody uniform, before it's too late, maaaaaaan!", to which Zappa retorts: "Every person in this room is wearing a uniform, and don't kid yourself!" The audience roars its agreement, but the heckler isn't through; he keeps on shrieking, and again it's indecipherable, so Zappa, frustrated, snaps: "*You'll hurt your throat! Stop it!*" I had originally thought that the segment was on *Weasels Ripped My Flesh* (the album after *Burnt Weenie Sandwich*), and I bought the Rykodisc CD, only to discover that the snippet was missing (or so I thought). I inquired to Rykodisc, who referred me to Barking Pumpkin Records (Rykodisc's CDs were made from Zappa masters; they did not do any editing). Writing to them, I was set straight by Jim Nagle of Intercontinental Absurdities, Ltd. (apparently an offshoot of Barking Pumpkin), and I appreciate his prompt, courteous response to my letter.

CANNED HEAT LIVE IN EUROPE: Another culture clash, in which the overrated American boogie monster was recorded doing a club date somewhere on the Continent. The late Bob Hite gamely tries to converse with the audience because "Larry's amp's not workin,'" and he's heard inquiring about "the Rag Queen" (who shows up before the album's over). Hite even threatens to do "my Jim Morrison impersonation" (this was recorded soon after the Lizard King's Miami bust). The latter comment is greeted with whoops from the crowd, followed by Hite's "Lookit this!!!", and subsequent derisive cackling from the audience. I guess you had to be there.

Naturally, there are quite a few other examples; some appear on old, obscure albums like one by the Grateful Dead (sloppy performance *and* sloppy recording) where, after a sidelong version of "In the Midnight Hour" (!), the audience at the Frisco concert hall is yowling for more, and one guy starts bellowing obscenities because the band won't do an encore, cracking up the rest of the crowd, at least that portion of the crowd which is still straight enough to understand what's going on.

Some record company like Rhino or maybe even K-Tel should market an album with nothing but live snippets like all of the preceding on it; in most cases the original concert albums cited are out of print and/or hard to find. It's not like the concept hasn't been done before; remember *Having Fun Onstage with Elvis?* Gimme the "800" number to call; I've got my Mastercard ready!

Lists

DIAMONDS IN A DUNG HEAP

Whenever I'm out of town overnight, usually at some point during my sojourn I end up wandering through the local mall in whatever city I'm staying (that is, if the burg is big enough to even have a mall), and naturally I'll make sure to hit the music stores (Record, tape & CD stores, not instrument stores. The latter are rarely found in malls, at least they aren't in my part of country). Bargain-hunter that I am, I'll of course rummage through all of the cutout and off-the-wall cassettes that are usually found a bit off the "regular price traffic" areas of the store, under a sign that says something like "SPECIAL VALUE!!!"

First and foremost, let me emphasize that I'm not talking about some major label's reissues (mostly from the Seventies) at a lower price, although there's a lot to be said for that particular marketing concept; I've been able to replace worn-out albums that are personal favorites of mine at a budget price. "Nice Price" and "Sound Savings Series" are examples of some major label reissues, and the cassettes can usually be had in the under-$6.00 range.

However, if you're really on a tight budget and are willing to do a bit of digging through mountains of tapes by such "artists" as Little Steven, Asia, Loudness, and other performers that nobody cares about anymore, occasionally it's worth the effort. There's a lot to be said as well for the $1.99-3.99 budget tape (a good bit of which is unprintable, since so much schlock is out there); ya just gotta roll up your sleeves. Some of the following were on such specialty labels as Relativity and Passport Jazz, but none cost me over $3.99:

INTO THE RAINBOW (MAX LASSER'S ARK): Lasser has been an associate of New Age electro-harpist Andreas Vollenweider, and it shows; this album is very lightweight, melodic New Age/jazz, and is actually superior to Lasser's later major label efforts. Pat Metheny (and the ECM label, for that matter) should have realized that the reason Metheny's first couple of albums in the late Seventies were so successful was that they were so *accessible;* my interest in Metheny declined swiftly when he began experimenting with his guitar synth, making rude, blatting, trumpet-like noises, and that's why Lasser's playing is such a breath of fresh air.

WHAT'S WORDS WORTH (MOTORHEAD): Recorded live (sloppily); I've seen this cassette with at least three different covers, one which shows the current four-man lineup of the World's Most Brutal Heavy Metal Band, which is false advertising in that the personnel when this was recorded consisted of Lemmy on bass & vocals, Philthy Animal Taylor on drums, and Fast Eddie Clarke on guitar (most metalheads agree that this was the band's best incarnation). While the vocals are sometimes unintelligible

25

Executive Rock

(due to the aforementioned sloppy production plus the fact that Lemmy ain't exactly Roger Whitaker), nevertheless the performance is chock full of riffs ("The Watcher", "On Parole") and there's even covers of "The Train Kept A'Rollin'" and "I'm Your Witch Doctor".

THE INTRODUCTION (STEVE MORSE BAND): This one is for everyone who, like yours truly, thought the Dixie Dregs' best album was their second, *What If*, because *The Introduction* cooks just as much as the 1978 Capricorn release did. Morse shows off his usual amount of virtuosity, but it's tempered with a bit more restraint than some of his other recordings, *plus* the songs are appropriately short enough to steer clear of boredom. Moreover, this all-instrumental effort beats another Morse cutout, *Stand Up*, in spades; the latter was a so-called "all-star" effort (including the apparently reclusive Eric Johnson) that didn't really work. This cutout is an example where I ultimately sought out and purchased the CD (which, unfortunately, *wasn't* on sale); for one thing, I was finally able to determine who the bass player was (Jerry Peek) since their *were* liner notes with the CD. I'd never heard of Peek, but his romping bass lines snare a listener's ear *immediately* on the first cut ("Cruise Missile"), and there's note-for-note riffing with Morse that preceded the much-heralded Gilbert-Sheehan efforts in Mr. Big by half a decade.

GREATEST HITS LIVE (FLEETWOOD MAC): The mighty Mac is now in its umpteenth incarnation, and nobody seems to remember that the original group was composed of British players that included ex-members of John Mayall's Bluesbreakers, so that's why stumbling across this live effort (recorded at the Boston Tea Party in 1970) was not only an unexpected surprise (it's by the original quintet), it shows how much the band has changed. In addition to Mick Fleetwood and John McVie, Fleetwood Mac's original guitar triumvirate consisted of blues god Peter Green, slidemeister Jeremy Spencer, and Danny Kirwan (actually, Kirwan came on board after the band had been in existence for a while, but he's considered to be a integral facet of the Phase One Mac). *Greatest Hits Live* contains classic songs, too: "Oh Well", the original "Black Magic Woman", and an over-sixteen minute version of "Green Manalishi". Ultimately, I've seen *Greatest Hits Live* on CD, along with other albums with songs culled from the live Boston sessions.

FULL HOUSE - ACES HIGH (THE AMAZING RHYTHM ACES): Another live one (seems like lots of full-time or even part-time players would be attracted to such) by the now-defunct country-rock band that had a major hit ("Third Rate Romance", circa 1974) and a few minor ones. At one point, this double set was supposed to be available only by mail order. Lotsa slick fretwork (including steel), plus boozy, sing-along honkytonk lyrics and terrific harmony. The ARAs were a vastly underrated combo

Lists

that could've held their own with the likes of the Flying Burrito Brothers and other bands.

THE OTHER SIDE (THE FENTS): Some quartet I've never heard of apparently put out a solitary fusion album some years back that's one of the genre's best efforts; almost every cut *burns*. I bought this because of the quirky song titles on the cover ("Where's My Producer", "I Don't Want My MTV"), and the music sorta reminded me of some old Return to Forever stuff with an Eighties edge.

SAY UNCLE (UNCLE FESTIVE): The only reason I'd ever heard of this band is on accounta their bass player was listed in an endorsement roster for a particular brand of electric bass. Well-produced instrumentals that sound somewhat like Dave Grusin/Lee Ritenour collaborations, and the over-ten-minute-long "Harvest" is worth the price alone because it sounds like an early Pat Metheny Group tune. While *Say Uncle* is a passable value from the cutout bin, I subsequently encountered (and purchased) some other Uncle Festive albums that ain't so hot.

INSTRUMENT LANDING (PRESTON REED): Normally, solo acoustic guitar albums don't excite the average listener, but this is an exuberant and melodic performance.

HOT ASH (WISHBONE ASH): Circa 1980 live stuff that was apparently released as part of an overseas effort called *Live Dates II,* if I remember correctly; methinks the Euro release was a double set. WARNING: I've had two copies of this cassette but both tapes went bad fairly quickly, so if you get this, dub it off to a more durable format as soon as possible. Obviously, if I ever encounter the CD I'll buy it, but I don't anticipate that'll ever happen. For further details, see the "Wishbone Asterisk" monograph.

STORYTIME (T. LAVITZ): Best of several solo albums by the Dixie Dregs' keyboard player. Snappy arrangements that are almost "hummable", and there's a guest vocal by Paul Barrére.

PENSYL SKETCHES #3 (The Emerald Sunrise) (KIM PENSYL): While this album could be lumped in with zillions of other instrumental cutouts under the "L.A. Happy Jazz" slur, it's better than #1 or #2, which rely way too much on MIDI. From what I can tell about the only things that are MIDI'ed on #3 are some horns. Overall this third volume sorta reminds me of Joe Sample's *Rainbow Seeker*.

UNTITLED ISLAND (RAY FLACKE): A brilliant guitar album by a fingerpicker who's a legend among his peers (he used to play for Ricky Skaggs). This eclectic offering doesn't have the first throwaway cut on it; Flacke even covers Deep Purple's "Wring That Neck" with ease. Don't overlook this one.

VISAGE (KEN WILEY): This one could also be prematurely pigeon-

Executive Rock

holed as L.A. Happy Jazz, but the unique thing going for it is that the featured instrument is a French horn, so it's a bit mellower but not quite New Age.

TWO HEARTS (DAVE MASON): A techno-pop excursion (of all things) for the venerable Worcester warbler. Initial misgivings are ultimately assuaged, since Mason's soulful singing and melodic guitar lines mesh better with the electronic keyboards and drums than one might think. Musical guests include Phoebe Snow and Steve Winwood; the squiggling signature sound of Winwood's synthesizer is *instantly* recognizable on "Something in the Heart". If you can look past the machinery and pay attention to the songs, this is palatable, quasi-Phil Collins-type fare. Other Mason albums have also been spotted in cutout bins; apparently he label-hopped quite a bit for some time before hooking up with Fleetwood Mac in the mid-Nineties.

ISLANDS (MIKE OLDFIELD): An interesting and slightly different concept ... for Oldfield, that is. Side One is a stereotypical Oldfield extended work with unusual rhythms and instrumentation, while Side Two consists of five songs with guest vocalists, including Bonnie Tyler and the remarkable Kevin Ayers.

THEME (LESLIE WEST BAND): I'm a bit ambivalent about this one, because on the one hand the new stuff on this apparent "quickie" isn't anything great, but there are also commendable remakes of "Theme from an Imaginary Western" and "Spoonful", plus a not-so-hot rendition of "Red House". So to what extent is this an effort to make a comeback versus another dumb time warp plunge? I dunno, but what made it worth the $2.99 I spent on it was the fact that I didn't know until I opened the cassette case and read the inside liner notes that the band's bassist (and vocalist on the first two covers I mentioned) was none other than *Jack Bruce,* and he's in *fine* form.

THE ENTIRE KING CRIMSON CATALOG (EXCEPT FOR TWO ALBUMS): That's right, I've encountered every album the British progressive rock icons ever recorded in some cutout bin at one time or another, save *Larks' Tongues in Aspic* and 1995's *THRAK*. Everything from *In the Court of the Crimson King* to *Three of a Perfect Pair*; the majority of albums are on the EG Editions label, while the final three (which were by the incarnation of the Crimsons that included Adrian Belew) are on EG/Warner Brothers. Here's your chance to find out why this band was critically venerated and excoriated so much. There are even a couple of anthologies available (*A Young Person's Guide to King Crimson* and *The Compact King Crimson*). *WARNING!* Side One of *Lizard* still sounds as muddled and confused as it did a quarter-century ago.

THE LAST EXPERIENCE - HIS FINAL LIVE PERFORMANCE (JIMI

Lists

HENDRIX): Beware! This one ain't a diamond; it's at best a zircon; at worst a waste. It seems like I recall another live reissue with an abbreviated version of "Wild Thing" that also fades out after 1:16, so maybe this is the same album with a different cover; at any rate, this Italian cassette is badly produced, and the performance is erratic and uninspiring, with Hendrix mixing up lyrics in "Fire" and practically mumbling his way through the rest of the tunes. There's no way to verify that this was indeed Hendrix's last performance, which if I remember correctly was somewhere in Europe rather than on the Isle of Wight, which many think was his swan song. Even if it *is* Hendrix's last hoorah, there's a temptation to say "big deal" since it's so lousy. I bought this for $3.99 and at the same time purchased Ryko's *Live at Winterland* cassette, recorded in October 1968, before Hendrix was in decline (and while Noel Redding was still bassist; this recording shows how much of an asset Redding was), and the difference in the coherence of Jimi's playing *and* singing over an approximately two-year period is chilling.

I listed the Hendrix live cassette in a effort to show how it's possible to waste your money, even at a cutout price. Another example might be the Sex Pistols' *The Great Rock and Roll Swindle,* the title of which is applicable to the album *and* Malcolm McLaren's "concept" of punk rock, as far as I'm concerned. John "Johnny Rotten" Lydon said it himself during the band's "cover" of "Johnny B. Goode" (I think it was an audition for Lydon): "Aw, ****; it's awful...."

One good thing about bargain bins is that you won't waste too much cash on an artist that you may have heard about or read about but never heard (I didn't care for Uli Jon Roth's *Electric Sun* at all, for example). And as might be expected, *The Introduction* wasn't the only album listed here where I ultimately sought out the Compact Disc version, and in some cases those CDs were themselves in cutout bins! Cassette or Compact Disc, there are still probably some gems in those bins that may make all of that rummaging worthwhile. Have at it.

Executive Rock

ROBINSON CRUSOE AND HIS WALKMAN

"What about your personal choices for a so-called 'desert island Top Ten'?" asked Malc.

"Albums or songs?"

"Albums."

"Would I have a turntable, boom box or Compact Disc player?"

"What's the difference?" snarled Malc.

"Under the circumstances, I'd want the best fidelity I could get, on accounta I'd have the time to listen for what each instrument was playing in each song. You know, picking out patterns and riffs."

"Oh. Anyways, what ten albums would you pick?"

"Lemme think about it and I'll get back to you. Such a list would require an awful lot of rumination, considering all of the choices I'd have. Any restrictions, like whether the album is still available or not?"

"Nope."

Later, when I showed Malc my list, naturally he had a plethora of questions and comments:

"Seems like a variety of styles."

"Yep. I'd want sort of an assortment, y'know?"

"No disco?" smirked Malc.

"Up yours."

"There's three double albums and a triple album on here!" he protested.

"You didn't say how many *records,* you said *albums.*"

"Why not *Chicago IV-Live at Carnegie Hall*? It's *quadruple*," Malc said, smirking again.

" 'Cause it's a lousy album."

"One of the live ones doesn't even exist!"

"Hopefully it will. Anyway, I could rig up an audio cassette deck to a stereo VCR and dub off the soundtrack of the videotape concert that's available."

"In that case you'd need a *boom box,*" chirped Malc. What VCR format would you wanna dub from?"

"Beta. It sounds better than VHS, but Beta's practically extinct, at least in the U.S.," I said.

"Mmph. Well, if you were on some desert island, most likely it wouldn't be U.S. territory," he said, nitpicking. For once I had the upper hand in one of our conversations, so Malc tried an alternate approach: "How come so many live albums?"

"Seems like I prefer live versions of tunes to studio versions. Maybe I like 'em live 'cause I still play in a combo... or maybe I'd want to fantasize that I was at a concert and bang my head against a coconut tree..."

Lists

"All in all, this is a weird list for someone your age."

"I know. How old is a guy supposed to be when middle-age craziness hits?"

So here are the selections, in no particular order:

YESSONGS (YES): The definitive British progressive rock album, and it still holds up after the genre is practically extinct. Some folks don't know that there was also a *Yessongs* movie, with alternate versions of tunes found on the album.

THE PAT METHENY GROUP (First album): This combo's first release from 1978 is a lightweight, uncluttered masterpiece featuring Metheny's bright 12-string guitar and Lyle Mays' moody synthesizer. Beautiful in its simplicity.

PHAEDRA (TANGERINE DREAM): "Breakthrough" 1974 album for the avant-garde German synth trio. Gimme some electronic-psychedelic mung to wallow in...

LIVE AT THE MONTEREY POP FESTIVAL - 1967 (JIMI HENDRIX AND OTIS REDDING): Here again, definitive performances by two doomed black men at opposite ends of that era's music spectrum.

MOTORHEAD LIVE - NO SLEEP TILL HAMMERSMITH (MOTORHEAD): Heavy metal doesn't get any more brutal than this, especially since the "singer" doesn't have a full set of teeth....

THE WALL (PINK FLOYD): When Fleetwood Mac's "Tusk" was released in late 1979, some critics were comparing it to the Beatles' "white" album, released at the end of the *previous* decade, while at the same time, *this* double set was generally dismissed as an autobiographical Roger Waters twilight-of-Empire nightmare, as was the subsequent film of the same name. However, *both* remain powerful (if depressing and unnerving) statements, and I'd still like to know how many acid flashbacks the movie version caused.

WHEELS OF FIRE (CREAM): This one is around three decades old, yet in some ways nothing's topped some of the material found on the studio sides *or* the live sides. Just imagine how it would sound if recorded today using modern technology... The trio of Baker, Bruce and Clapton is considered by many to have been the ultimate rock band, incapable of ever being topped in the innovation and talent depts.

POLICE LIVE (POLICE): This album was indeed nonexistent when Malc and I had the conversation noted at the outset of this essay, but lo and behold, a double-CD set was finally released in the summer of 1995. I'd based my portion of our dialogue (and my decision as well) on having seen and heard the *Synchronicity Concert* video, which was taped at the Omni in Atlanta, and that November 1983 show does indeed comprise one of the two discs. The other disc is a November 1979 Boston gig, which is

Executive Rock

leaner but just as listenable. I consider the Bottle Blonds to have been the most innovative rock trio (or perhaps even the most innovative rock band of *any* size) since Cream, and these performances simply reinforce my opinion.

LOCAL HERO SOUNDTRACK (MARK KNOPFLER): Not only is the lead guitarist of Dire Straits one of rock's latter day guitar heroes, he's also an excellent instrumental composer. This is the best of his several soundtracks, featuring uncomplicated melodies, Scottish folk tunes and nifty arrangements. Like the film itself, it's a simple pleasure.

EXPOSED (MIKE OLDFIELD): A limited edition British import by the founder of so-called "new age" music, who composed and performed "Tubular Bells" when he was 18 years old. This live double set features both "Tubular Bells" and the unreleased-in-the-U.S. "Incantations" (abbreviated), and was recorded live in Europe in 1979, featuring a 12-piece rock band, 4 trumpet players, 2 flautists, 18 string players, and a 11-voice choir. Somewhat unusual but well done.

ALTERNATES (In case I couldn't find some of the older, out-of-print ones; might as well make it an even dozen...):

LOGOS-LIVE AT THE DOMINION 1982 (TANGERINE DREAM): Gimme some *live* electronic-psychedelic mung to wallow in. Outstanding fidelity.

METALLIC K.O.-THE LAST EVER IGGY & THE STOOGES CONCERT (STOOGES): This is the most dangerous album ever recorded. Taped with a small portable cassette recorder, it's obviously hideous soundwise, but nevertheless it keeps an iron grip on the listener as the proto-punk Stooges lurch through an out-of-tune, stoned-out nightmare, while "singer" Iggy destroys the idea that a rock concert should be *enjoyed*. Dodging ice cubes and eggs (and ultimately, glass bottles), the Ig threatens and cajoles the audience ("Lissen, I been egged by better than you"), all the while making up his own obscene lyrics to the group's "songs". The album ends, as one might expect, with "Louie Louie" (which the Ig intros with "I never thought it'd come to this"), and of course it's got every four-letter word you thought you might have heard in other versions. The last thing one hears on the album is the sound of a bottle crashing onstage ... Y'know, come to think of it, I might pass on this album after all, 'cause if I heard it while stranded on a desert island I might climb to the top of the aforementioned coconut tree and jump off.

Malc was fuming. "How come no Beatles, Led Zeppelin, or Stones albums?"

"Because you wanted a list of *albums*. Now as for songs..." (that's another story).

Lists

THE COVER STORY

These days, it's almost embarrassing for some people to admit that they were fans of the Vanilla Fudge back in the Sixties. Critically excoriated then and now, the Fudge nevertheless carved their own niche in the annals of pop music history with their innovative versions of other songs. Hailed as a harbinger of the progressive music "glory days" of the late Sixties and early Seventies, the quartet of Mark Stein, Tim Bogert, Carmine Appice, and Vinnie Martell was also slagged by others as producing music that was pretentious and boring. Bogert stated in an interview with *Vintage Guitar* that he preferred doing the band's cover songs to their original stuff, and also listed the terms by which the Vanilla Fudge's music was known back then, including "pompous bull****".

Count me among those who were fans then, and I still like hearing their stuff now, even if it sounds a mite dated in some respects. Yet in the Spring of 1968 I heard a version of the Supremes' "You Keep Me Hangin' On" unlike anything I'd ever heard before, and purchasing the first album by the Vanilla Fudge also turned me on to heavily re-worked Beatles tunes; "Ticket to Ride" began with an announcement about "400 cycles per second", and "Eleanor Rigby" was interspersed with snippets of works by *Beethoven!* The Vanilla Fudge put out a total of five albums, and there was at least one cover tune on each of 'em.

A recent trend in current recordings involves a buncha artists doing cover versions of songs by other particular artists or songs from a particular genre, such as Disney movie tunes. Actually, this "trend" isn't all that new; I recall an all-star version of *Tommy* (with Ringo Starr, Stevie Winwood, etc. plus a symphony orchestra) as well as an anthology of Beatles songs by other artists called *All This and World War Two*, both of which date from the mid-Seventies.

Now, what if one could assemble his/her own album of all-time favorite cover tunes? In many respects the cover is superior to the original, in my opinion, and some of them were bigger hits than the original versions, if the originals *were* hits at all.

Obviously, "tribute" albums would be an excellent source for songs on this list, but they've been omitted from consideration here, because they're too much of a "convenience", for lack of a better term. Despite the success of albums like *Common Thread: Songs of the Eagles*, it might be a more meaningful experience if a listener accidentally stumbles across a unique version of a song he/she has heard previously, instead of having such tunes conveniently prepackaged in one album; at least, that's been the case for me.

What's more, some of the tribute albums that are out these days might

Executive Rock

be commendable efforts, but in some cases an average listener may not be familiar with the honoree (Richard Thompson, for example). The flipside with which knowledgeable music fans can retort is to dis certain covers as inferior to the original; for example, what's so special about Ugly Kid Joe's version of Harry Chapin's "Cat's in the Cradle"?

At any rate, my own custom-recorded cassette would probably feature the following tunes:

"WE GOTTA GET OUT OF THIS PLACE" (BLUE OYSTER CULT): A 1977 live version of the Animals' hit, from the *Some Enchanted Evening* album, which was not only a fine effort, but production-wise it beat BOC's previous live album, *On Your Feet or On Your Knees*, in spades. On the other hand, *Some Enchanted Evening* also contains an attempted cover of the MC5's "Kick Out the Jams" which is nothing less than heresy.

"SUNSHINE OF YOUR LOVE" (ROTARY CONNECTION): One of *three* songs from Cream's *Disraeli Gears* album found on Rotary Connection's *Songs* LP; the other two were "Tales of Brave Ulysses" and "We're Going Wrong". Featuring orchestrated arrangements and the late Minnie Ripperton's umpteen-octave voice, Rotary Connection was probably pigeonholed into the same place as the Fudge, but their music was a good bit different and usually worth a listen. How much (if any) of Rotary Connection's stuff is available on Compact Disc?

"THIS WHEEL'S ON FIRE" (JULIE DRISCOLL, BRIAN AUGER, & THE TRINITY): Token Dylan tune. This British aggregation usually featured Driscoll's plaintive vocals and Auger's crisp, up-front keyboards. However, the Dylan cover was a good bit "heavier", with whooshing, flanged sound effects. Among the other covers JD, BA & TT did were "Light My Fire" and Richie Havens' "Indian Rope Man". I can't recall seeing "This Wheel's On Fire" on any albums by Julie Driscoll, Brian Auger & The Trinity; was it just a single?

"BLACK MAGIC WOMAN" (SANTANA): Originally a Peter Green song done by the first incarnation of Fleetwood Mac, of which Green was the focal point. This is an obvious example of the cover being more popular than the original, and I recall one local garage band doing a commendable version of the Fleetwood Mac original at an early Seventies "battle of the bands". However, since almost everyone in the audience (as well as the judges) were only familiar with Santana's cover, everyone thought the band was *awful.* Sometimes sticking too close to home and/or being a purist ain't too smart from a show biz perspective....

"SUMMERTIME BLUES" (BLUE CHEER): "The Road Kill of Cover Tunes", as far as I'm concerned, on accounta the Eddie Cochran chestnut has been bludgeoned, run over, and stomped on so ferociously it bears no resemblance to the original except for the lyrics. Other covers this brutal

Lists

trio did on their first album (released in 1967) were "Parchman Farm" and "Rock Me Baby". I wonder if they figured they had to pay royalties or not? They might could've gotten away with not paying, considering the way their covers sounded.

"I WANT CANDY" (BOW WOW WOW): Cited in an earlier essay. It has a Bo Diddley beat, in case you're interested.

"FANFARE FOR THE COMMON MAN" (EMERSON, LAKE & PALMER): Token instrumental symphonic work, composed by Aaron Copland. A choice such as this should be able to stand *on its own,* rather than being mixed in with other stuff, such as the aforementioned Beethoven licks on the Fudge's version of "Eleanor Rigby".

"SATISFACTION" (DEVO): Token New Wave weirdness.

"HIGHER AND HIGHER" (JIMMY HALL): I fell in love with this song, originally done by Jackie Wilson, which is found on one of Charlie Daniels' *Volunteer Jam* live albums. Hall was/is the singer for Wet Willie, and he showed some class by dedicating the song to Wilson ("Gawd blessim"). Hall also sang on Jeff Beck's "Ambitious", the video for which showed Hall auditioning in front of Beck along with the likes of Donny Osmond and the late Herve What's-His-Name, who played Tattoo on the "Fantasy Island" TV series.

"I'VE GOT THE MUSIC IN ME" (HEART): An early live number that blows away the original version by Kiki Dee; as far as I'm concerned it's one of the best songs the Wilson sisters and associates have ever done.

"STOP! IN THE NAME OF LOVE" (HOLLIES): Another Supremes cover, from an Eighties reunion album. If I remember correctly it's in a different key, but its loping beat and inimitable harmony vocals make it a lotta fun.

"I'M A MAN" (CHICAGO TRANSIT AUTHORITY): Within a couple of years after the Spencer Davis Group's follow-up hit to "Gimme Some Lovin' ", here came a horn band with a cover that featured a drum solo and rousing guitar chords from Terry Kath. One of the main reasons their first album is one of their most listenable.

"HUSH" (DEEP PURPLE): About half of their first album (*Shades of Deep Purple*) was comprised of "heavy" cover tunes.

"CALLING OCCUPANTS OF INTERPLANETARY CRAFT" (CAR-PENTERS): An odd choice for this list, perhaps, *especially* since it was rumored that the musicians who recorded the original version in the mid-Seventies were actually the Beatles. Turned out to be a Canadian band called Klaatu, who apparently milked the Beatles association for all it was worth and offered some interesting music while doing so, even if a listener already knew about the bogus Beatles rumors. The Carpenters' version was a bit more radio-ready (as might have been expected), and featured a

Executive Rock

hilarious dialogue at the outset between an alien and an adrenaline-rush AM radio deejay.

"ALL I HAVE TO DO IS DREAM" (THE NITTY GRITTY DIRT BAND): Lighthearted, whimsical version of the Everly Brothers chestnut that relies primarily on bluegrass-type instrumentation.

"THE TRAIN KEPT A ROLLIN'" (AEROSMITH): Half-studio, half-live variant of a Yardbirds song from the mid-Seventies *Get Your Wings* album. In those days, Ol' Fish Lips sounded like he *meant* what he was singing.

"WALK ON BY" (ISAAC HAYES): Ain't tokenism terrific?

"CAN'T HELP FALLING IN LOVE" (COREY HART): Doesn't even have a beat, and it's gorgeous.

"THE GREEN MANALISHI" (JUDAS PRIEST): Son-of-a-gun. Another Peter Green tune. A live version of this was found on Judas Priest's *Unleashed In The East* album, but a superior version is found on the *Priest Live* video, *but not on the live album that was released at the same time!* "Green Manalishi" was also one of the tunes Priest performed at Live Aid.

"IT'S A SMALL WORLD" (ANDY KAUFMAN & THE B STREET CONGA BAND): Yeah, right. I want my dada.

"LEAN ON ME" (MICHAEL BOLTON): I'm embarrassed to admit it, but I got fooled on this one, and will give credit where credit's due. The Missus knows how much I loathe Bolton's chock-fulla-phony-angst vocal stylings, but when this song wafted out of the speakers of a jukebox in a barbecue restaurant that we patronize on a regular basis, I was so intrigued that I walked over to the machine to discern the name of the artist. This singular gem doesn't necessarily make up for Bolton's past atrocities, however.

"ATLANTIC CITY" (THE BAND): Easily tops the Springsteen original from the sparse *Nebraska* album. The Band's *Jericho* album should have gotten more attention; "Atlantic City" is only one of several outstanding songs on it.

"BEAT ME DADDY EIGHT TO THE BAR" (COMMANDER CODY & THE LOST PLANET AIRMEN): Something that the parents of Boomers can relate to, and more than one generation could find this ditty enjoyable.

"THE MAN WHO SOLD THE WORLD" (NIRVANA): For those music fans who have never been into the chameleon-like David Bowie's efforts, this keystone selection from Nirvana's *Unplugged* performance might come as a surprise. In spite of Cobain's introductory disclaimer of "I can guarantee you that I will screw this song up", the tune suits his slightly-ragged mumble perfectly, and the instrumental ending of this song is utterly fascinating; Cobain's guitar (an old Martin electric flat-top with those

Lists

great-sounding DeArmond pickups) sounds just like Lori Goldston's cello.

"AIN'T THAT A SHAME" (CHEAP TRICK): A definitive example of how a rock band oughta cover an R & B tune.

"SHOTGUN" (VANILLA FUDGE): Tim Bogert's favorite Fudge cover is also mine. Basically a one-chord rocker, on which each member gets to briefly show off his chops. They leave out a verse, but so what? There's one mystery I'd like to clear up, however: Listen real close to the buildup intro, which was a feature of a lotta Fudge tunes. Someone in the background of the mix is heard saying something like "Martin". Whazzat all about???

There may be some other tunes that I really like that might actually be covers and I'm not aware of such, and in some situations (particularly blues tunes) the originals may be decades old, from a time when there were such things as "race records", etc. Yet failing to give an original artist his/her due in such situations is probably a case of ignorance for most folks, and there are many modern artists who are active in trying to make the public aware of such historically important yet often overlooked parts of American music; the Delta Blues Museum is a good example.

I'm sure there are many other covers that are favorites of readers; the ones listed here probably just scratch the surface of commendable updates of earlier songs. Two last points of irony regarding cover songs: I seem to recall reading a story about some audience members at a rock venue (was it a Fillmore?) getting excited when Albert King began playing "Oh Pretty Woman"; "He's playing a John Mayall song!", they exclaimed. Trouble was, "Oh Pretty Woman" is an Albert King original.

The other oddball occurrence was when Rod Stewart recorded a version of "You Keep Me Hangin' On". Y'see, he did a cover of the Vanilla Fudge's cover of that song! That ain't full circle; that's more like a Mobius Strip!!!

Executive Rock

SOLE SURVIVORS OR TIME WARP BANDITS?

One of the things with which I have a bit of difficulty when it comes to the ongoing interest in the "classic rock" phenomenon concerns bands that are still in existence and that are still playing concert clubs, but there's only one original member left in the combo. For the most part, bands with a "sole survivor" seem to have been relegated to what might be called "journeyman" status, but that's not always the case; many groups such as Santana still have a respectable amount of viability when it comes to current recordings and concerts.

The thing is, I've interviewed some of the guitar players who fit into such a category, and some of 'em (Kim Simmonds, Hughie Thomasson, etc.) have been forthright with me when I've brought up the fact that the interviewee is the only original member left. An honest response to such an inquiry is always appreciated if I've ever asked; I can't think of any interviewee who's ever tried to evade such a question.

Many of the "sole survivors" I can think of happen to be focal points of their respective bands (lead singers, lead guitarists, whatever), so many consumers might not be concerned about the turnover of other personnel. What follows is a list of bands that at one time or another (including the present) have had one original member in their lineups. One point that needs to be made at this juncture concerns the use of the term "original": In some of the following examples, there may have been a difference in the literally "original" membership of a band and what the lineup was when the band came into prominence; many longtime fans of a particular combo would probably consider the latter to be the "classic" version of a band, and such fans may not be aware of an earlier incarnation. For instance, I bet a lot of Motorheadbangers would consider the version of the World's Most Brutal Heavy Metal Band that consisted of Lemmy, Philthy Animal Taylor, and Fast Eddie Clarke to have been the "classic" lineup of Motorhead, whereas the original lineup consisted of Lemmy, Lucas Fox, and Larry Wallis. It gets a bit nebulous, eh?

THE OUTLAWS (Hughie Thomasson): Thomasson noted in his *Vintage Guitar* interview that even the personnel that made the band's first album in the mid-Seventies weren't all original members. Although "The Florida Guitar Army" never achieved the success of some other Southern rock bands, a live 1993 "concert club" album called *Hittin' the Road* is an excellent effort, in my opinion.

PAUL REVERE & THE RAIDERS (Paul Revere): From what I can tell, this group has pretty much become sort of a Vegas-type lounge act. The last time I saw 'em was on some gawdawful Boomer dance show on the Nostalgia Channel (hosted by former MTV veejay/airhead/bimbo/

38

Lists

ditsoid Nina Blackwood), and ol' Paul seemed to be a bit befuddled about where he was.

QUICKSILVER (Gary Duncan): Nee Quicksilver Messenger Service, I guess. I think this was a mid-Eighties attempt to resurrect the name, and the resulting album, *Peace by Piece*, was a far cry from QMS's first album or *Happy Trails*. I found a cassette of *Peace by Piece* in the cutout section of a Camelot Music store, and bought it for $3.99. Popping it into my car's tape player, I only made it halfway through the third song before hitting the Eject button and throwing the piece/peace of **** out the window.

SAVOY BROWN (Kim Simmonds): May hold the record (along with Santana) for the most turnover in personnel, but Simmonds has been around with his aggregation for about three decades. My perception is that Simmonds is a more astute businessman than most veteran guitarists, and one of Savoy Brown's more recent efforts (*Live and Kickin'*) was another example of a fine "concert club" recording; it featured the redoubtable Dave Walker in his second go-round as lead vocalist.

WHITESNAKE (David Coverdale): Check, please.

JOHN KAY & STEPPENWOLF (John Kay): Note the name difference, which Kay addressed in his *Vintage Guitar* interview; it involved some "bogus" Steppenwolf bands, according to Kay. At one point in the Seventies there was also a bogus Fleetwood Mac, if I remember correctly.

MOTORHEAD (Lemmy): "Lemmy *is* Motorhead, period", said Malc. Maybe so; the chord-based bass playing, piledriver-like riffs, and phlegm-coated "singing" are certainly inimitable to most longtime listeners. I was going to list Hawkwind in this essay (guitarist Dave Brock being the sole survivor) but Lemmy (who's a former Hawkwind member himself) told me that another original member was back in the band with Brock. Hawkwind is the band that A Flock of Seagulls wanted to be when they grew up... come to think of it, A Flock of Seagulls may now have one original member, but who gives a ****?

FOGHAT (Lonesome Dave Peverett and Roger Earl): The reason two individuals are listed is because for a short time a while back there were actually *two* bands sporting the Foghat moniker! One contained Peverett and was handled by a Florida organization, and the other band had Earl in it; they were hooked up with a New England-based booking firm, from what I could determine. "Forget all that", guitarist Rod Price told me at the 1994 Dallas show (he was at the *VG* booth signing autographs). At that time the original Foghat lineup of Peverett, Price, Earl and Tone Stevens were back together, and were rehearsing and planning on recording. That's a bit easier to understand than it had been at one point, obviously, and it seems ironic that with the exception of Price, the original members of

Executive Rock

Foghat were ex-members of Savoy Brown.

SANTANA (Carlos Santana): Probably the most successful example on this list, yet the mid-Nineties *Sacred Fire* live album left me a bit unsatisfied (possibly because I'm not a Third World resident). Nevertheless, the version of "Black Magic Woman/Gypsy Queen" on *Sacred Fire burns* (pun intended). Another interesting facet of Carlos' recent efforts is his appearance in a Ben and Jerry's ice cream ad along with some other activists; Mr. Santana is doing an admirable Gene Simmons impression...

ZZ TOP (Billy F Gibbons): It might surprise a lot of folks to see "The Lil' Ol' Band From Texas" on this list, since its lineup has consisted of Rev. Gibbons, Dusty Hill, and Frank Beard since *ZZ Top's First Album* was recorded about a quarter-century ago. But prior to that, there were various other short-lived incarnations of the band; one version even put out a single, "Salt Lick", on the Scat label.

WISHBONE ASH (Andy Powell): As of this writing, guitarist Powell is the only original member of this respected British aggregation; guitarist Ted Turner departed for a second time in early 1994. Andy Powell's Gibson Flying V guitar has practically become the band's logo, anyway.

BLACK OAK ARKANSAS (Jim Dandy Mangrum): Who?

When it comes to entertainment, there may be very little difference between "Buyer Beware" and "Keep the Customer Satisfied"; there may be very little difference as well between admirable ongoing efforts by veteran rockers versus something that's chock fulla hype or an outright con. *Vintage Guitar* readers would probably be more astute about the lineup of a band that's got a moniker which has been around for some time, and while the seriousness with which such a combo should be taken depends on each listener, I tend to admire such efforts by such veterans if they've got a "this-is-what-I-do-for-a-living" attitude.

There *have* been some exceptions for yours truly, and perhaps the most unfortunate example occurred some time ago: I showed up at a concert club where a band with one remaining original member was scheduled to perform that evening. The roadies were already setting up equipment, and after they perused the samples of *VG* that I'd brought they advised me to stick around until the tour bus arrived; that the player would probably be glad to do an interview. Once the tour bus arrived, however, I approached the tour manager (whose hair was too long for somebody his age), and after looking over a copy of the magazine, he advised that the "star" didn't do interviews, adding a smirk to punctuate his statement.

It should go without saying that the term "has-been" was bouncing around in my mind as I huffed out of the club after waiting around for over two hours....

Lists

BATTLE OF THE ULTRA-BOOGIES

One of my all-time favorite sketches on the late, lamented "SCTV" show was an editorial commentary by Rick Moranis, made up to look like David Brinkley, in which the squinting, stone-faced "reporter" was decrying the change in personnel in some of his favorite Fifties doo-wop groups; I remember the first line of the bit was something along the lines of "What the *hell* ever happened to the original Coasters?"

Sometimes I tend to take the same attitude in pondering the extinction (for all intents and purposes) of the sidelong rock song. Seems like nowadays whenever a critic reviews a new release, anything that exceeds 6-7 minutes gets noted (a long cut on Metallica's *Master of Puppets* is somewhat of an example of a modern song that got cited when the album came out), whereas nonstop jams, segues a-plenty, and lumbering boogies were a staple of many bands of the late Sixties and early Seventies. What few *disco* tunes I listened to circa 1979 were usually long, Latin-tinged covers of old Animals songs done by some group called Santa Esmeralda.

To qualify for membership in this particular genre, a song should be more than ten minutes long and should have the same basic riff to anchor it. Segues are allowed *if* the tune returns to its original turf *or* the segue leads in to yet another long song. Obviously, most folks would tend to feel that the Allmans and the Grateful Dead wrote the book on this concept, but there were a lot of extended cuts that never did seem to get pretentious or boring, and so help me, they're *still* quite listenable. Also, almost all of 'em were *live* versions.

The aforementioned guidelines would of course disqualify such commendable efforts as Side Two of *Abbey Road* or the title melange from Be-Bop Deluxe's underrated *Modern Music* album of the mid-Seventies. What's more, there might even be some debate about which songs (if any) by such progressive behemoths as Yes or ELP would qualify; at any rate, here's a list of "stretch versions" that ought to keep the listener's interest, as well as remind him/her of a type of rock music idea that ain't around too much these days:

"DREAMS OF MILK AND HONEY" (MOUNTAIN): This tune was previously cited in the paragraph about Leslie West in the "Time Warp to the Tone Age" essay; its main two sections consist of a guitar and bass "ping pong" riff duel between West (with his squealing Les Paul Jr.) and the late Felix Pappalardi's buzzing Gibson EB-1, followed by a speeded-up jam that lurches all too awkwardly to a halt. There was so much music crammed onto the LP side on which "Dreams of Milk and Honey" is found that the record company enclosed a small flyer advising the listener that the volume would have to be turned up.

41

Executive Rock

"SAVOY BROWN BOOGIE" (SAVOY BROWN): Boy, did they name this one appropriately. Recorded in a club circa 1969, this monster is perhaps the definitive example of what this British blues band could do, made all the more sad since there's still a combo around sporting the Savoy Brown moniker, although guitarist Kim Simmonds is the only original member (and it's been that way for who knows how long). Besides Simmonds and what would later become the core of Foghat, this incarnation of Savoy Brown had a lead singer named Chris Youlden, an *incredibly* gifted yowler. Youlden was apparently so ugly, however, that his photo on the cover didn't reveal much of his face; he was sporting a stovepipe hat (the shadow of which covered his eyes), a large stogie, and pancake makeup over his acne. That didn't stop the band from arrogantly but rightfully giving this sweat-drenched workout their name, though. Snippets of other songs heard in the middle include "Whole Lotta Shakin'", "Purple Haze", and "Hernando's Hideaway"(!!!). Moreover, the band cranks up again after one ending, and fades out with Youlden's staccato yelping, so who knows *when* they got through.

"WHO DO YOU LOVE" (QUICKSILVER MESSENGER SERVICE): Already noted in a previous essay about audience participation. Yet the first version I heard of this Bo Diddley tune was by some One-Hit-Wonder band in the Sixties named the Woolies. I'd loved QMS's first album, which contained a long, primarily instrumental song called "The Fool", so the second album (entitled *Happy Trails*) picked right up with this sidelong, live nugget, which shows why the first two or three albums by Q.M.S. were their best: Cippolina's trademark guitar, David Freiberg's underrated bass, Gary Duncan's second guitar (rhythm most of the time but some lead as well) and Greg Elmore's rock-steady drumming plus strong vocals made for a classic Frisco sound.

"I CAN'T KEEP FROM CRYING" (TEN YEARS AFTER): Actually, this is an old Blues Project tune, and on *their* live reunion album from the early Seventies, Al Kooper is heard muttering about how royalties from Ten Years After's performances of this song "paid for my car this year", to which another Blues Project alumnus (I think it's Danny Kalb) retorts: "Al has a VW." The listener has two versions of Ten Years After's cover from which to choose: One is found on their obligatory live double set, but the other (and preferable) take appeared on a live triple-set called *The First Great Rock Festivals of the Seventies*, which was apparently Columbia Records' would-be response to the success of the Woodstock soundtrack. This version predates the one from TYA's own live album, but naturally both feature Alvin Lee's rapid-fire guitar histrionics, with snatches of "Sunshine of Your Love", "Cat's Squirrel", etc. thrown in. When Lee showed up many years later on IRS's *Night of the Guitar* live

Lists

album, one of his songs featured many of the same riffs. Some things never change....

"(TURN ON YOUR) LOVELIGHT" (GRATEFUL DEAD): For the record (no pun intended), this is Side Three of the first *Live Dead* album, and is a segue from the first two sides, which consisted of "Dark Star" (Side One) and "St. Stephen" and "The Eleven" (Side Two). "Lovelight" is a two chord romp, including an appropriately short drum duet, witty banter from the stage ("Take yo' hands outta yo' pockets"), and Garcia and Lesh in definitive form. They shoulda ended the album there, on accounta Side Four is a waste.

"FEEL SO GOOD" (JEFFERSON AIRPLANE): Ya notice how a lotta tunes from this genre belong to Frisco bands? I can't remember if Kaukonen and Casady were already into their Hot Tuna offshoot when the Airplane's second live foray, *Thirty Seconds Over Winterland* (on which "Feel So Good" is found) was released, but Jorma and Jack are the featured players on the song. I still have yet to decide whether Papa John's Creach's fiddle is an asset or an annoyance.

"ECHOES" (PINK FLOYD): Definitive Floyd, period. Mysterious, brooding, and downright scary at times (I refuse to use the term "psychedelic" despite the fact that it's the term everyone has always applied to the Floyd throughout the years, and admittedly I've also utilized the cliché), "Echoes" is found on the 1972 album *Meddle* , and should come with a warning sticker on the shrink wrap that says: "WARNING! DO NOT LISTEN TO THE MIDDLE PORTION OF 'ECHOES' IF: (1) YOU ARE ALONE IN THE DARK, (2) YOU ARE UNDER THE INFLUENCE OF ANY TYPE OF CONSCIOUSNESS-EXPANDING SUBSTANCE, (3) YOU ARE RECENTLY DIVORCED, OR (4) ANY COMBINATION OF (1), (2), OR (3)." The banshee-like saxophone will scare the *bejeezus* out of anyone who's even the least bit unstable, for whatever reason.

"FREEBIRD" (LYNYRD SKYNYRD): Awright, call me a bit wishy-washy since the original studio version fades out after 9:08, but I still think it's preferable to the live cut. As a born and bred Southerner I'm outraged that this song was cut in two just to make it fit onto the cassette version of the first album.

"MOUNTAIN JAM" (ALLMAN BROTHERS): Admittedly, almost any cut from the *Fillmore East* live double set would also qualify, but for some reason I've always liked this two-sides-long jam (based on an old Donovan tune) from the follow-up *Eat A Peach*, I guess because there's plenty of Allman/Betts double leads, plus everyone else has solos that aren't long enough to get boring.

"TELEGRAPH ROAD" (DIRE STRAITS): Well whaddaya know: a token Eighties example. The first song on Dire Straits' *Love Over Gold*

43

Executive Rock

album (which is sonically superior to lots of their other works), this is sort of an opus that tells a story, and the last few minutes contain some classic Knopfler guitar licks.

"LOST WOMAN" (THE JAMES GANG): The title of Joe Walsh & Co.'s first release, 'Yer Album, was enough to snag my interest, and this reworking of a semi-obscure Yardbirds number has solos from each of the trio's members, but *all three solos stay within the beat,* and as a result a listener stays hooked. Jim Fox is one of the most underrated drummers of the Seventies. "Lost Woman" clocks in at 9:04. Humor me.

"GREEN GRASS AND HIGH TIDES" (THE OUTLAWS): Critically dismissed as Lynyrd Skynyrd clones (which in a way they deserved since they either chose or allowed themselves to be nicknamed "The Florida Guitar Army"), this tune was of course inevitably compared to "Freebird", since it was the last song on each band's first album, and both begin in one tempo then abruptly shift gears, accompanied by guitar solos comin' at ya from all directions. Nevertheless, "Green Grass and High Tides" is actually a bit raunchier than the Skynyrd anthem was, and the final guitar lick heard as the song crashes to an end (as opposed to "Freebird" fading out) represents one of the *rudest* Stratocaster runs ever encountered.

"HAMBURGER CONCERTO" (FOCUS): Probably one of the most listenable things the Dutch band ever did. This extended work does indeed sound sort of like a concerto played on rock instruments; all of its passages/ movements/segments/whatever make sense, and guitar god Jan Akkerman is in fine form. Another plus is that there's a minimal amount of that damned operatic yodeling from Thijs Van Leer. Unfortunately, Focus's next album, *Mother Focus*, sounded like the soundtrack to a porn film, so perhaps to opine that "Hamburger Concerto" was their zenith isn't too far off the mark.

SIDEBAR: As more of the extended cuts cited here have become available in the Compact Disc format, it's been interesting to attempt to ascertain which ones that were originally longer than one side (medleys or individual songs) have been placed on CDs as *extremely* long tracks; i.e., the uninterrupted versions as originally recorded. The Allman Brothers' "Mountain Jam" clocks in at a mind-boggling 33:40 on the *Eat A Peach* Compact Disc, while the three-side Grateful Dead medley that concludes with "Turn On Your Lovelight" is nonstop (but the songs in the medley are still set up as individual tracks). However, other albums such as Hawkwind's interminable *Space Ritual* still fade out and back in just like their vinyl LP predecessors did.

One last point: Purists will be annoyed that I didn't list Cream's "Spoonful"; that's because it's such a classic that I consider it to have reached Emeritus status and its number has been retired, so to speak.

Lists

So don't expect to hear too much of this kind of music anymore, but time was it was a staple of many groups. I suppose one reason longer songs aren't around much nowadays is the apparently shorter attention span of most listeners; seems like we're stuck with nothing but musical "sound bites" (to borrow a stoopid term from politics), and sometimes I really miss tunes that tend to "snowball".

THERE ARE NO WORDS

"You ever come up with a list of 'desert island top ten *songs*'?" asked Malc (we'd already discussed 'desert island albums').

"Not yet."

"What's the holdup?"

"There's so many to choose from. Does it have to be strictly ten songs?"

"Why shouldn't it be? You thinkin' about other criteria?"

"Howzabout cover songs?"

"Nope."

"What about ten songs within a particular genre, like country or heavy metal?"

"You know good and well you'd want an assortment, like your album list."

"Well, that's true. Instrumentals?"

"Uh..." Malc flinched, so I dove:

"Bingo." (And at the same time, I was thinking to myself: "Whew; there's at least one more column." Our conversation occurred during a time when I felt like I was in a "dry spell" or was perhaps "jogging in place", writing-wise.)

Seems like instrumental music has always been sort of an odd stepchild within the popular music spectrum. Certain genres like surf music (which is now practically extinct) and jazz (which doesn't command the largest section of a record store these days) are primarily wordless, and it also seemed like a lot of instrumentals that made the *Billboard* charts over the

45

Executive Rock

last couple of decades had something else going for 'em, like a movie or event ("Chariots of Fire", "Nadia's Theme", etc.).

It should be noted at this point that as of this writing *Billboard* has a New Age chart, and of course that genre is not only almost *entirely* instrumental, it's a lot more nebulous as well... and maybe that's part of the hype.

Rock instrumentals seem to be an even rarer phenomenon these days, and while some efforts like IRS's "Guitarspeak" series and recordings by veterans like Ronnie Montrose may be of interest to other players (armchair-types included), since when has an album of that ilk been on the charts?

Malc was right; what I tried to come up with was indeed a melange of many musical styles. Most of 'em were indeed guitar or bass guitar songs:

"GREENY" (JOHN MAYALL'S BLUESBREAKERS): Let's go ahead and get the expected token Peter Green song taken care of here at the outset. The curious thing is that Mayall himself ain't even on the track; it's just Green, bassist John McVie and drummer Aynsley Dunbar doing a loud blues jam, but it cooks, of course. My friend Rogene will occasionally try to envision lyrics from certain song's applied to certain other songs with a similar chord structure, which is relatively easy if blues tunes are utilized. He says the lyrics from the Doobie Brothers' "Snake Man" would sound neat if plopped on top of "Greeny", but longtime Peter Green fanatics would probably consider just the *thought* of doing such to be blasphemy. However, sometimes Rogene doesn't have anything better to do with his time (or his mind)...

"MERE IMAGE" (MANNHEIM STEAMROLLER): Many years ago I was a salesman for a wholesale electronics distributor, and I got to hear Mannheim Steamroller's *Fresh Aire* series when such recordings were only retailed in stereo shops. This tune is from *Fresh Aire III*, and I ended up using it to demo some of the audio equipment I was peddling. From what I can tell, it starts out with a simple, singular recorder playing a lilting melody that tends to conjure up a mental image of a small child playing in a field. The recorder is slowly joined by a harpsichord, an oboe, strings and percussion until it sounds somewhat like a "medieval" song (as least, that's the case for me, or maybe I've got my centuries and/or ancient musical genres mixed up. B.F.D.). Then, a drum kit and one of the fattest synthesizers ever heard kick in to bring the effort into a more modern format, yet the oboe is the first instrument taking the melody once the modern instrumentation is heard. It's a brilliant, fascinating and irresistible work, and I probably sold more copies of *Fresh Aire III* than audio items on which "Mere Image" was played, so as far as I'm concerned American Gramaphone Records owes me some commissions.

46

Lists

"CAN I MAKE IT LAST" (BOZ SCAGGS): From the *Moments* album; simply a pretty and melodic song that relies on a guitar plugged into a Leslie speaker (one of those rotating gizmos usually utilized by organs). There's also a nice string arrangement, and overall the tune has a minor Oriental flavor. This one is great to slow-dance to.

"GRAND FINALE" (PROCOL HARUM): From a live album done with a symphony orchestra and a choir; this one is a bit of a stretch in that "Grand Finale" (which the last part of a multipart work called "In Held 'Twas In I") *does* have some "Ooooos" and "Ahhhhs" from the singers, but there ain't no lyrics. This is possibly the most enthralling piece ever done by a rock hand collaborating with a symphony; the arrangement will give you chill bumps.

"WORK SONG" (BUTTERFIELD BLUES BAND): A version of the tune that was popularized by Herb Alpert and the Tijuana Brass. It's found on the classic *East-West* album, and is one of many examples found on there as to why Paul Butterfield and Mike Bloomfield were masters of the instruments they played and the genre of music they purveyed. Elvin Bishop and Mark Naftalin get to solo as well.

"COUNTRY MUSIC (A NIGHT IN HELL)" (STU HAMM): A jaw-dropper. What's intriguing is to watch the reaction of any listener who's never heard the song (and usually they haven't heard of Stu Hamm, for that matter); what's more, sometimes it's necessary to explain to non-musicians that it's a *bass* doing the melody here, not a guitar. Regardless, a neophyte listener will sit there with a ho-hum countenance while Hamm runs through two verses of root-five, root-five, but when he launches into "Foggy Mountain Breakdown" a stereotypical result is that the new listener's eyes bug out like he/she has a goiter, and he/she subsequently stays hooked for the duration. Sure, Hamm and players of his ilk each have a bag fulla chops as deep as the Grand Canyon, but few "show-off" tunes are as much fun as this is, and the, uh, "commentary" from the guy in the audience is a bonus that any musician who's ever played in a bar band can relate to.

"ZERO TO SIXTY IN FIVE" (PABLO CRUSE): Actually, I'd rather hear the longer "Ocean Breeze" by this band, on accounta Corey Lerios' piano is showcased more than it is in "Zero to Sixty in Five"; however, there's a verse of two of singing right at the end of "Ocean Breeze", so I guess this one will have to do. "Zero to Sixty in Five" *does* have a short bit of scat-singing, but no lyrics (a la Procol Harum's "Grand Finale") so it qualifies, as far as I'm concerned. It also rocks a bit more than "Ocean Breeze" and there's some slick slide guitar work on it.

ALMOST ANYTHING BY PAUL JOHNSON & THE PACKARDS OR THE HEPCATS: Veteran surf guitarist Paul Johnson of Bel-Aires

Executive Rock

fame has two aggregations that he activates on occasion; the Packards are a modern surf band, and their *California* album is a don't-miss. The cover describes the contents as "high energy guitar instrumentals", and that's putting it mildly; this stuff is great fun and extremely melodic to boot, so it should be quite appealing to most listeners. There's a Link Wray medley, a sharp cover of "Day Tripper", and sort of a time-warp song called "Mr. Moto", which the Bel-Aires recorded, only to have the tune covered by the Ventures, who had a bigger hit with it than the Bel-Aires did! Johnson's other venture (pun intended), the Hepcats, is an acoustic guitar multitrack effort that's also entertaining; the Hepcats' Christmas album is especially noteworthy.

"PURPLE HAZE" (MICHAEL MANRING): Between this cover and Mannheim Steamroller's "Mere Image", methinks that might be enough New Age stuff for a list such as this; furthermore, another bass "show-off" tune might seem redundant as well, but this solo piece is as amazing as Hamm's goofy fun. When someone is as gifted as Manring is, it seems like sometimes the unaccompanied pieces are more intriguing than the player's efforts with other musicians.

"POPPY" (FRANK MARINO & MAHOGANY RUSH): This is from the *Double Live* album, which I think was recorded in the mid-Eighties (I found the cassette in a cutout bin for a buck; there's no recording information on it at all). Marino's in fine shape here; it's obvious that he's still inspired by Hendrix but he seems to have, er, "matured" to the point that he ain't as much of a clone as he used to be. "Poppy" features some nice octave chording and one segment that blatantly rips off the Doors' extended version of "Light My Fire". Can't say that the album is worth an extensive search, but if you stumble across it like I did, it's worth the cutout price (up to $3.99, in my opinion).

"WIPEOUT" (THE VENTURES): Specifically, the live version from *The Ventures On Stage*, not so much for the guitar licks, but to spotlight Mel's Taylor's impeccable drumming. This guy was rock-steady but every time he added a bit of flash, it was exactly what was needed; no more, no less. Interestingly, "Caravan" (another drum solo-oriented song) is on the same side, and the latter features a primeval bass solo from Bob Bogle.

"SEQUENCER" (AL DIMEOLA): Knowledgeable guitarists know that DiMeola has a much-more-varied and larger arsenal of chops than this dance tune might indicate, but on the other hand it's probably one of the most accessible efforts (for an average listener, of which DiMeola probably doesn't have too many) that the erstwhile Return to Forever guitarist has ever done. It's melodic and fun, yet it also hints at DiMeola's immense talent. The video for "Sequencer" showed him going through a buncha martial arts moves.

Lists

That's an even dozen instead of ten (as was the case with the desert island-album commentary), and Malc was a bit nonplussed: "I can't believe you didn't cite any Alan Parsons Project stuff, as much as you listen to them."

"A lot of their instrumental stuff sounds a lot alike; I was disappointed with that anthology called *The Instrumental Works*. I use a lot of those tunes to end a side of a blank cassette where I don't have enough tape for another song; I'll put on an A.P.P. instrumental and fade out the music as the counter shows how close the tape is to ending. It's gotten to the point where if the Missus and I are listening to something I've dubbed off, and a song like "Hawkeye" or "Mammagamma" cranks up, she'll opine that the side must be fixin' to end."

"You think that's about all such songs are good for?"

"Not necessarily; instrumental songs can be a bit of a refreshing break on some albums. The thing is, if Rogene was trying to transpose lyrics onto Alan Parsons Project instrumentals, hopefully he could come up with some that were a bit more meaningful than some of Alan Parsons tunes that *do* have lyrics; critics have always excoriated the "band" for so-called lyrical banality, among other things."

"Maybe somebody like Keith Reid or Peter Sinfield would be interested in actually writing some lyrics for 'em."

"Don't think so. And in some respects, I hope I don't listen to the Alan Parsons Project as much as you seem to think I do."

WHO'DA THUNK IT?

As the Compact Disc format of recordings began its inexorable encroachment into the record stores of America around the mid-Eighties (and the phenomenon was worldwide, I suppose), I purposely refrained from getting a CD player until I felt like the situation regarding the format had stabilized. Students of marketing concepts know that the initial segment of consumers that "takes the plunge" first on a new product are known as

Executive Rock

"innovators", and I'd been in that group of buyers before, only to end up frustrated. I'd bought a Beta format video recorder, only to see Beta end up as "the Eight-Track of the Eighties", in spite of the fact that it was a better format than VHS from a technical standpoint. I knew all about the differences between U-load and M-load mechanisms, but the format to which I committed ultimately lost the war, at least in the U.S. marketplace.

I'd also bought a particular brand of automobile, and was well pleased with its performance, but the manufacturer abruptly withdrew from the American market. I ended up selling the car to a Polish Air Force officer who was at a one-year school for foreign military personnel at the local Air Force base; I betcha it's changed owners once a year since then, and after that episode I resolved never to be an "innovator" again.

So I didn't opt to purchase a CD player until early 1989. I'd already begun hearing some minor criticism of the format; some listeners opined that Compact Discs didn't sound as "warm" or "fat" as LPs; that CDs were "sterile"-sounding, but since more of the older stuff was becoming available on the new format, I figured it would be worth the investment to be able to have a practically-indestructible copy of something like *The Wall* or *Abraxas*.

As I expected, my CD collection pretty much began with albums that I already had in the LP format. A few new offerings were purchased when they were released, but in some cases I bought the cassette album first, before committing to the CD version, just to be sure the new release was worth it. Tangerine Dream's *Livemiles* is an example of this latter, uh, "concept".

So I've gradually made the switch over the last several years, just like umpteen other consumers. I've joined a mail-order CD club off and on, and have had a card or two punched at a local mall retailer any time I've made a purchase. As is the case with guitars, these days I figure I've just about "maxxed out" on the CDs I've been buying, for several reasons: First, I've just about got all of the "classic" albums on CD that I've been seeking. Secondly, I don't have as much time these days to listen to music, and last, there ain't much modern stuff out there that's all that appealing (ruminations concerning current musical trends will be found elsewhere).

Yet an interesting facet of the *first* reason cited involves certain albums that have finally been marketed on Compact Disc that many people never would have thought were in demand enough to merit the new format. It seems like more and more, the answer to an inquiry if a particular album by So-and-So is available on CD is "Yes".

Most longtime popular music fans have probably wondered at one time or another if some of their personal all-time favorite albums would ever be available on CD (*especially* if their LPs were getting more worn and/or scratched). I can't say that any of what follows would make a revised "desert-island-top-ten" list of mine, but at one time or another I had each of these

Lists

albums in a "twelve-inch licorice pizza" format, and it was a bit of a minor surprise to discover that each one was now available on Compact Disc:

KICK OUT THE JAMS (MC5): Lemmy was right; this doesn't sound as good on CD as it does on record. For some reason it tweaks the tweeters on my bookshelf speakers, and even though it would be unreasonable to expect such a brutal recording to sound crystal-clear on CD, it ended up seeming a bit "murky", for lack of a better term.

But Got-Taw-Mitey is the *energy* still there. From the opening exhortation from the stage (*"Brothers and sisters! I wanna see a sea a' hands out dere! Lemme see a sea a' hands!"*) to the fading applause when the spacey "Starship" tapers down, this decibel-laden juggernaut practically *incinerates* a listener. Songs like "Rambling Rose", "I Want You Right Now" and the immortal "Kick Out The Jams" spew out primeval guitar chords in nothing less than an aural firestorm. And by the way, the introduction to "Kick Out the Jams" comes unedited on the CD; i.e., it's the original twelve-letter obscenity.

It's easy to see why the MC5 inspired Lemmy; listen closely to the end of any song that comes to a crashing climax. The reverberating nanosecond that's heard when the cacophony explodes into silence not only sounds like the tail end of a Godzilla roar, the same resonant "honk" can be heard at the end of any number of Motorhead tunes on *No Sleep 'Til Hammersmith*, which was recorded about a dozen years later.

The raw force of this initial offering from the MC5 made any follow-up anticlimactic; their studio albums were just ho-hum. Forty percent of the band (singer Rob Tyner and guitarist Fred "Sonic" Smith) are now deceased.

FLEETWOOD MAC IN CHICAGO: While some of the songs on this double-set ended up on a CD anthology or two (the imported *Like It This Way*, for example), it's great to see (and hear) these recordings issued in their original presentation; i.e., complete with in-studio banter between the musicians and the control booth, two false starts to "Sugar Mama", etc. Jam session recordings were issued a good bit back in those days (and sometimes certain ones were nothing more than a con), but few were as important (then *and* now) as this one. Hearing the peerless Peter Green as well as Elmore James disciple Jeremy Spencer making music with blues legends from the Windy City is an enthralling experience, just as the British players were enthralled while they were recording these tunes. The reason such an album is important *now* is obvious when one considers what happened to Green and Spencer (and to Danny Kirwan as well, for that matter).

Greg Martin was the guy who told me in 1994 that *Fleetwood Mac in Chicago* had finally been released as an unedited, double-CD set, and I owe him *big time* for that bit of information.

BACKSLIDING FEARLESSLY (MOTT THE HOOPLE): You take what

51

Executive Rock

you can get, I suppose. Technically, I didn't own *Backsliding Fearlessly* on a twelve-inch LP, since it's only been released as a CD anthology, but I *did* own all four Atlantic albums (the self-titled debut, *Mad Shadows, Wildlife*, and *Brain Capers*) from which the songs on *Backsliding Fearlessly* were culled; all four albums were produced by the now-deceased Guy Stevens. Personally, I'd rather have all four albums on individual CDs, but the only example I ever encountered was a solitary copy of *Brain Capers* (which of course I snapped up immediately). The anthology's liner notes even mention songs from the albums that *aren't* on *Backsliding Fearlessly*; what I wouldn't give to hear the likes of the live "Keep A' Knockin' " or the Hoople's instrumental version of "You Really Got Me".

Nevertheless, this is a potent melange (so potent, in fact, that some songs on this CD tweak the tweeters on my bookshelf speakers as well). Mick Ralphs's guitar tone is *awesome;* I don't think he's ever sounded better. Check out "Thunderbuck Ram" or "The Moon Upstairs"; you'll see what I mean.

THE CHARLATANS: Hailed by lotsa folks as the progenitors of Frisco acid rock; their album had a cover painting by Globe Propaganda (which also did covers for San Francisco area bands like Quicksilver Messenger Service and It's A Beautiful Day). This isn't really bona fide psychedelic music; it's more of a mixed bag of all sorts of styles (including covers of "Folsom Prison Blues" and "Wabash Cannonball") along with guitar tones which most likely inspired certain Bay Area players. The Charlatans' first album comes on CD with some follow-up album called *Alabama Bound,* a stoopid hodgepodge of outtakes and extraneous material that could only be considered important by long time, hard-core Charlatans fans (all three of 'em).

LAST OF THE RED HOT BURRITOS (The Flying Burrito Brothers): Apparently I got "under the wire" on this one, because I ordered it out of an ad in *Goldmine;* the dealer had it listed in an "out-of-print CDs" section. The Byrds begat this offshoot early country rock aggregation; they'd be right at home on TNN or CMT these days. This live performance is a definitive sampler: Rip-roarin' licks, bluegrass ditties, a commendable cover of "Six Days On The Road" and the funniest (and sneakiest) song about draft-dodging ever recorded.

PEAKS (KLAATU): As was the case with *Backsliding Fearlessly,* this is an anthology rather than a reissue. I'd owned Klaatu's *3:47 E.S.T.* (their debut), *Hope* and *Sir Army Suit* on LP, and while it's not surprising that the debut album was released on CD (it has the original version of "Calling Occupants of Interplanetary Craft" and was the subject of media speculation/hype that the musicians were actually the Beatles), *Hope* was possibly a better overall effort, with a sidelong saga about a lighthouse-keeper.

Lists

At one point it too was available on Compact Disc, but is apparently now out of print. This anthology is exemplary; it is indeed a collection of what probably have been considered "the best" of Klaatu, and it's replete with songs that show why the Beatles comparison (or con) was inevitable. It's interesting pop music, and well done. Even though that suite from *Hope* isn't on *Peaks*, this is a better anthology than many others.

CHILDREN OF THE FUTURE (Steve Miller Band) and *QUICKSIL-VER MESSENGER SERVICE*: Cited here as a two-fer on accounta these were debut albums by Frisco-based bands that were released in 1968, and in some respects they're definitive performances, not to mention the fact that getting ahold of CDs of these albums was more of an effort than originally expected.

I'd ordered each (at different times) from a record store, only to be advised that the albums were no longer available on Compact Disc. *Children of the Future* turned up on a Japanese CD that I found at the Dallas guitar show (cost me twenty-five bucks); it's still the most unusual and mysterious album Miller ever did. It's got very short songs, very long songs laced with lush Mellotrons, and straight blues like "Key to the Highway"; all in all a very eclectic mix but it's quite listenable. The CD turned up in that record store's inventory after I'd bought the imported disc, so apparently it's available once again.

On the other hand, Ouicksilver's debut turned up as a $6.99 CD made in Canada after I'd been advised it wasn't available anymore, so any extra amount spent on the import version of *Children of the Future* was offset by this purchase. To me, John Cippolina will always be the standard-bearer of the genre of guitarists in which he was pidgeonholed. His searing style was ultimately inimitable (and QMS's first album shows why), but Gary Duncan, David Freiberg, and Greg Elmore were just as important in this hand's sound: Duncan's singing and second guitar (as opposed to "rhythm guitar") were quite expressive; Freiberg had a unique bass tone compared to the likes of Jefferson Airplane's Jack Casady and the Dead's Phil Lesh, and Elmore's drumming was rock-steady. Great tunes like "Pride of Man" and "Dino's Song" plus "Gold and Silver" (an instrumental that lopes along at a jazz-like tempo reminiscent of Coltrane's cover of "My Favorite Things") as well as a remarkable extended song called "The Fool" make this album a definitive work. Even if the Canadian cutout isn't available anymore, this debut is worth finding. Curiously, legend has it that singer Dino Valenti was going to be this band's lead singer but he got busted (Valenti ended up joining the band circa the *Just For Love* album). If he'd been the vocalist from the outset I wouldn't have been a fan; Valenti's singing voice is an annoying whine that alienated me once he *did* join QMS.

Executive Rock

SPACE RITUAL (HAWKWIND): Outer space drone-rock at its finest! A live two-fer from 1973 that was perhaps the band's finest hour. Chock fulla seemingly endless riffs, Lemmy's unique bass stylings (such as they are; after Ol' Snaggletooth was sacked he formed the World's Most Brutal Heavy Metal Band), and bizarre monologues and poetry recitations(?!?). Hey swinging bachelors! Got a first date that isn't working out? Just plop the spoken-word track called "Sonic Attack" on your CD player; she'll he out of your apartment so fast she'll leave a vapor trail (which seems appropriate, considering Hawkwind's musical forte)!

Everyone has all-time favorite albums that they never expected to end up on a digital format, so the discovery of such a CD is probably not only a surprise but a minor delight as well. It would be interesting to determine the age (as well as other demographics) of the purchasers of such semi-obscure reissues, but I don't know how such a survey would be accomplished. Suffice to say that if someone cared enough about a certain band or musician to peruse the pages of *Goldmine* on at least a semi-regular basis, said fan is "into" the artist(s) enough that his/her pronouncements and/or opinions about said artist(s) are probably worthwhile.

IN SEARCH OF...

The obvious follow-up essay to the preceding commentary would be a listing of albums that a consumer might still have on LPs, but he/she has yet to see 'em on Compact Disc. As was the case with the previous list, such "still seeking" choices are probably as individual as the person who's still wondering if he/she will ever see such albums in a digital format.

It goes without saying that some albums noted in other essays besides the one right before this one would need to be cited herein as well (*Hot Ash, Into the Rainbow*, etc.). Add Klaatu's *Hope* and for me that's a good start to noting some favorite albums I still have yet to see on CD.

Another thing that needs to be noted here is that I don't peruse *Goldmine* on a regular basis, so at one point certain albums noted here may have

Lists

been available as CDs (if only as imports), and in some cases they may *still* be available. But when was the last time you walked into retailers like Tower, Camelot and Turtle's (now Blockbuster) and encountered on one of the following albums on Compact Disc?

LIVING WITH THE ANIMALS (MOTHER EARTH): An underrated blues-based aggregation featuring the remarkable Tracy Nelson on vocals. This debut album featured a guest guitarist named "Makal Blumfeld" (uh-huh; sure) on the song that's also the name of the band (and Nelson's passionate shriek at the end of "Mother Earth" will curl your hair). "Down So Low" is simply Nelson and a piano, and it has more feeling to it than a symphony orchestra and a choir combined.

ELEGY (THE NICE): The final release (as the title indicates) from the innovative trio that featured Keith Emerson prior to his ELP association. There's only four cuts (two studio, two live, all of 'em extended) and the cover looks like something Pink Floyd would've considered for one of their albums. The cover of the Byrds' "My Back Pages" is an acquired taste, but the live tunes are commendable. Seems like I saw this on cassette in a cutout bin some time ago...

LEVEE BLUES (Potliquor): If this ain't swamp rock, I'd like to know what is. Creole and other bayou-based musical influences pervade this second album from a band that generally wasn't cited in the echelons of Southern Rock (probably because they weren't on the Capricorn label, for one thing...). The leadoff cut, "Cheer", got a bit of airplay, but the lusty singing and energetic playing on covers like "Red Rooster" and "You're No Good" are still viable.

ZACHARIAH SOUNDTRACK: I never saw the bizarre "Rock & Roll Western" from which these tunes by the likes of the James Gang are culled, but if it was as weird as some of the dialogue that shows up at various points on the soundtrack seems to indicate, it might oughta be sought out at a video store.

THE WORST OF HOMER AND JETHRO: These guys were to Country music what Spike Jones was to Big Band (and what Frank Zappa was to Rock, I suppose). Homer Haynes and Jethro Burns were supremely talented musicians, but their overall presentation was to lampoon anything and everything they got their hands on. This, uh, "anthology" features collaborations with June Carter and the aforementioned Spike Jones, and will have you laughing out loud even if you're not a fan of humorous re-workings of hit tunes. Haynes and Burns did release an album that demonstrated their chops; not surprisingly, it was titled *Playing It Straight*.

ALMOST ANYTHING BY THE DICTATORS: Especially *Manifest Destiny*. Any band that let itself be fronted by a so-called professional wrestler deserves to be heard at least once.

Executive Rock

STREETNOISE (JULIE DRISCOLL, BRIAN AUGER & THE TRINITY): This band was noted in "The Cover Story"; this double-set is their definitive release.

TRIUMVIRAT: Just when Emerson, Lake & Palmer were getting a bit too artsy in the mid-Seventies for some of their fans, this clone band from the Continent appeared, sounding like ELP's earlier efforts. The debut album was satisfactory, but Triumvirat's follow-up, *Spartacus*, indicated that the band was pretty much a flash in the pan.

LESTER "ROADHOG" MORAN AND HIS CADILLAC COWBOYS LIVE AT JOHNNY MACK BROWN HIGH SCHOOL: An offspring of Homer and Jethro, as far as most listeners would be concerned, on accounta this is a comedy album by the Statler Brothers. Anybody who grew up listening to small town radio stations will be swept up into a time warp with this one. There are basically three programs; one is the concert noted in the title (with fights breaking out in the audience), an audition tape sent to Mercury Records, and a short Saturday morning radio show that is nothing less than quintessential Americana. It takes talent to recreate something this *bad*, and it's hilarious.

There have been others that might have ended up on this list, but I've recently been made aware that they're now apparently available on CD. The Bubble Puppy's album is an example; I'd seen some albums by their International Artist stablemates the Thirteenth Floor Elevators in CD cutout racks, but repeated rummaging failed to unearth the Puppy's offering, and in mid-'95 I noted that there was a Bubble Puppy European CD available. Since the band was a One-Hit-Wonder (and "Hot Smoke and Sassafras" can be found on more than one oldies anthology), paying a higher-than-usual price for the album might be a regrettable experience, in spite of the presence of a tune called "Elizabeth", which has some seminal twin/harmony lead guitar work on it. I just don't remember enough about the Bubble Puppy album to know if it'd be worth the price, but if and when I *do* happen to find it in a cutout bin, I'm sure I'll buy it, but I'm not really *looking* for it. Such an encounter would be accidental and unlikely, since as noted in the previous essay I've pretty much stopped collecting CDs.

Nevertheless, there will be occasions where something will waft out from a "classic rock" radio station that will not only bring back certain recollections for some listeners, the song will cause many people to wonder if attempting to find the album by the artist(s) who made such music would be a worthwhile effort. As is the case with a list of songs or albums that would be sought by certain individuals, the *reasons* for seeking out such music are probably as unique as the person doing the "research".... as are the memories that such songs can revive.

OCCURRENCES

TWO 1968 "FAREWELL" CONCERTS:
A Study in Contrasts

I was feeling a bit rocky. The previous night I'd graduated from high school, and had stayed out until almost sunrise celebrating. Woods (who was a year older than me) was already home from college, and why my mother woke me up to tell me he was on the phone (when I'd only had a couple of hours of sleep) I'll never know; the only thing I could figure was that she didn't know what time I'd gotten in, which was probably for the better.

"You goin' to the Yardbirds concert tonight?" Woods asked.

"Mglthphft." My tongue felt like it was wearing a wool sock. I'd heard on the radio that the British Invasion group was coming to town to perform for two nights at the ridiculously named "Montgomery International Speedway", which was a half-mile asphalt oval out on the Old Selma Highway. Around the beginning of the Sixties, we used to badger our parents to take us out there on Saturday nights to watch Modified Sportsman drivers like Friday Hassler, Red Farmer, and the Allison brothers (Bobby and Donnie) roar around the track, creating a din so loud that conversation was impossible, even if we were screaming at each other. There was also the opportunity to laugh at and berate a local perennial also-ran named Bill Bazzell, who was sort of like a redneck grease-monkey version of Bob Uecker.

One memorable Saturday night, Bazzell actually won one of the qualifying heats. This must have excited him terribly, because in the next race he wrecked, totalling his car.

"You goin' or not?" said Woods.

"Patti won't want to go", I opined.

"Yeah, well, you were out with her until all hours last night anyway," Woods

57

Executive Rock

said, "and besides, who knows when you'll get a chance to see 'em again?"

If I'd had a crystal ball I could've told Woods that the correct answer would've been "Never", because it turned out the 1968 "tour" was the swan song for the 'Birds, and I guess that's somewhat understandable, considering some of the locales they played.

So Woods, a couple of other college boys, and yours truly showed up at the racetrack on the first evening. The band's equipment was set up on a semi-trailer on the front straightaway, facing the grandstand. There probably weren't more than a few hundred people in attendance.

The last studio album the Yardbirds issued was called *Little Games*; the title cut had gotten a moderate amount of airplay, and the album's cover photo showed the faces of the four band members who were on this tour: Singer/harpist Keith Relf, drummer Jim McCarty, bassist Chris Dreja, and guitarist Jimmy Page.

Clapton had been gone from the band for years, and when original bassist Paul Samwell-Smith left, rhythm guitarist Dreja moved over to bass to make room for Page, who for a short period of time shared guitar duties with Jeff Beck (as seen in the movie *Blow-Up*). After Beck's departure, the band carried on as a foursome.

Jimmy Page..... I'd heard that this skinny Limey sporting the Telecaster around his kneecaps was supposed to be every bit the hotshot guitarist that Beck was; I hadn't heard any of their most recent LP except the aforementioned title cut on the radio. As it turned out, I guess I'd have to say Page and the rest of the band did the best they could for a group in decline.

In person, Keith Relf sounded like he did on recordings: loud, plaintive, and always just a bit flat, plus he was also a passable harmonica player. McCarty appeared to be an affable bloke who was enjoying himself; he was quite energetic but rock steady. Dreja, on the other hand, didn't put on much of a show at all, musically or visually. While he was watching the others quite closely (for cues?), about all he did was thump one note at a time.

Naturally, most of the aspiring musicians in the audience couldn't take their eyes (or ears) off Page. He appeared to be *squeezing* the neck of the Tele, ferociously *wringing* notes out of it. The violin bow trick on "I'm Confused" (which never did appear on a Yardbirds studio album but instead showed up on the first Led Zeppelin album as "Dazed and Confused") drove the crowd bonkers. Page's Telecaster appeared to have a pearloid pickguard; every now and then while Page was on the move the scratchplate would catch the light, sparkling and flashing in an unintentional minor special effect that added to the music somewhat, especially since there wasn't a light show....

The Yardbirds made the best use of what they had to work with, I guess, tromping through all their hits plus a couple of blues jams. We left the concert feeling like we'd gotten our money's worth, yet somehow sensing that this band was indeed on its last leg.

Occurrences

Later on we heard that the local radio station that had sponsored the Yardbirds concerts had gotten the band to play a few extra songs the second night for a *dance contest*, of all things.

Page, of course, went on to the zenith of rock with Led Zep; Relf (who's now deceased) and McCarty were in the first incarnation of Renaissance(!), and who knows what happened to Dreja. A while back there was even some Yardbirds reunion group called "Box of Frogs", but the song or two I happened to hear by them were so uninspiring I didn't even make the effort to determine who was in the band.

For aficionados of rare recordings, there was actually an album released (more than once) in the early Seventies of a concert recorded on that final tour. Titled *Live Yardbirds featuring Jimmy Page*, it was marketed to capitalize on the success of Led Zeppelin, and was the subject of threatened litigation. It too is not particularly inspiring, but is nevertheless an accurate representation of what the Yardbirds sounded like in their final days. For fans of Jimmy Page, it might be desirable as a curiosity item; otherwise forget about it.

I still carry an old Polaroid "Swinger" photograph in my wallet that I took in October of 1968; "Swinger" cameras, for those who may not recall, were very low-priced Polaroid outfits that took small black-and-white pictures, and the user had to coat the newly developed print with some hideous-smelling fluid from a sponge-like accessory to protect it. Battered and worn, the photo has nonetheless held up through the years, as has the music of its subjects, because one weekend that Fall, Woods and I hitchhiked to Georgia to see the Cream on their final tour.

I'd only been in college for a few weeks, and it was about 200 miles from Tuscaloosa to Atlanta, but I'd already worn out my copy of *Wheels of Fire* over the summer, so I was bound and determined to see Clapton, Bruce, and Baker on their last hoorah (unlike the Yardbirds concert, this was being billed as part of the "farewell" tour).

As it turned out, the Alabama Highway Patrol took us most of the way on the outward journey, and Woods's sympathetic relatives (with whom we stayed) loaned us bus fare to get back rather than see us thumb, but despite getting back on campus at 3 AM Monday morning, I'm still glad we went, because to this day I *still* have not heard that much musical power come from three individuals in concert (and that includes the bombast of Emerson, Lake & Palmer).

The concert was held in Chastain Park, which sort of reminds one of a junior version of the Hollywood Bowl, except there's no moat. There were to be two shows (we went to the earlier one), and tickets were available at the gate for $4.50 (those were the days).

Executive Rock

The warm-up act was the Terry Reid Group; Reid was an over-hyped British singer/guitarist who had a high-pitched-but-raspy-and-plaintive voice. He tended to specialize in his own unique covers of such tunes as "Bang Bang" and "Season of the Witch" (that made *three* versions of the latter tune, written by Donovan, which were out around that time; the others appeared on the Vanilla Fudge's third album and the Kooper/ Bloomfield/Stills *Super Session* album). Reid was politely received, but he never went on to any particular commercial success.

In between acts, I wandered down in front of the stage and milled around with other camera-toting fans, gawking over to the sides of the stage to see if I could spot anyone or anything worth shooting; I felt a bit inferior with my dinky plastic Swinger while most of the others were sporting expensive-looking units with large lens attachments. Ginger Baker appeared offstage, and some guy who sort of resembled Clapton was also seen; the most recent photos I'd seen of Clapton showed him with a thick mustache and a shag haircut way past his shoulders, and this fella kinda looked like that, except he was a bit chunky and had a beer gut. I had a feeling this wasn't the guitarist because I thought Clapton was thinner, so I didn't take any pictures, but I was in a minority; most of the others were firing away so rapidly, the front of the stage sounded like a field of crickets.

Ultimately we were shooed away, and out walked the trio; Baker and Bruce pretty much resembled their publicity photo images, but Clapton's appearance was a *shock* compared to previous pictures I'd seen: He'd cut his hair to where it now had sort of a "Pageboy" style and he'd also shaved his mustache. He looked like a scrawny, anemic girl. Bruce donned his usual Gibson EB-3; Clapton strapped on a single pickup, "reverse" Gibson Firebird I. Both of them had two Marshall stacks each.

The opening number was another shock: I never would've figured Cream would have tried to pull off "White Room" live since the tune was so heavily produced with strings, etc., but Bruce and Clapton wailed in harmony vocals instead, and the song crashed into the audience like a sledgehammer.

The band surged through their most popular songs in admirable fashion, just as the Yardbirds had done some months earlier. Eric Clapton was of course the center of attention, but *he barely even moved during the entire concert.* That didn't dampen the crowd's enthusiasm, of course, and I couldn't imagine how in the world he got all of those sounds out of a single pickup guitar. Jack Bruce, on the other hand, was a dynamo; stomping around onstage, grimacing, jerking. Ginger Baker was *all over* his drum kit, his red ponytail flapping madly. By the way, the most requested song from the audience was "Toad", and Baker delivered when it was played...

Clapton kept breaking strings on his Firebird; it happened so often that at one point Baker chuckled: "Eric Clapton will now do a tap dance...". Rather

Occurrences

than replace another one, however, Clapton handed the Firebird to a roadie in exchange for a beautiful late Fifties cherry sunburst Les Paul, for which he requested a round of applause; the audience responded appropriately. I was mildly surprised he didn't play this terrific-sounding instrument during the entire concert, but since he'd already had a similar guitar stolen around the time of the *Fresh Cream* album, I can understand why he'd only want to have another one on hand just in case of such an "emergency".

And so it was that the sun set about the time the first of the two shows ended; seemed somewhat appropriate to Woods and me. I got into trouble for missing a post-football game fraternity party while we were in Atlanta, but I didn't care. I came back from Georgia with sounds and images branded into my brain that I've never forgotten.

A few weeks later Cream did their final concert in England, and the farewell has been preserved on video, although I don't own a copy (yet). I hope the viewers of this concert will be as similarly blown away as Woods and I were in Atlanta. The music these three men made was phenomenal; since they were constantly pushing, nudging, and challenging each other, it's now clear to me why this band was so fragile: When something takes that kind of pounding on a regular basis, cracks are bound to appear.

Some say Cream took music to places that will never again be reached. Rumors are constantly flying around about a possible reunion tour; I don't think it'll ever come about, but if it does I'll be there, at least in spirit if not physically, since the new addition in the Fall of 1989 has kept me closer to home.

Meanwhile, I occasionally pull out the Polaroid to show to some younger upstart musician; I usually preface displaying the photo by remarking something like: "Oh yeah? Well look who I got to see in 1968." *That* usually takes 'em down a notch or two.....

Executive Rock

LIVE AID AND FARM AID RE-EXAMINED — HALF A DECADE LATER

I stumbled out of bed at 2 AM and staggered into the den to see what the beginning of the much-heralded Live Aid benefit for world hunger was like; it was at that time that the Australian feed began. "Oz for Africa" didn't exactly get me going at that hour, because after 75 minutes I still hadn't seen one Aussie band with which I was familiar: No AC/DC, INXS, not even the Little River Band. I might have gone ahead and set the VCR, but at the time the model I owned wasn't a stereo version, so I suppose I figured I wasn't missing much, and I decided not to tape anything while I caught some more shut-eye.

About three hours later it was up again, this time for good. I'd missed the opening set by Status Quo at Wembley, but caught the end of Style Council's performance. I was fortified with caffeine and several blank cassettes, hoping that the effort and expenditure would prove worthwhile (and, I suppose, also hoping that the effort and expenditure of the *participants* would prove worthwhile as well). I also wondered how many other viewers were in my situation, as the media had reported that blank audio cassettes and blank video cassettes had been selling at a brisk pace in the last few days prior to the event.

The Missus had to work that particular Saturday, and she recalls the excitement in my voice when she called home a couple of times during the day as I told her about such things as the Phil Collins/Sting collaboration and the Who reunion. Son-of-a-gun, this was actually working.

When it was all over late that evening, and I finally had time to digest everything, I decided that certain acts or individuals should be cited for their respective accomplishments (good, bad or ugly). Accordingly, the following awards might jog a memory or two for those who didn't tape any of the proceedings:

THE EVENT/LOGISTICS

BEST PARADOX: Wasn't it difficult to accept the fact that humanitarian extraordinaire Bob Geldof was the same individual that portrayed the brooding, paranoid rock star in the movie *Pink Floyd-The Wall*?

WEIRDEST PRONOUNCEMENT: Joan "Pinko" Baez's "This is your Woodstock". *PHFFFFT.* Live Aid was, as advertised, a tightly organized "global jukebox", while I've already rendered my humble opinion on the so-called Sixties milestone in the first paragraph of "The Guitars of Woodstock" in the September 1989 issue of the *NMT*, so I see no need to get repetitive here (I can't stand redundancy, and if I've said that once I've said it a thousand times...).

Occurrences

MOST VALUABLE PLAYER (GELDOF EXCEPTED): Phil Collins.

BEST PROOF THAT GELDOF WAS RUNNING A TIGHT SHIP: U2 getting the hook for running overtime.

BIGGEST LOGISTICAL DISAPPOINTMENT: The loss of the satellite signal during the Who's set.

FAILURE TO CHECK EGO: Madonna. Did you see those backstage shots?

STOOPID PROGRAMMING MOVES: Tie between cutting away from performances for commercials, and showing those bozo MTV veejays staring ga-ga at monitors during certain groups' sets. Dishonorable mention: The ad-hoc radio network broadcast wasn't completely live; some performances were replays.

THE MUSIC

MOST UNUSUAL TIMING: Judas Priest. 10:30 AM was a bit early for that much leather and Rob Halford's banshee shriek, but they were well received.

BEST SET: Queen. I didn't know they still had it in 'em.

WORST SET: Madonna. Like watching those humanoid robots at Disney World.

INTRODUCING A CLASSIC: Live Aid marked the first time I heard Dire Straits' "Money for Nothing".

BEST COLLABORATION: Paul Young and Allison Moyet.

WORST COLLABORATION: Mick Jagger and Tina Turner. More strutting than a peacock convention. Runner-up: Bob Dylan with Ron Wood and Keith "Zomboid" Richards.

MOST PATHETIC: David "Land Whale" Crosby. The cameras were hardly ever on him during both the CSN *and* CSNY reunions.

HURRY UP AND WAIT (FOR NOT MUCH): Thompson Twins.

BEST NEWCOMER: Power Station. Even with an alternate lead singer, they delivered as promised. Tony Thompson oughta scare the bejeezus out of every drummer on the planet.

BEST REUNION: Black Sabbath. Surprisingly, the Sabs get the nod over the more-anticipated Who and Led Zeppelin sets. The Zeps' performance in particular was incredibly sloppy, but they had a nostalgia factor going for them.

WITH A LITTLE HELP FROM MY FRIENDS: George Thorogood showed some class by bringing on Albert Collins and Bo Diddley. Runner-up: Santana, who pulled in Pat Metheny.

FUNNIEST MOMENT: The chants from the Philadelphia audience during Bette Midler's introduction of Madonna.

MOST MEMORABLE VISUAL MOMENT: The Wembley audience's hand choreography during Queen's "Radio Ga-Ga". Runner-up: Bono

Executive Rock

dancing with an unknown female during U2's set.

COMEBACK AWARD: Teddy Pendergrass. Runner-up: Eric Clapton.

BETTER FINALE: Wembley by a mile. The British climax was fitting, since they closed with "Do They Know It's Christmas", the progenitor of the whole musicians-united-for-humanitarian-causes concept, and the tune was an appropriate length. On the other hand, Philadelphia's "We Are The World" slogged *on and on and on* like some arthritic behemoth, and while Patti LaBelle has got the pipes (her rendition of "Whiskey Blues" in *A Soldier's Story* will give you goose bumps), her vocal histrionics here got very annoying very quickly.

Post-Live Aid disappointments include of course the fact that Geldof was reported to have been considering reneging on his vow not to market a Live Aid album and/or concert video, but nothing ever materialized, except for a commendable photo album of the day's proceedings. More importantly, it turns out there's a lot of questions about how much good Live Aid actually accomplished. I'm not about to get into the socio-political ramifications of this event, but a chilling exposé was later found in the usually hipper-than-thou and boring *Spin* magazine. Some post-concert occurrences in Africa appear to bear out the misgivings of the likes of Huey Lewis & the News, who pulled out of the Philadelphia lineup (being lambasted by Geldof for doing so).

Now as for Farm Aid (two months later), I'll admit I wasn't anticipating that event as much as I had been looking forward to Live Aid; my lack of enthusiasm was due to the feeling that Live Aid would be hard to top, plus there was an abundance of ambivalence in the pre-concert publicity. Farm Aid and certain other subsequent all-star events have seemed to get into the dreaded "gray area" when something that's supposed to be benevolent starts spewing out political rhetoric (usually one-sided and alienating), thereby putting off who knows how many potential donors.

So what were these ominous signs prior to the concert? Geldof, when asked about the copycat event, opined that he was more concerned about someone losing his life rather than losing his livelihood (that didn't stop Kris Kristofferson from yelping from the Farm Aid stage: "God bless Bob Geldof and Bill Graham for showin' us how to pull this off!"). What's more, TV interviews with many concert-goers showed a great deal of apathy concerning the purpose of Farm Aid; a stereotypical comment sounded something like: "Naw, man, like I'm just here for the *music*."

And sure enough, there were several denunciations from the stage, an example of which was Tim Hutton's reading an open letter to President

Occurrences

Reagan from Neil Young (correct me if I'm wrong, but Young's *Canadian*). Such occurrences were made even more awkward by an embarrassed and befuddled Brenda Lee(!), who was co-hosting; she had to ad-lib a disclaimer each time such statements were heard.

Nevertheless, there were some memorable musical moments at the first Farm Aid as well, and I'd be doing the performers a disservice if I didn't note certain acts at this event as well:

MOST VALUABLE PLAYERS: John Mellencamp's band, who backed up several performers throughout the day, including John Fogerty and Bonnie "I'm Almost Famous" Raitt.

TROUPERS AWARD: Tom Petty & the Heartbreakers, who performed fine sets at both Live Aid and Farm Aid.

NAME THAT TUNE: What was the title of the song Don Henley sang while standing in a greenish spotlight? I'd never heard it before, nor have I heard it since, but it was quite meaningful in its attempt to address the farm issue.

COMEBACK AWARD: John Fogerty, natch. Ol' Flannel Shirt is back! Runner-up: Roy Orbison, although his guitarist's wild, Van Halen-esque solo in the middle of "I Gotta Woman" was incredibly out of place.

SHOWSTOPPER!: B.B. King, who's been doing "How Blue Can You Get" for *decades,* and I swear, it never gets tiresome; I always whoop whenever he gets to the part about "I gave you seven children.... and now you wanna give 'em back!". Technically, King also appeared at Live Aid, albeit from neither Wembley nor Philadelphia; his set was a satellite feed from Holland.

THUMB YER NOSE AT BILL GRAHAM: Foreigner, who were rebuffed by Graham in an attempt to sign up for Live Aid, delivered a strong set at Farm Aid, which included a fully-robed choir being shuttled onstage to back them up on "I Want To Know What Love Is".

COMING ATTRACTIONS: Eddie Van Halen sat in with Sammy Hagar's band.

I'LL NEVER FORGET WHAT'S-HIS-NAME: Some country singer, in a lame attempt to get the audience to remember him, introduced one song by blurbing: "Here's the first song I've released since I left Pure Prairie League."

APPROPRIATE DRESS REQUIRED: It was a hip touch to see Mellencamp as well members of Alabama sporting blue corduroy Future Farmers of America jackets.

WEIRDEST SEGUE: Lou Reed's performance being followed by Kenny Rogers. Like going from a zombie to Santa Claus. The older Lou gets, the more he looks like some kind of bug.

INAPPROPRIATE DRESS REQUIRED: It's my understanding that

Executive Rock

the band known as Southern Pacific became entrenched in the upper echelons of country music, but I wasn't familiar with them back in '85, so it raised my eyebrows to see a *country* band whose male lead guitarist was sporting a pink solidbody guitar, dropped earrings from both ears, pseudo-hip sunglasses, a visor, and a George Thorogood-type sneer.... turned out it was ex-Doobie Brother John McFee.

I won't comment on all of the other all-star events that were inspired by these two 1985 happenings (including more Farm Aids); suffice to say that the concept has just about run its course, and maybe that's for the better. Live Aid and Farm Aid were, however, pioneering examples of how music and technology are capable of making people *worldwide* of aware of certain situations that may need addressing from a benevolent standpoint (hands off for me, though, if things start turning political). I'm unsure if I'll ever make a concerted effort to tune in such goings-on again; I know for sure it won't be at 2 AM to view a buncha Aussie bands.

MTV'S DECADE OF DECADENCE

QUICK! Gimme the names of all five of the original veejays on MTV! Now, I know this might sound like a question one would possibly encounter on one of those "900" telephone trivia games (or worse yet, on MTV's own "Remote Control" quiz show), but for those who might have forgotten (and you have my utmost respect if you have), the original lineup of hosts and hostesses for Music Television when it appeared in 1981 was a blatant exercise in tokenism: Nina Blackwood (blond-maned airhead/bimbo/ditsoid), Mark Goodman (stocky, curly-haired; had sort of a dark complexion and resembled Epstein on "Welcome Back Kotter"), Martha Quinn (wide-eyed, gee-whiz ingenue; showed up in 1990 as a cast member of "The Bradys," which seemed appropriate), J.J. Jackson (jovial black with a stage name if I ever heard one), and Alan Hunter (scrawny, sandy-haired WASP).

There's a large Army base about seventy-five miles southeast of my

Occurrences

hometown; it's the headquarters for Army Aviation (meaning helicopter training). My business travels have taken me into that area frequently over the years, and although several different types of choppers can be seen in the skies over Fort Rucker and surrounding communities such as Ozark and Enterprise, whenever I see a "Huey" model darting along the treetops, I always hear (mentally) the intro to the Doors' "The End" (Krieger's sitar-like guitar drone and Morrison's disembodied vocals). The connection between the Huey and my silent singalong is of course the appearance of "The End" on the soundtrack to Francis Ford Coppolla's film *Apocalypse Now*.

Accordingly, I wonder how many people who've watched MTV on a relatively regular basis over the last ten years can't hear a song on the radio without immediately visualizing the video that accompanies it? I submit the following tunes and their, uh, "unforgettable" images as examples:

"SOME LIKE IT HOT" (POWER STATION): Day-Glo bras.

"DREAMS" (VAN HALEN): U.S. Navy Blue Angels aerial acrobatic team.

"KEEP YOUR HANDS TO YOURSELF" (GEORGIA SATELLITES): Yokels in the back of a flatbed truck playing Ampeg/Dan Armstrong instruments.

"RIGHT ON TRACK" (BREAKFAST CLUB): Trash-trimmed guitars (a la Devo, circa 1978), and women dressed up as chickens.

"MEXICAN RADIO" (WALL OF VOODOO): Stan Ridgway's head poking up from a bowl of beans, chanting: "Radio, radio...."

"TRUE FAITH" (NEW ORDER): Live characters in a cartoon-like scenario (this one was just plain *weird*).

The main problem I have with music videos is the danger that yet another portion of the human brain's "Creativity Section" may be stifled, in much the same way that other brain sections which were fully operational before the advent of *television itself* might now be permanently hobbled. Think about it: How many older relatives have told you about listening to the likes of "The Shadow" or "The Lone Ranger" on an Atwater-Kent or Philco radio half a century ago? Surely each person listening to radio programs back then was conjuring up visuals in his or her own mind to accompany the narration, so radio (or for that matter, *books)* ought to stimulate the ol' gray matter better than TV.

Now, before anyone thinks I should have titled this article "I Don't Want My MTV", let me advise the reader that such a title has already been used *twice*. An underrated fusion group called the Fents had a tune called "I Don't Want My MTV" on their (only?) album *The Other Side*, and a certain sanctimonious Motor City writer also wrote a critical essay with

Executive Rock

the same title when MTV first began to be noticed.

Actually, there are some aspects of MTV that appealed to yours truly in times past. There were some videos were almost like very short art films (a brilliant concept, since most people can't stand *full-length* art films). For some reason, a disproportionate number of these were in black-and-white; examples include Springsteen's "Atlantic City", Don Henley's "Boys of Summer", and "Every Breath You Take" by the Police.

What's more, some of the humorous videos have been worthwhile, *especially* if they lampoon other videos, films or TV shows. Dave "The Human Whoopee Cushion" Roth's visuals for "Just a Gigolo/I Ain't Got Nobody" had him hosting something called "Dave TV"; Roth was shown barging in on sound stages occupied by such luminaries as Michael Jackson, Billy "The Human Q-Tip" Idol, and Willie Nelson. In an classic example of video one-upmanship, Phil Collins' video for "Don't Lose My Number" even topped Roth's; the Singing Cabbage Patch Doll was shown auditioning video concepts to accompany the tune. Among the ideas that were demonstrated were videos resembling the Cars' "You Might Think" (Collins as a flying bug), and a clone of *The Road Warrior* (Collins and other band members as post-nuclear Apocalypse bikers chasing a fuel truck; Phil's sporting a Mohawk). What gives Collins the nod in this category is the fact that he even lampooned a Roth video, "California Girls", in a definitive electronic version of "in yo' face".

Regrettably, some performers were more into using visuals to sell their albums *from the outset,* letting looks count for more than the music. The insufferable Duran Duran is the hands-down winner here; although there are many examples in all music categories. Moreover, the music video scene quickly (and not unexpectedly) acquired its own version of Spike Jones or Homer and Jethro (who recorded comedy versions of songs in the Big Band and Country & Western fields, respectively), but Weird Al Yankovic's video offerings pale in comparison to the arrangements of these musical ancestors.

Critically excoriated in the beginning as too limited in their format (even being called "racist" by some for not programming enough black videos), MTV ultimately tried to become all things to everyone, showing heavy metal segments, rap segments, call-in request segments, etc. They also came up with a weekly Top 20 Countdown of videos, and I wondered how they came up with the rankings; at one point it seemed like the Christian metal band Stryper was getting a lot of airplay due to some call-in requests, but I don't recall seeing the same video(s) on a Top 20 Countdown during the same weeks they dominated the call-in segments. While I've stated before that I think Stryper's gimmicks (including bumblebee outfits) were corny, something doesn't quite add up here.

Occurrences

On Sunday, April 15, 1990, I de-programmed MTV from my TV set. The day also happened to be Easter, and on any weekday would have been IRS deadline day. Yet those two occasions had nothing to do with my decision to see if I could do without music videos 24 hours a day.

Turns out that as of this writing the only times I've programmed the channel back in was to catch some special concert events. 1990's Knebworth concert was worthwhile, but 1991's "Rock in Rio" was as boring as MTV itself seems to have become. So I've learned that I don't need to let a music video take the place of my own cerebellum whenever I hear a certain tune. However, anytime I happen to hear "Doin' It All For My Baby" by Huey Lewis & the News, I immediately start thinking about a mad professor in a castle trying to jump-start a Frankenstein monster...

RATING THE MTV CONCERTS

One of the best things about Music Television as far as viewers who were also *musicians* were concerned was most likely the series of concerts MTV used to show on Saturday nights. 'Course, any musician who was sitting at home on a Saturday night instead of playing a gig might be subject to ridicule from working players.... At any rate, many of the players I know (full-time *and* part-time) seem to have a disproportionate amount of *live* albums in their LP/cassette/CD collections, so it's understandable why they'd be oriented towards concert videos; equipment and stage moves could be checked out, interesting licks picked up, etc.

MTV didn't make it to my local cable system until 1984, and from what I could tell at the time, the Saturday night concert series had been a staple for quite a while. I tried to set the VCR every week, even if I didn't particularly like the group. Sometimes I got surprised, sometimes disgusted, sometimes delighted; I rarely got bored by the proceedings.

Many of the concerts were made for release on video software, and are available in most video stores. In some cases I went out and purchased the concert video outright after having seen in on MTV; I was that impressed.

Executive Rock

Some shows weren't really bona fide concerts; they were documentaries with some concert footage, and that probably miffed quite a few viewers; I know I for one got p.o.'ed by the likes of *Dire Straits in Israel* and others.

Seems like the Saturday night concerts began winding down with a "Live at the Ritz" series, taped for MTV at a New York club. Among the participants was the then up-and-coming Guns 'N Roses, and I lost interest around this time. It's my understanding that MTV still shows a concert every now and then, but I'm usually not aware of it, since as stated in last month's column I de-programmed MTV from my set in April of 1990. Nevertheless, there were some memorable moments from some of the Saturday night concerts, and some of them need to be cited:

ERIC CLAPTON LIVE IN HARTFORD, CONNECTICUT 1985: Released in software as *Live Now*, this is the best Clapton I've ever heard, period. Grand versions of "Motherless Children", "Tangled in Love", and a spectacular medley of "Badge" and "Let It Rain". What's more, the closing song is the absolute, definitive version of "Layla". A must-see/hear.

BANGLES LIVE IN PITTSBURGH: Fodder for feminists; the Bangles can indeed play their instruments, but I defy any male viewer to keep any sexist thoughts out of his head when Susanna Hoffs does an oh-so-slow split onstage right in the middle of one song.

BANDS WHO WERE BETTER LIVE THAN ONE MIGHT HAVE THOUGHT THEY'D BE: The Fixx, the Cars, and Mr. Mister (who were taped at the Ritz).

BANDS WHO STUNK LIVE: The Cult (from the same Ritz show as Mr. Mister, which was one of the weirdest double bills of all time), and Y & T. I opted to pay no attention to the Cult after seeing them in concert on MTV, then did a considerable about-face when "Sonic Temple" came along. Y & T's riffs are better than many heavy metal bands, but their stage dialogue was predictable and boring.

BEST CONCERT BY AN OFFSHOOT GROUP: David Gilmour's Hammersmith-Odeon concert from 1984. In many ways I prefer this concert's version of "Comfortably Numb" better than any Pink Floyd versions. The other guitarist in this band was none other than the redoubtable Mick Ralphs.

HOW'S THAT AGAIN?: "What's she saying?" asked the Missus. The "she" in question was Christina Amphlett of the Divinyls, whose singing voice is somewhere between a hiccup and a burp, and neither the Missus or I could understand the lyrics. Taped in concert at the Ritz, the Divinyls were *ferocious,* and I think Amphlett mooned the audience at the end of one tune. Runner-up in the unintelligible category is Big Country, since I

Occurrences

couldn't understand the stage patter.

GOLDEN EARRING LIVE IN HOLLAND: I'm almost embarrassed to admit that I liked this concert. Consisting of grand total of six songs over sixty minutes, the Dutch Boys win the "Old Warhorse" award, since they were competent and tight, despite salt-and-pepper hair. Of particular note was the drummer, whose drum kit sounded like tuned cardboard boxes. He was mugging for the camera, and during his solo on "Radar Love", ol' Caesar stood up wearing an outfit with a bunch of touch pads wired inside of it, and, uh, played with himself. And yes, he leaped over the drum kit at the end of the last song.

DON'T MISS THESE: The Police's 1983 Synchronicity concert (taped at the Omni in Atlanta), and INXS's 1985 concert in Melbourne, Australia. Both are definitive performances, and both are available in software.

COMPARISON INVITED: The Tears for Fears "concert" on MTV was actually one of the aforementioned documentaries, titled *Scenes from the Big Chair*. I never saw their bona fide concert video *In My Mind's Eye* on MTV, so if you're looking at your video store, be sure to look for the latter tape. Tears for Fears is perhaps the most intellectual pop band since Steely Dan, and they're good at their craft in concert.

WORST EDIT ON A LIVE ALBUM: Judas Priest released a live double album and a live concert video from the same tour, but the live album doesn't have their thunderous cover of Fleetwood Mac's "Green Manalishi". I saw the concert video on MTV and bought the live album without bothering to check the list of song titles, thinking the contents were the same. Lesson learned.

MOST MEMORABLE AUDIO-VISUALS: A song called "The Voice" from Ultravox's *Monument* concert film. At the conclusion of this tune, drummer Warren Cann kept the beat going, and the guitarist, bass guitarist and keyboard player (Midge Ure, Chris Cross, and Billy Currie respectively) came out front to three hexagon-shaped Simmons electronic drums spaced a few feet from each other, and began pounding out electronic polyrhythms with drumsticks. Neat stuff. All of the band members were wearing black uniforms, and the staging was pretty elaborate (the concert was recorded in 1982). I found an import LP of the soundtrack, but I'm unsure if a videotape is available.

I'LL BUY THE CD OR VIDEO IF EITHER ARE AVAILABLE: The third incarnation of King Crimson (Robert Fripp, Adrian Belew, Tony Levin and Bill Bruford) recorded a live concert in Japan just after releasing their third (and last) album, and showed that they had the chops in performance as well as in the studio. It was intriguing to be able to determine who got which outworldly sounds out of their respective instruments, and Tony Levin can indeed play a mean Electric Stick.

Executive Rock

WORST CONCERT: Traffic live at Santa Monica. Apparently this was released to capitalize on Steve Winwood's success, and if I was him I'd be embarrassed.

Readers may have other memorable things that stick in their minds from MTV's Saturday concerts, but all in all I'd have to say that it was one of the best things MTV had going for it as far as my viewing was concerned. If and when they crank up another concert series I may program MTV back into my set, but don't hold yer breath. If the day never comes when I say "I want my MTV" I won't be surprised, and I won't consider myself as an intellectual cripple simply because I ignore music videos and their relevance.

MOSH DIVE INTO ETERNITY

If he chose to do so, Jim Fuller of Big City Productions could blackmail me with an "outtake" from his *Vintage Guitars in America, Vol. 2* video, so I'm gonna defuse that potential controversy right here and now:

Y'see, when Fuller and his associate Brian Wilson came through my hometown in early 1992, the videotaping session that involved my comments was done at Hank Williams' grave. Fuller wired me up with a lapel mike, then he let me do an introductory commentary about where the segment was being shot; I noted that Montgomery was also the home of such musical luminaries as Nat King Cole, Toni Tennille, and Tommy Shaw. Then I did an impromptu anti-drug commercial. I wheeled around to face Williams' tombstone and launched into a Sam Kinison-ish diatribe; as I recall, it sounded something like: *Hank, you drunken junkie! What the hell did you hafta o.d. for? You coulda made millions of people happy with your singin' and your playin' and your songwritin', but you blew it, you DUMBASS REDNECK!!!"*

Longtime fans of Luke the Drifter would probably want to organize a lynch mob upon hearing such raving and ranting, but those who think I needed to be a bit more reverent in such a place need to be advised that

Occurrences

sitting in front of the Williams plot was a 55-gallon drum that was full of empty beer cans; a solitary pool cue was also poking out of the container.

The point is, I really felt that way about Williams' self-inflicted demise, and that particular opinion is usually applicable whenever I hear about some entertainer whose death is for the most part due to the fact that he/she didn't take care of himself/herself, regardless of whether or not I was a fan of the recently-departed star.

Accordingly, I'd have to admit that my reaction when I heard about Kurt Cobain's suicide was to wonder what he could have accomplished if he'd had his act together (umpteen others have probably had similar ruminations about umpteen other dead rock stars, so such contemplation isn't anything new).

The grunge "phenomenon" came charging out of Seattle after I'd already de-programmed MTV from my television, but I still heard some occasional Nirvana or Pearl Jam tunes on a local radio station. I bought *Nevermind* after seeing and hearing the "Lithium" video, and what I heard on the album was quite potent. Not only did I seem to hear the snarling anger of Seventies punk (whether or not such anger in *both* musical genres was/is legitimate is another matter), there also seemed to be pain and/or angst as well (and how much credence should be given to such so-called pain and/or angst is also another matter). Nevertheless, the sound and fury of Nirvana's riffs were of definite interest.

Cobain seemed to be a master at coming up with songs that had brooding, low-volume verses followed by a chorus that would practically *detonate* right in front of a listener. Examples of such tunes included "Heart-Shaped Box", the aforementioned (and appropriately titled) "Lithium", and to a lesser extent, "Smells Like Teen Spirit" and "In Bloom".

So while I respected most of Nirvana's music that I heard, I wasn't a fan; therefore when I heard about Cobain's death, I didn't get on the phone to the *Vintage Guitar* home office and ask them to bump the column that was scheduled for the next issue 'cause I was sending 'em a "dated" column that had priority (such *was* the case when I found out about the deaths of Semie Moseley and Toy Caldwell). Besides, it's hard to have any strong feelings about the loss of a player in a musical genre that I wasn't "into" all that much, particularly since I do feel so strongly that Cobain's demise, which was self-inflicted like Hank Williams', was also *stupid and inexcusable* like Williams'.

Before somebody starts slinging "old fart"-type invective in my direction (Cobain was born the year before I graduated from high school), let me ask how often during the media coverage of Cobain's death (particularly the verbal hand-wringing on MTV) it was pointed out that Cobain and Courtney Love (who ain't exactly a role model either) had a nineteen-

73

Executive Rock

month-old daughter? What kind of future can that child look forward to, and what kind of legacy did Cobain leave *her*?

One reason I find myself grousing so intensely about this particular aspect of such a sordid story is the fact that I know of a local situation where a child was suddenly a member of a single-parent household due to the irresponsibility of the other parent. 'Nuff said; I don't feel it's necessary to go into details.

As alluded to earlier, I did watch some of MTV's "coverage" (for lack of a better term) when Cobain died; it was basically a melange of older Nirvana reports, Nirvana videos, and a couple of interviews. It marked the first time I'd ever seen the "Smells Like Teen Spirit" video in its entirety; I noted that most of the cheerleaders had tattoos.

Nirvana's *Unplugged* concert was also presented, and there was a haunting moment right at the end of the last song ("Where Did You Sleep Last Night"). Cobain sang most of the tune in a near-mumble, bumping his voice up an octave to a near-shriek towards the end. The song lurched to a stop, and just before singing the final lyrics, Cobain opened his eyes (which were closed for most of the near-shriek portion), and the look on his face was one of bewilderment and terror. Whether it was staged or not I'm not sure, but that splitsecond image of Cobain's countenance seems to speak volumes about his stability, especially now. He may have played old left-handed Mustangs and Jaguars, but that moment on *Unplugged* now seems to have been prophetic at the very least.

Less than a week after Cobain's body was found, I talked with a 26-year-old Seattle resident about the reaction to Cobain's death out there. This guy doesn't consider himself to be a so-called Generation X member; he has a decent job and works hard at it. Like me, the only Nirvana album he has is *Nevermind*. He likes it because of its "hard edge"; he says it's "aggressive" (my opinion too). He also says he doesn't identify with the lyrics, calling them "very negative" (my opinion too). Moreover, he opined that the stereotypical reaction among his peers in the city of the Space Needle concerning Cobain's death was something along the lines of "what a dumb ****."

So a southpaw, so-called god of grunge has gone to the grave. I suppose I'll give a listen to further Nirvana material that happens to get released, but don't gimme none of this "hero" or "martyr" ****, 'cause I ain't buyin' into *that* particular facet of the Kurt Cobain "legend". As far as I'm concerned he's left an extremely dubious legacy, not just for Frances Bean, but also as to what his place in the annals of popular music should be.

Occurrences

BULLFROG BLUES/IN TERMS OF TWO

I can tell you the exact date and location where I made the discovery: Monday, September 12, 1994, on I-10 East near DeFuniak Springs, Florida.

It had been three and a half weeks since my thyroidectomy; my recuperation seemed to be progressing fine, but this was the first overnight trip I'd made in my "legitimate"/"day" job since the operation. I'd stayed home a week, then had gradually begun puttering around to my accounts, working half-days, then a few full days as my strength, mobility and endurance began to improve.

I'd finished making sales calls for the day, and was tooling towards my motel room. I'd popped Cream's *Wheels of Fire* into the cassette player, and as the live portion began, I realized that I hadn't really felt like doing any singing since my surgery, and I'd always been able to do a passable job on the vocals to "Crossroads" whenever my bar-band had opted to play it (which was usually at practice instead of at a gig). Admittedly the song's vocal histrionics were at the upper end of my range, but I could usually pull it off without embarrassing myself. As the cassette went through the introductory instrumental verse, I planned on singing along once the vocal portion came up (as most people traveling by themselves would probably do). When Eric Clapton began warbling "I went down to the crossroads", I was right in sync with him.

And what came out of my throat was a croak that sounded worse than Wendy O. Williams, ex-"singer" for the Plasmatics.

Worse than Christina Amphlett, "singer" for the Divinyls.

Worse than whoever the "singer" is for that gawdawful grindcore group called Morbid Asshole ('TRADITIONAL VALUES' READERS PLEASE NOTE: I'm pretty much one of ya, but I feel so strongly about the repugnancy of this band, which in reality goes by the moniker of Morbid Angel, that I feel the sardonic lampoon of their name is appropriate. The "vocalist" sounds like Regan, the possessed little girl in *The Exorcist*. Humor me.).

Worse than Marianne Faithful when she belched out "Broken English" on "Saturday Night Live" some years ago.

I mean, I was so mortified, the hair stood up on the back of my neck. I rewound the tape to the beginning of "Crossroads", waited again for the first verse of vocals, took a deep breath and tried again.

Same result.

I hadn't expected this facet of after-effects from surgery in any way, shape or form. I'd known going in the I might be a bit hoarse afterwards, perhaps permanently, but it still came as a shock to discover that my so-called singing voice was for all intents and purposes no longer in exist-

Executive Rock

ence. The thyroidectomy *had* to be done, and I didn't regret having such surgery, but I slipped into a minor funk because of the obliteration of my singing capability. A couple of weeks later I was doing a telephone interview, and had established enough of a rapport with the interviewee that I admitted to him that I got a bit down in the dumps on occasion because of the surgery's effect on my singing. The interviewee advised me not to be depressed, but to try and "work around it; come up with an alternate approach."

"Yeah, but there ain't much of a market for Tom Waits impersonators", I muttered, which evoked a chuckle from the interviewee.

As it turned out, there wasn't any permanent damage to my vocal cords, but since the surgery was more "extensive" than expected (but not more "serious"), it's taken longer for my voice to recover. As I write this, it's been about six months since the thyroidectomy, and my voice still cracks on occasion; as for singing, I've gotten to where I can pretty much handle songs in the key of G ("Crossroads" is in A, so that's the next goal).

I realize that such a minor problem like a change in one's voice is insignificant when it comes to health (especially if the most profound result is an inability to sing in a part-time bar band), but the circumstances made me wonder about how a big-name entertainer would react if he/she had the same problem. I bet it'd be pretty traumatic.

Even before the unexpected discovery about my voice, I'd already pondered how my lifestyle was going to be different due to the surgery. I thought about such changes before the thyroidectomy and while hospitalized as well, as anyone who has major surgery would probably do during his/her post-surgery hospital recuperation. Let me tell you something: If you're horizontal and wired up to oxygen, an IV, a catheter, and pneumatic doo-dads on your legs that contract every thirty seconds or so, and *you don't care,* then you're where you need to be, and you've got a plethora of time to ruminate.

1994 was a fairly tumultuous year; lotsa big things happened in the socio-political arena as well as the entertainment field.... and sometimes one couldn't tell the difference. As for my family, the number '2' was involved in more than one facet of how we fared in 1994. We moved twice, and ultimately I had to have surgery twice. Another personal facet was the fact that I actually attended two rock concerts, the first ones I'd attended in seven years.

And one way that the number '2' might figure into a perspective on 1994 for many readers of *Vintage Guitar* might be to consider reactions (personal and collective) to the suicides of Kurt Cobain and Danny Gatton. The demographics of this magazine's readership lead me to believe that most people who read *VG* on a regular basis probably experienced more

Occurrences

angst due to Gatton's death than Cobain's, but I'd also bet that the *total* number of persons that miss Gatton's playing is *far less* than those who profess to be Cobain devotees.

Hell, Cobain's demise turned out to be an international media event that was milked for the balance of the year. Some weeks after he shot himself, *Rolling Stone* and *Spin* sported near-identical Cobain portraits on their covers, and one article in one of those issues actually compared Cobain to Jesus Christ (Don't ask me whether it was in *Rolling Stone* or *Spin*. I forgot, and such an item isn't worth researching to clarify as far as I'm concerned). *Rolling Stone*'s editors also marketed a Kurt Cobain book before the year was over.

MTV weighed in with a four-hour Nirvana special some weeks after Cobain's death; it consisted of a well-produced documentary plus two live Nirvana shows (*Unplugged* and the New Year's Eve '93-'94 concert). It was fairly straightforward and not nearly as maudlin as their "coverage" had been immediately following the suicide. Did anybody notice that Pat Smear's guitar of choice for most of the New Year's Eve show appeared to be an old Hagstrom? And while Krist Novoselic's pogoing looked amateurish (he looks like a second-string high school basketball player), he held down the beat impeccably.

Sardonic condemnations of Cobain were heard from expected sources, including Ted Nugent. Da Nuge's invective was countered by such intellectual luminaries as Bobcat "Smokey" Goldthwait, who told "Later" host Greg Kinnear that "Nugent hasn't had a hit since before Cobain was born." The hype seemed to slog on for the entire year; around Christmas Courtney Love was doing interviews and was back out on the road.

This essay is slated to appear in the issue of *Vintage Guitar* that will be released around the time of the first anniversary of Cobain's death, but the 'timing' factor is not the main reason for writing it. Ain't it curious that the primary prattle herein is about Cobain, not Danny Gatton? The demons that plagued Gatton were every bit as monstrous as Cobain's, and in my opinion that's the case for *anyone* who successfully opts to check out early.

Yet Danny Gatton's demise caused barely a ripple in the mainstream media. Both of these guitarists played great music, *within their respective genres,* and therein lies part of the problem (or con): While Gatton's expressive Telecaster tricks defied categorization, Cobain's ranting was part of the so-called 'Generation X' phenomenon, which amounts to nothing more than overblown media hype, according to a lot of folks with whom I've talked, and that's pretty much my point of view as well... considering the minuscule amount of time I've paid attention to such a so-called phenomenon.

Executive Rock

The point is, I had my own health problems in 1994, and took the proper steps to get better, but my health problems were physical, not emotional. I stand by my opinion that Cobain left a dubious legacy, and while I'm not going to say the same thing about Danny Gatton, I wish Gatton had taken the proper steps (if he could have) to get better. And quite frankly, I wish Kurt Cobain had done the same thing. Circumstances like the deaths of these two leave too many people asking "Why?", and such is the case for any person who takes his/her own life, famous guitar player or not.

One last (possible) facet where the number '2' may have figured into 1994 on a personal basis is the fact that after I spent years looking for old instruments in pawn shops, flea markets, and vintage stores, the bulk of my collection is now on display on two walls of my new office. The assortment of instruments pretty much fulfills the goals I set for my own collection efforts, yet I sometimes find myself thinking: "Okay, Mose, you've just about got what you wanted; now what are ya gonna do with 'em besides stare at 'em?"

But that's another subject for another column.

A FEW MOMENTS WITH THE MASTER

The initial instructions I received from B.B. King's tour manager seemed simple enough... *too* simple, in fact.

He'd phoned a few days before Mr. King was due to play in my area, advising me to show up at the band's bus about an hour or so before showtime (Mr. King was closing out one evening of a three-day festival at a medium-sized burg; other performers included John Anderson, Jr. Walker & the All-Stars, Confederate Railroad, and blues guitarist Debbie Davies). It was a family-oriented event replete with arts & crafts exhibits, kiddie rides, etc., and almost every town the size of this one has such an event each year, right?

I was a bit nonplussed, wondering how I'd make my presence known to the tour manager if the bus had already arrived by the time I got to the

Occurrences

concert venue. I'm still naive about some of the facets of putting on live events; my usual procedure has been to show up at a concert hall quite a while before my appointed time to interview artists, but this was a multiple-act venture, with performers and equipment being shuttled on and off more than one stage. While I was sure it was quite well organized, I had a bit of (ultimately unfounded) trepidation that somehow I'd get lost in the shuffle, but it was a case of "fear of the unknown" on my part, I guess.

Attempts at helping out my situation in advance included arriving at the venue *before* the tour bus, and hand-lettering a sign with the tour manager's name on it (to flash at the bus driver, I supposed; such notices are often seen in airports). However, while I was waiting for authorization to enter the performers' area, a long white limousine pulled up; the driver advised he was on the way to pick up Mr. King, so I knew then and there that Mr. King himself wasn't on the tour bus (it made for some intriguing observations later).

Once I was cleared to hang around the backstage area, I chatted with some of the promoter's security personnel (I remembered some of 'em from a ZZ TOP concert in the Fall of '94). As the tour bus pulled in, dozens of people who had backstage passes crowded around it, brandishing album covers and posters for autographs (there was even a guitar or two). I stayed out of the way and positioned myself by the door that was the entrance to the performers' lounge and dressing rooms, hoping that the fact that my hand-lettered sign was bright yellow was a plus.

Musicians piled out of the bus and made their way into the lounge area. A man with a calm-but-organized countenance stopped on the way in and told me he'd be with me in a few minutes; it was immediately obvious who he was. The tour manager returned and advised me to go on in, saying: "B.B.'s going to do a press conference when he gets here, then you can talk to him."

The lounge area featured a buffet set up for the band; the fare included meat loaf and butterbeans. I chatted with one guy about their previous night's engagement (turned out it was Mr. King's son Willie; apparently several members of Mr. King's family accompany him on tour).

I ambled back to the area where the press conference would be held. I sat down next to a news reporter for a local TV station, who I immediately alienated by referring to her as a "talking head" (turns out folks of that ilk consider it to be a denigrating term). There were perhaps two dozen people in the room, and from what I could discern they were all from what might be termed "general" media (print *and* electronic).

Soon, the aforementioned limousine pulled up outside; the entrance to the press conference area wasn't the same one where the musicians on the

Executive Rock

tour bus had entered, so apparently the backstage gawkers weren't aware that Mr. King had arrived (and that's probably for the better). Accompanied by his tour manager and a couple of security people, in walked soon-to-be septuagenarian guitarist Riley B. King.

I did a double-take. If Mr. King hadn't been wearing glasses, I'd have sworn I was looking at Chester "Howlin' Wolf" Burnett. Mr. King's hair was closer-cropped and a bit grayer than his publicity photos indicate, and he was wearing a loose-fitting, brightly-colored short sleeve shirt. In fact, his entire band was attired in such shirts (which they all wore onstage; a smart sartorial move since it was a humid Southern night in late May).

Greeting the press conference with a "How's everybody doin'?", the King of the Blues settled into a chair behind a table and immediately began fielding questions. Most of the inquiries were of the "softball" type, but Mr. King had ready and eloquent responses to anything the press asked. Soon, the appearance of the tour manager next to the table made it obvious it was time to wrap things up, and as the media began dispersing the tour manager gestured for me to follow him as he escorted Mr. King from the area. Thirty seconds later, I was sitting in a small, curtained-off dressing area, talking one-on-one with a man who was making blues records before I was born (I'm 45).

Doing "in-the-flesh" interviews is obviously preferable to telephone conversations; an interviewer can pick up on some nuance that would be unknown if the interview was being done via long distance, and whether such a nuance is verbal or in the form of a facial expression or gesture, it can be a definite plus when an interview is done. B.B. King was no exception, and his relaxed demeanor put me at ease, making my task all the more enjoyable and hopefully worthwhile. And I'll have to say this: Of all the interviews I've done with notable guitarists and bassists, Mr. King came across as the most self-effacing yet confident player with whom I've conversed, and in my opinion that's yet another reason why he's earned the position of respect that he has among fans and other players as well.

I had approximately thirty minutes with Mr. King, and attempted to make the most of it; I suppose it might have appeared that I was jabbering a bit rapidly at times, but I knew the time I had was limited (of course, I also tend to talk fast when I'm excited, so I'm sure that was a factor as well). Once again, the appearance of the tour manager made it obvious it was time to wrap things up. After packing my tape recorder back into my briefcase, I headed outside to watch the show backstage.

B.B. King's approach to keeping things simple with his equipment is also applicable to his entire band. There were, however, *two* drummers; I looked forward to hearing how their interplay meshed. A minimum of lighting (simple colored stage lights, a couple of spotlights behind the

Occurrences

audience) also seemed to add to the "no frills" ambience.

As is the case with many entertainers, the band did a couple of warm-up numbers before the star was introduced; they proved themselves from the outset to be competent and professional. Various players soloed, and the drummers had their act together every bit as well as, say, Butch Trucks and Jaimoe.

Ultimately Mr. King was escorted to the rear of the stage, and strode front and center when he was introduced, a black Gibson "Lucille" model strapped onto his frame. The guitar looked like it belonged there and nowhere else in the world. The first stinging note that B.B. King evoked from his instrument brought a roar of approval from the thousands who had gathered for the show. I've often conversed with guitar players about famous players who could hit *one note,* and you'd know who it was. Who thinks that B.B. King *doesn't* belong on such a list???

And you know who I was thinking of while I was watching Mr. King ply his trade? The late Arthur Fiedler, of all people.

Years ago, "60 Minutes" did a profile of the Boston Pops conductor that came off as less-than-flattering; Fiedler let himself end up being portrayed as a cantankerous curmudgeon who was so feeble he could barely make it to his position in front of the orchestra. Yet when he was conducting, he was somehow transformed into an energetic master of his craft.

The point is, B.B. King is not a grouchy, doddering old man like "60 Minutes" purveyed in its Fiedler profile. But chronologically, Mr. King *is* a senior citizen, and while he has full mobility, he seems to go at his own pace when he's not onstage. As his interview hopefully indicates, he's also very eloquent and erudite.

But something almost magical happens when Mr. King is in front of an audience. He's in his element, and knows it. His theatrics add to his music immeasurably: Mugging, grimacing, wiggling his hips; he even began flapping his arms like a bird when he got to the line in "Stormy Monday" about how "the eagle flies on Friday". His energy was *absolutely contagious.*

It's obvious that Mr. King is in charge of his band when he's onstage, but it's a "loose dictatorship", for lack of a better term. He allowed all of the other band members to solo, and at one point stretched out a certain tune, turning his back to the audience momentarily and calling out "One mo' time!" to his associates.

For a while, Mr. King sat down in a chair that was brought onstage, but that didn't stop him from playing, and the meaningfulness of his music wasn't affected one iota. As noted at the conclusion of the interview, the performance lasted almost twice its scheduled time.

Since that memorable evening, I've already thought of umpteen other

Executive Rock

questions I'd like to ask Mr. King should the opportunity of a follow-up interview transpire; keep your fingers crossed that such will eventually happen.

Among the decorations on my office walls is a limited edition print of B.B. King (advertised in *Vintage Guitar* some time ago). It's #206 of 650, and was signed by the artist and Mr. King; it was a gift from some good friends. It's all the more unique because my father made the frame for it out of some old barnboard from Lowndes County, Alabama. To say that I look at that print differently since 27 MAY 95 is an understatement.

I've gotten into discussions with musicians and music fans about the terms "musician", "artist" and "entertainer", and how each term (or any combination of them) might apply to specific performers. Such a "concept" often makes for some spirited conversations.

And for what my opinion's worth, B.B. King is a consummate example of all three of those terms. Anybody wanna debate it?

IN MEMORY OF RORY GALLAGHER

The title of this essay is straight to the point; there's no subtitle with a meaningful or catchy phrase, and there's no oblique hook to it as was the case with "In Memory of Peter Green" (some people might have considered the Peter Green essay title to be pretentious).

The point is, the type of music purveyed by the late Rory Gallagher was straight to the point as well. Whether fronting the "heavy/psychedelic blues" band known as Taste (which first brought Gallagher to public notice) or his own solo aggregation, the Irish guitarist's searing, evocative licks and no-frills vocals earned him a longtime position of respect and admiration among other guitarists.

The self-titled Taste debut album was loud, unpolished, and more or less unheralded among the general public when it was released in 1969; it was probably lumped in with umpteen other British blues bands' efforts despite the fact that Gallagher hailed from the Emerald Isle. But more

Occurrences

than one player I knew back then got *awfully* excited by the band's renditions of blues standards like "Sugar Mama" and "Catfish", not to mention their original material. There was also a unique cover of Hank Snow's "I'm Movin' On" and something called "Hail", which was simply Gallagher and an acoustic guitar; I have yet to figure out how he managed to coordinate his singing and playing on that song. So imagine the Who paying homage to Delta and Chicago blues musicians and you've kinda got an idea what Taste's approach was; the album's available on CD and is worth finding.

The follow-up album, *On the Boards*, took a slight jazzoid approach on some songs (including the title tune); a saxophone was heard on more than one track. I don't think Taste's *Live at the Isle of Wight* was released in the U.S.; it's available on CD as well. That's all of the Taste albums I ever heard about. Ultimately Gallagher embarked on a solo career that was more or less that of a journeyman musician, and I agree with Eric Shoaf's comment (in the notice of Gallagher's demise that was in *Vintage Guitar*'s August 1995 issue) that the live albums from his solo career were standouts. One tune purveyed when Gallagher appeared on the old "In Concert" series was called "Hands Off"; my then-girlfriend and I were watching the show, and I wisecracked that she'd been telling me that a lot lately (she broke up with me a few weeks later). I don't think "Hands Off" was on either of those live albums, but it was a potent tune.

I'm not trying to sound maudlin, or like I'm trying to take a "now-it-can-be-told" line, but the fact is that at one point an interview for *VG* with Rory Gallagher was in the offing. The folks at I.R.S. sent me a copy of his early Nineties album *Fresh Evidence* (he looked and sounded great, and was sporting that old familiar Stratocaster on the cover), and they put me in touch with Gallagher's manager (his brother) in London, who opined that Rory would be glad to do an interview.

But I never heard from him again, in spite of my occasional mailing of a then-current issue of *VG*, showing the folks in London how much the magazine was growing. I just plain couldn't understand why such an initially positive reaction from Rory Gallagher's brother would be followed by absolute silence from the other side of the Atlantic.

It was ironic that I discovered the apparent reasons for no further contact from Gallagher's management company in a letter from a *VG* reader in Pennsylvania, who wrote to me concerning the Peter Green column. He mentioned almost in passing that Rory Gallagher, who (according to the writer) had been slated to be on a Green tribute album, had died the previous week.

Technically, Rory Gallagher did appear in *Vintage Guitar*, albeit in a photograph only. One part of Randy Bachman's interview in early 1992

Executive Rock

showed Gallagher backstage at a B.T.O. concert, examining Bachman's much-modified Stratocaster known as the "Legend"; the first part of the photo's caption read: "Battered Stratocaster Lovers Unite!"

I'll bet many *VG* readers already feel like Gallagher was to blues/rock Strat players what Peter Green was to blues/rock Les Paul players; i.e., a consummate example. Both were capable of some of the most passionate playing on the planet, utilizing classic/icon (and very different) vintage guitars.

And Rory Gallagher's hideously-worn '61 Strat can be viewed whenever it's convenient for many fans, as is the case with the magnificent sounding Les Paul formerly owned by Peter Green (as noted in the column on Green, the 'Burst is in Tony Bacon's Les Paul book). Rory Gallagher's Strat is on Page 75 of *The Ultimate Guitar Book*, and many guitar lovers would probably opine that it sounds just as magnificent as the Peter Green Les Paul. Count me among the folks with such an opinion.

Yet another possible basis for comparison between Rory Gallagher and Peter Green might be to speculate as to what extent each player "lived the blues" in addition to playing blues music, but that facet of those musicians' respective lifestyles won't be examined or discussed herein (this ain't no supermarket tabloid).

A night or two after I found out about Rory Gallagher's demise, I had a mild case of insomnia. I got back up (the Missus and the Princess were way into Dreamland), turned on the stereo and donned the headphones. Then I slid Taste's first album into the CD player. Without even realizing it at first, I began playing air guitar, whomping out the "E" and "D" power chords that introduce "Blister On The Moon". It felt good.

GENRE-MANIA!

DO THE COLLECTIVE GUILT BOOGIE!

One of the earliest episodes of the old "Don Kirshner's Rock Concert" television series was called "Saturday Night in Macon"; it featured concert hall performances by the Allman Brothers Band and the Marshall Tucker Band, as well as some outdoor tunes from Wet Willie (their backup singers were known as the Williettes....).

Also included (apparently as literal comic relief) was a monologue from the then-up-and-coming Martin Mull. "Let's talk about the blues", he said to the camera, flashing that smug, condescending smirk of his. Mull's ruminations, as I recall, included an admission that he used to think the blues could only be played by "five skinny English guys with long hair, with a horn section on one side of the stage plus a trio of black female backup singers on the other side." After a few minutes of commentary about so-called roots of blues music, Mull pulled out a baby bottle and a ukulele, then began playing and singing what was supposed to be a parody, but due to the ludicrous scenario (the baby bottle was being used as a slide), the sketch didn't seem to be all that funny, and I think the laughter was "canned".

And that performance happened over twenty years ago.

Many tomes have been written about the evolution of blues music, its Delta and Chicago variants, and its heroes and heroines. It's always interesting to read some author's assertions about how such a uniquely-American brand of music came about, particularly since the author probably hasn't "lived the blues" himself/herself. The reason "lived the blues" is in quotation marks is on accounta the "concept" can be as unique as each individual who may think he/she is affected. B.B. King's been commenting about such for years, and his observations would make more sense to an average music

Executive Rock

fan than any number of books written by (primarily white) academics.

The point is, since music is a form of entertainment (therefore a form of "escapism" and/or "optional"; this proposition will be dissected further in the introduction to "The Rock & Roll Curmudgeon"), it can be a dubious achievement if and when a performer is supposedly "living the blues" in an effort to make his/her presentation supposedly more authentic. It isn't necessary to list certain performers and their malefactions at this point, and when I mentioned the idea that some musicians and singers let their personal lives get so out of crank that it affects their performances, my friend Rogene sought to refine such a generalization:

"Well, then, what kind of so-called prerequisite do blues performers need?"

"How should I know? What matters is the performance! I'm talkin' about *playing* authentic blues music versus a *lifestyle*. Granted, if a person's been through some troublesome times, it can, and perhaps *should* affect the meaningfulness of his/her songwriting and/or performance. What I can't stand are juice-outs, no-shows, and lackluster gigs by musicians that your average working stiff paid good money to see and hear. Said stiffs deserve a decent performance."

"Such subpar performances due to the reasons you cited aren't necessarily exclusive to blues musicians," Rogene observed.

"Absolutely. "Living the blues" could be applicable to musicians playing anything from "Little Brown Jug" to "Lithium", as far as I'm concerned."

For some reason, it seems like the popularity of blues music has been somewhat "cyclical", for lack of a better term. Foghat's Lonesome Dave Peverett once observed that the blues always seems to come around and shake things up a bit whenever such is needed. Being as how Peverett has been a pretty good student of the John Lee Hooker school, he's in a position to know..... but on the other hand, he also fits the stereotype proffered by Martin Mull.

But other players fitting the Martin Mull stereotype have indeed "lived the blues" at various times in their respective careers, and may still be doing so, for that matter. Peter Green is an obvious example, as is Eric Clapton. However, Green's withdrawal from the popular music scene occurred over a quarter-century ago, and Clapton's career has probably been considered spotty by blues guitar lovers who were enraptured by his fiery technique when he was the guitarist for John Mayall's Bluesbreakers.

At least E.C. came out with a blues homage album called *From the Cradle* in 1994 (but I know more than one Peter Green aficionado who wasn't too impressed). While Clapton's offering was a new recording, around the same time ZZ TOP released an anthology called *One Foot in the Blues*, which brings up another facet of the fathers-and-sons concept of blues roots:

Y'see, Texas is for all intents and purposes its own musical *planet,* from

86

Genre-Mania!

what I can tell, and that includes the type(s) of blues music emanating from the Lone Star State. It may be influenced by Delta and Chicago blues, but the likes of Lightnin' Hopkins, T. Bone Walker and Freddy King begat the likes of Rev. Billy Gibbons, the Vaughan Brothers, and others, and it's definitely a different diversion. The sheer size of Texas and its polyglot musicality should make it understandable why Texas blues would be something with its own hot-and-raucous style.

And to their credit, the Lil' Ol' Band From Texas has been instrumental in attempting to make folks aware of the debt owed to earlier blues musicians by becoming involved with the Delta Blues Museum project in Mississippi; they also salvaged some timber from the birthplace of Muddy Waters and had some "Muddywood" guitars built with the wood. Such actions are positive examples of acknowledging musical roots without laying a guilt trip on somebody, and it ought to be appreciated by fans of both blues *and* rock.

Indeed, so much of rock music has been blues-based for so many decades that many blues disciples probably feel that such a debt never will be repaid, so that's why it's been refreshing in recent times to see smaller labels like Black Top and Alligator dedicating themselves to modern blues artists as well as veteran players (Black Top's roster has included the likes of Ronnie Earl and Earl King).

A lot of blues "fathers" as well as "sons" who are now deceased can still inspire new generations of listeners through their recordings; that is, hopefully such inspiration would be musical rather than seeming to advocate a self-destructive lifestyle, as unfortunately seems to happen all too often (examples range from Robert Johnson to Mike Bloomfield).

And those two individuals show how diverse blues interpreters can be: Johnson was a rural black; Bloomfield was a Jewish kid from Chicago who used to sneak into South Side blues clubs with his guitar to learn from black mentors. Yet these two legends also apparently "lived the blues" to the extent that it cost them their lives.

Perhaps a definitive editorial about the relationship of blues music to race was Dan Forte's "In Defense of Bluesmen of All Color", which appeared in the October 1990 issue of *Guitar Player*. Forte, a veteran and erudite music journalist (who's younger than me), held forth concerning a previous article in the same periodical by one Lawrence Hoffman. I didn't read the Hoffman commentary, but can well imagine its contents, considering Forte's response. The title of Forte's monograph is an accurate description of its subject matter; the writer offers an excellent rebuttal to what he terms as Hoffman's "academician's reverse-racist slant". Mere fans of blues and rock music need to defer to authorities on such genres on occasion, and Dan Forte knows such subjects well.

So it's obvious that efforts have been made in recent years to make the

Executive Rock

average rock fan more aware of the blues roots facet of American music. As stated near the outset of this essay, if the awareness of such roots is acknowledged by a more passionate (i.e., authentic) performance, that's a positive step each and every time a guitar player bends a note, a la B.B. King.... or a la Jimmie Vaughan.

ERNEST TUBB IS TURNING OVER IN HIS GRAVE

The singer in the performance video was out in front of his band, whomping his prop guitar with abandon. His hair was almost down to his bohunkus, and was at least partially contained with a headband. The aforementioned bohunkus was being manipulated in a manner that would of course raise the blood pressure of not only female viewers, but many a fundamentalist minister as well, for entirely different reasons.

Er, trouble is, the singer was Ricky Lynn Gregg, and this video was on Country Music Television (CMT), not MTV.

It seems a bit of a paradox that on the cable system in the town from which my family moved to the country in '94, MTV was sandwiched between TNN (The Nashville Network) and CMT. Such a juxtaposition is all the more ironic since CMT broadcasts nothing but videos, just like MTV used to do before it tried to become electronically egalitarian (In early 1995, one veteran music publication referred to MTV as an "old warhorse"... *Oooooo*...).

Does anybody really want to debate the opinion that what is referred to as "Country" these days can just about pass for pop or rock, particularly among Boomer listeners? I don't think there'd be many naysayers, and I've heard more than one current Country star say something like "Thank God for rap, because it's sending so many listeners to *us*."

Musically *and* visually, what's called Country these days is a far cry from cowboy hats, Nudie suits, and steel guitars. You'll still see and hear some of that, but in 1993, when I was interviewing Alabama lead guitarist Jeff Cook, the subject of this transmogrification came up; the Fort Payne, Alabama-based

Genre-Mania!

quartet had been at the forefront of the genre during its, uh, "transition".

In particular, I cited Billy Ray Cyrus's gazillion-selling "Achy Breaky Neck"; it's one of the most banal songs I've ever heard, but I opined to Cook that it sounded almost exactly like "Keep Your Hands to Yourself", the solitary hit for the Georgia Satellites some years ago.

"Exactly; those two songs are in the same vein", said the guitarist.

I followed up: "My wife's first comment on hearing one of your more recent singles, 'I'm In A Hurry', was that it didn't strike her as a country song. It starts with acappella vocals and seems to be a pop song designed to appeal to a wide audience."

"That's an excellent example", said Cook. "In 1968 that tune could have been a Number One pop song. If we put out something without fiddles or a steel guitar and somebody still wants to put a Country label on it, so be it."

Other examples of this metamorphosis I've heard discussed include Travis Tritt; "He ain't nothin' but good ol' Southern boogie" is a comment that more than one of my musical peers has uttered. And Tritt figured into what I thought was something of a tempest-in-a-Pabst-can controversy awhile back, involving the aforementioned Billy Ray Cyrus. It seems like Tritt was critical of Cyrus's "hunk" status, opining that the exploitation of such demeaned the Country music business. Then Tritt showed up on his video of "T-R-O-U-B-L-E" (a rollicking remake of one of Elvis's last hits), holding his Stratocaster in his crotch and twisting his hips. Yeah, right.

Not that Cyrus doesn't deserve being singled out; every time he's made an appearance in an interview or on a talk show, he's come off looking like an airhead. One particular appearance on "Arsenio" was definitive: Seemed like every time he had something to say to Mr. Hall, Cyrus would punctuate his remark with a sincere look up at the audience, almost as if he was saying to them: "You believe me, don't cha?"

There've been some throwbacks to an earlier time that have come along in Country from time to time; Dwight Yoakam being a handy example. Yet Yoakam has appeared onstage and in videos sporting leather pants that looked they're painted on, and ain't it curious that he too had some success with a latter-day Elvis cover ("Suspicious Minds").

Country *does* still have its share of distinctive voices; Randy Travis is to the genre what Stevie Winwood is (and has been) to pop/rock. Either person could sing one line and you'd know who it was (and some time ago, Winwood moved to the Nashville area). Travis's "Forever and Ever, Amen" is one song that any fan of any musical genre ought appreciate; it contains the classic line that the singer is going to love the person who's the subject of his crooning "as long as old men sit and talk about the weather.... as long as old women sit and talk about old men." That sort of songwriting is timeless, as is Travis's interpretation.

Executive Rock

Another interesting phenomenon has been the advent of Country dance clubs, and certain dance instructors I knew during the Disco days of the late Seventies are now teaching line dancing moves.

Since my family's move to a rural area, we haven't gotten a satellite dish, and we're too far from the nearby town to get cable; in fact, I've wisecracked to one friend that instead of getting umpteen channels via a satellite dish, maybe I'm getting a life instead. The lack of cable or a dish means of course that about the only time we get to see Country artists in performance on TV is on PBS's "Austin City Limits" or a syndicated show called "The Road." The Missus likes the latter, but I prefer the former, because of its "unadorned" ambience; no matter how big a singer or musician is; he/she is on equal turf with other performers who've been on ACL's stage.

And it's been on "Austin City Limits's" stage that many of the current Country stars have demonstrated that they do indeed deserve their status, for what my opinion's worth. While I might not be a fan of second-generation singer Pam Tillis, I thought her appearance on ACL was expressive, passionate and confident.... plus, her backup band had a cool moniker (the Mystic Biscuits).

Of course, "Austin City Limits" has had an eclectic mix of performers in its history; musicians from Dr. John to Timbuk 3 to the amazing Eric Johnson have plied their trade on the Texas stage, but the Country genre seems to be the one that's featured the most.

And it goes without saying that the musical stylings of the younger performers that stride the stage at the Grand Ole Opry are probably quite different from those of the veterans, particularly the ones that played at the Opry when it was located at the Ryman Auditorium. Not only that, but the sartorial aesthetic is interesting; I wonder what the likes of Little Jimmy Dickens and the ageless Bill Monroe think about male performers with long hair and/or pierced ears.

Country and Rock have always been symbiotic, so it really shouldn't be all that surprising that what's heard on Country radio stations would indeed have been equally at home on a Top 40 station some time back. As the trend in rock music over the last decade or so has been to let itself become more "segmented" (thereby becoming more fragmented and confusing), it's really not surprising that the Country format has indeed become more attractive to mainstream listeners, and Country's transition to a more modern sound may simply be a reaction to the wants of such alienated rock fans.

The thing is, if the Kentucky Headhunters are a Country & Western band, then I'm a brain surgeon.

90

Genre-Mania!

SHRAPNEL

Rogene was trying a different tack. Instead of trying to put lyrics from one song on top of some instrumental tune (see "There Are No Words"), he was speculating what certain songs would sound like if they had an alternate lead vocalist.

Rogene is a bit more buffoon-like than most people I know; he laughs a bit too loudly at his own humorous comments or jokes. He has what would probably be termed a blue-collar job, and has never married. On the other hand, Malcolm is divorced with two kids and is a harried salesman. Double R is divorced with one kid and like Rogene has a blue-collar job; he still plays in a bar band and his current girlfriend is about half his age.

So of the peers with whom I converse about music on a regular basis, Rogene has the least amount of responsibilities (but that's not to say he's the most irresponsible of such peers, eh?). He can listen to music on a regular basis more often than most people I know; he's "into" certain bands and trends more than most people I know.

I don't recall most of the examples he cited curing a 1993 conversation at Dimitri's pub, but one of 'em really stuck in my mind: "You take two of the songs that were on MTV's "Countdown to the Ball" program this summer, "Plush" by the Stone Temple Pilots and "Only" by Anthrax, and put Ozzy Osbourne in on lead vocals instead of Scott Weiland or John Bush, and you'd swear you were listening to Black Sabbath."

His assertion was brilliant. "Plush" slogs along like an older mid-tempo riff by the Sabs; it's dangerously reminiscent of "All Moving Parts (Stand Still)", and it's also quite easy to imagine Ozzy fronting the rapid-fire roar of "Only" as well.

Which brings up an interesting point: MTV's "Countdown to the Ball" was a one-hour program citing the ten most popular heavy metal videos of the week, and was followed by a two-hour "Headbanger's Ball" program of assorted metal videos (that this particular programming was offered late Saturday night says something about the genre and its viewers/listeners as well).

The Stone Temple Pilots have been cited as a so-called "grunge" band ("grunge" and so-called "alternative" music will be discussed later), and Anthrax has always been designated as a Heavy Metal aggregation, yet I've also heard one or more of the following terms applied to Anthrax: "Speed Metal", "Thrash" "Soft Metal", "Death Metal" "Neo-Classical", "Hardcore", "Grindcore". These are names of specific sub-genres of Heavy Metal, and if I've left some out, or some of 'em are already extinct, who gives a ****?

All of the guys mentioned at the outset of this essay were legal age

91

Executive Rock

when "Smoke On The Water" came out, and it seemed like during those times anything that had a loud, melodic "crunch" to it was lumped under the "Hard Rock" label. It's questionable if a term such as "Hard Rock" would even be applicable to music these days, given the propensity of the media to pigeonhole.

Personally, I think bands like the Cult and Mr. Big might be considered as Hard Rock bands rather than Heavy Metal, yet the opposite consideration would be an attempt to determine where Hard Rock ends and music that is simply loud rock & roll or pop begins.

Take the Smithereens, for example. Here's a quartet that has been churning out dependable (if predictable) albums for years; they simply dispense reliable, well-crafted songs that rely heavily on loud guitar chords (again, the term "blue collar" comes to mind). So what kind of band does that make 'em? (NOTE: Apparently the Smithereens were making an attempt to bust out of their predictability when they released a 1994 album called *A Date with the Smithereens* that had two potentially controversial songs, "Sick of Seattle" and "Gotti", but I'm not sure it worked for 'em).

And what made the Cult exciting when *Sonic Temple* was released was probably partially attributable to a less-than-sublime Jim Morrison fixation by lead singer Ian Astbury. Between song titles such as "Sun King", "Fire Woman", and "American Horse" (*and those are the first three tunes!*) and the fact that Astbury showed up on the video for "Edie (Ciao Baby)" sporting snakeskin pants, such an obvious tip of the hat seemed to get very tiresome very quickly. Still, *Sonic Temple* seemed to represent a turning point for the Cult, since it beat their previous efforts in spades. I'm not sure how subsequent albums have fared for 'em, however (*Ceremony* showed up in cutout bins pretty quick).

But the Heavy Metal subcategories are something else. I've heard of "Speed Metal", which as I understand it is a style that comes on so loud and fast it's barely musical (much less *melodic*). Come to think of it, maybe that's the *intent*: To pound away so incessantly the listener *can't be distracted*... or maybe the listener will pay close attention because he/she would like to ascertain if the song even has a melody.

I've also heard "Thrash" being cited as something that's close to Speed Metal, but I ain't gonna take the time to determine the differences. Admittedly, however, some of the "no frills" ideas associated with bands such as Metallica did seem to have a certain appeal, particular when compared to the music *and visuals* of other so-called sub-genres (more about that later).

Whaddabout "Neo-Classical", which is apparently the term for the lightning-fast, instrumental guitar sub-category in Heavy Metal? I think a better name might be something like "Subliminal Guitar Races", on accounta the music goes by so fast a listener sometimes can't absorb it all, and I'll

92

Genre-Mania!

tell ya this: Anytime someone has to explain *in writing* what the differences are in the playing styles of Yngwie Malmsteen, Vinnie Moore, Tony McAlpine, *et. al.*, something's wrong, and I've seen such commentaries more than once! Paganini aside, and regardless of whether you're talking about hammer-ons or other playing gimmicks, Eddie Van Halen's comments circa 1986 (on an MTV special) about other players mimicing his style weren't too far off base.

"Soft Metal" is/was an appropriately dorky term for recycled pop with a loud guitar and a pretty-boy lead singer; offenders include Bon Jovi, Cinderella, and White Lion.

Regardless of the so-called subcategories, what about the music itself? It got to the point with me to where by the end of the Eighties it was difficult to find a memorable Hard Rock/Heavy Metal riff outside of Motorhead, AC/DC or a couple of Judas Priest tunes. The genre used to be defined by sensible power chords and gritty vocals instead of speedball guitar races accompanied by Wagnerian shrieks. While Black Sabbath was excoriated by music critics on a regular basis for *years* (and quite frankly, some of their God vs. Satan imagery now seems a bit redundant and silly), at least the Sabs' earlier albums were chock fulla riffs; I still get a kick out of hearing "Tomorrow's Dream" or "Paranoid".

Even before MTV got into "compartmentalizing" their presentations, the Hard Rock *videos* were equally depressing, and I've seen nothing since the advent of the Saturday night Metal hours to indicate otherwise. There's a lotta head-banging performance clips with cameras diving and swooping to such an extent that if the Missus attempted to watch 'em it would drive her astigmatism crazy, but this "dig out the Dramamine" idea is equally applicable to other facets of MTV as well. It seems like if and when there's any imagery it usually tends to be in a quasi-science fiction/fantasy setting, featuring buxom women removing their clothes. How novel... An exception for a long time was Metallica, who steadfastly refused for years to put out a video, letting their music speak for itself. I admired them for such a stance; however, when they finally did release a video, it was a morbid, uninspiring black and white performance clip interspersed with scenes from the anti-war movie *Johnny Got His Gun*, which was about a soldier whose war wounds turn him into an armless, legless, blind, mute vegetable. *Urgh.*

Ya say ya want gimmicks? We got gimmicks! Yup, some folks have tried almost anything in an effort to distinguish themselves from every other pouting, haystack-haired batch. Examples include female impersonators such as Vinnie Vincent and Steve Stevens, and Stryper, an apparently now-extinct Christian rock band that used to dress up in bumblebee outfits. Musically, Stryper came across as Styx impersonators, which I

93

Executive Rock

believe is a felony in some states (if it ain't it should be).

So I've seen nothing since de-programming MTV to indicate that Metal and its hyped-up facets have, um, "matured". Suffice to say that I knew I was getting permanently alienated by mid-1989, when a musical friend of mine returned to California, where he reported that lots of aspiring bands that used to sport the aforementioned "haystack" hair styles plus lotsa Spandex were now appearing with tattoos and a much-more-seedy wardrobe, apparently as a nod to Guns 'N Roses. Helluva role model, folks. While some of their riffs are interesting, W. Axl Rose persists in demonstrating that he's an intellectual cripple, given the content of some interviews I've heard or read, not to mention the lyrics to "One in A Million".

And ultimately, I don't trust any band whose lead singer has *hair* and *teeth* that are the *same color* (and I bet Left Coast dentists celebrated if they thought this was a trend). I've seen no reason since then for any amount of optimism at all; I know that the so-called "grunge" phenomenon may have had at least a portion of its roots in the Metal genre, and what sense I have been able to make of so-called Nineties musical phenomena/genres will be examined elsewhere.

THE GODFATHER: PARTS 1, 2, 5, 7, 19, & 23

You've probably seen the photo; it's part of the Michael Ochs Archives, and often appears in historical perspectives on pop and/or R & B music. I once cut a large copy of it out of *Rolling Stone* and framed it; the picture still has a place of prominence in my office.

The singer who is its subject is shown in what is almost certainly a posed publicity shot that makes him appear to be in the middle of a passionate performance. His tuxedo's bow tie is askew; his processed pompadour pokes out so precariously one might think he'd be off-balance if he stood upright and stood still (an unlikely occurrence). His eyes are closed, his hand delicately-but-firmly grips a now-antiquated-style microphone, and he appears to be evoking a meaningful message in song.

Genre-Mania!

It can't be determined whether the singer is crooning softly, mournfully moaning, or yowling like de debbil has ahold of him.... but does it matter??? Because after all of his personal and legal problems, after all sorts of fads have blossomed on the pop charts and flamed out like so many musical meteorites, and after he's appeared innumerable times on Letterman Top Ten lists, there always was, is, and always will be James Brown.

The only three CDs I have by The-Hardest-Working-Man-In-Show-Business are all live efforts, because to me that's where James Brown lived up to the slogan at the beginning of this sentence (other hype lines through the years have included "The Godfather of Soul" and "The Founder of Funk"). Brown's arrangements for his studio recordings are legendary, but to witness Brown in concert during his physical prime (I understand he doesn't do knee drops anymore) was to be in the presence of an unleashed monster.

Whoever patched together the historical collage for the "Papa's Got A Brand New Bag" video some years ago (it was first seen when the *Star Time* boxed set was released) knew what he/she was doing; watching the old concert films is a treat, but whenever that stop at the end of each verse happens (after which Browns sings the title acappella, after which there's a solo chinka-chinka guitar lick, followed by a mighty roar from the horns), the video producers showed Brown doing one of his fabled knee drops as the horns kicked in. It's an incredible, indelible moment of popular music history that remains permanently etched into a viewer's mind.

(SIDEBAR: I once heard a story about a once-famous white singer who is now pretty of a "journeyman" but apparently still active. Seems that when he was up-and-coming, he used to do knee drops a la the Godfather, and he damaged his legs permanently, only to discover years later that James Brown used knee pads. I don't know if that's a true story or not, but it's still noteworthy.)

At any rate, examining Brown's performances (visually and aurally) can be an awesome experience. One interesting facet of the aforementioned portions of the "Papa's Got A Brand New Bag" video is to use the Pause and Frame Advance controls on a VCR; the height of Brown's leaps before he crashed to the stage floor in a split is mind-boggling.

What's more, when Prince and the Revolution went out on their "Purple Rain" tour in the mid-Eighties, the seventeen-minute-or-so concert clip that MTV purveyed borrowed so heavily from a James Brown concert (right down to the "Good-Gawd!" yelp) that the Godfather could've sued for plagiarism.

The three live James Brown CDs I own are taken from performances at the Apollo in 1962 and 1967, and Atlanta's Chastain Park (supposedly) circa 1980. The '62 concert is hailed by many as the greatest live album of all time (Oh yeah? Howzabout B.B. King's *Live at the Regal*?), but the

Executive Rock

'67 show is actually superior. By then, Brown had been crossing over onto the pop charts for some time, and such hits are sampled here, but a romping, extended workout of "There Was A Time" is a highlight. It'll make you sweat by simply listening to it; it's *that* potent.

On the other hand, the circa 1980 show remains a bit dubious. It's one of those "truck stop cutout" albums that has been proffered with different covers and different song sequences, and I think it was actually recorded a few years after the turn of the decade, on accounta at least one of the deceased popular music stars that Brown salutes during one of his stage raps wasn't dead in 1980... Nevertheless, the fidelity is much better than the Sixties concerts (expected), and the performance still smokes and appears to have been executed in a professional manner. Even some of Brown's then-current singles like "It's Too Funky in Here" sound better in concert. The bass player's got some hefty chops as well.

Eddie Murphy's lampoons on "Saturday Night Live" not withstanding, James Brown remains an icon of entertainment. The point is, there's a lot of guitar players that get cited by other players for their tone; i.e., "So-and-so could hit three notes and you'd know who he was." However, the Godfather's domain includes an even-more-popular example of such instant recognition: The vast majority of folks who have heard popular music on the radio from the Sixties on would probably know that a certain unaccompanied panther-like shriek was not only James Brown, they'd also know that it's the kickoff to "I Feel Good", and the screeching "*EEEEYOW!*" would be an enticement to the majority of the vast majority to boogie.... at least mentally.... Good-Gawd!

As is the case with blues music, the debt owed by white musicians to soul, funk, and R & B is acknowledged here as well, and won't be examined. The main facets of Sixties soul and R & B (including the Motown and Memphis Stax/Volt "rivalries") as well as earlier musical history are better documented in other efforts by other writers.

Anyway, my senior year in high school, when the majority of my peers were listening to Otis and Aretha, I was checking out the Airplane and the Dead... yet nowadays it seems like the Memphis and Motown classics have stood the test of time better, and I betcha "Dock of the Bay" gets more airplay on Oldies stations than "Somebody to Love".

Perhaps a defining moment about the durability of R & B and soul music occurred at my twentieth high school reunion in 1988, when a drunken ex-jock opined (after hearing my bar band warm up for a reunion of a group that had specialized in soul music): "Ah always figgered you'd turn out to be a

Genre-Mania!

hippie" (punctuating his remark with a belch). My band was much better than the hastily-thrown-together reunion, but naturally the nostalgia numbed out any notice that they were sloppy as hell, and I found myself singing along with everyone else at the country club on songs like "Shotgun".

One final aspect of the race factor in popular music (if one opts to pay attention to such things) that needs to be noted is the advent in the Eighties of something called the Black Rock Coalition. Even its name might strike some folks as potentially controversial, but apparently it was founded to show consumers that black musicians could also rock and roll instead of purveying stereotypical black music (whatever that is).

However, one guitarist with whom I conversed about the B.R.C. also stated that it was a reaction to the narrow format MTV adhered to in those times, which seems like a logical and commendable move. On the other hand, as stated previously it seems like MTV ultimately has attempted to become everything to everybody who might happen to tune in. Zzzzz.

The Black Rock Coalition was co-founded by Living Colour guitarist Vernon Reid; that band was described by one publication as "Vernon Reid's vision of a black rock band with a jazz-funk soul and a sociopolitical consciousness." Reid does seem to fancy himself as somewhat of a philosopher (as do many activist musicians), and when I said such to the afore mentioned guitarist, he said: "Well, that's where Vernon's head's at", going on to question whether the B.R.C. (if it's still in existence) now has any relevance in contemporary music.

Doesn't matter to me; in what I've seen of Vernon Reid's pronouncements, it seems like he plays the race card a little too quickly. That having been said, however, I think Living Colour needs to be commended for showing an admirable amount of restraint on the "Arsenio" show some years ago, around the time of the controversy over Guns N' Roses' tune called "One In A Million", which contained some racial and ethnic slurs. Living Colour had the forum (an appropriate one at that, considering some of the other "Arsenio" programming moves during that show's history) to snarl right back, but refrained from doing so, which was a classy move; if it had been me, I'd have wanted to kick Axl Rose's ass. What's more, Living Colour sounded better live than on record.

Activism by musicians will be addressed later, but the guitarist with whom I conversed about the B.R.C. agrees with me that ultimately the *music* ought to count more than anything else, including the color of the musicians making the music.

Oh, by the way, guess the race of that guitarist... or does it matter???

Executive Rock

THIS AIN'T "THE OLD RUGGED CROSS"

One evening in the Fall of '94 I was channel surfing (we still had cable television at the time), and I happened to encounter a show on the Family Channel called something like "America's Christian Music Video Awards". It was an event staged in a large venue with an enthusiastic crowd of young, mostly white kids yelling in approval as certain nominees in certain categories were cited and the winners announced. It was like any number of nationally-televised awards shows, except that the artists were probably not too well known on a national or international basis except to followers of the genre, which is of course applicable to almost *any* musical genre, from Thrash to Big Band. But this was a pretty elaborate production.

Among the hosts of the award show was a trio that went by the name of d.c. Talk. I could've sworn I was looking at celebrity look-alikes of Kurt Cobain, Corey Glover (Living Colour's lead singer), and whoever the guy is who's the lead singer for the Spin Doctors. So help me, the Cobain clone even acted spacey, just like the real Cobain did.

Watching the video segments was intriguing as well, particularly with the volume turned off. Such clips looked exactly like what would probably be termed "mainstream" or "secular" videos: Lotsa hair, swooping camera angles, and guitars with angular shapes and pointy headstocks. Bringing up the volume simply averred that such a comparison was valid, since a lot of the male singers seemed to specialize in high-pitched, Valkyrie-like vocal stylings. One video even showed a live concert with a mosh pit.

The "Contemporary Christian Music"/"Christian Rock" phenomenon seems to have come into its own over the last decade or so, from what I can tell. There have been modernistic interpretations of Biblical stories around for quite some time, including musicals like *Godspell* and *Jesus Christ Superstar*; not surprisingly some of those efforts were condemned by some groups as blasphemous.

Some artists who have been mega-stars within the CCM genre may have ultimately achieved a bit of fame (i.e.; a hit record) within the secular music market (an obvious example would be Amy Grant), while other supremely talented musicians seem to stay pigeonholed in the Christian Music section of mall record stores (provided such stores even have a religious music section). Gifted guitarist Phil Keaggy has been around for years, but I wonder if his instrumental albums would have sold better if they'd been located in another section.

Genre-Mania!

Then there's the smattering of musicians who might have been successful at one time in the secular music arena, and are now making a name for themselves within CCM. Secular cynics might be tempted to use terms like "has-beens" to describe such folks, but that fact is, Dion's been the definitive example of such an individual for decades. He seems at peace with himself whenever he does interviews, and three guitarists I've interviewed who had secular success then a born again experience were both eloquent about their past, and managed to get their convictions across without sounding like they were proselytizing.

On the other hand, some *local* guys I know claim to have had the same experience; I'm more familiar with their, um, tumultuous pasts than I would be with the turbulent personal history of some rock star. Yet more than one conversation with such local musicians has ended up as an alienating experience: Even if said musician led a more raucous lifestyle than I ever did, his conversion seemed to make him confident that he now had more of an inside track to salvation than somebody who might have stayed pretty much on the straight-and-narrow all along. Sometimes such so-called "witnessing" has been accompanied by bug-eyed Scripture recitation and finger-jabbing, and I know of one example where the individual is no longer in a born-again mode; he's back to his former ways. 'Nuff said.

Another odd facet has been Little Richard, who has ping-ponged back and forth between rock & roll and Christianity more than once.... pass the Dramamine.

Given the advent of Christian bookstores in recent times, it's interesting to browse through the section where CDs and tapes are located in such an establishment. Many stores have demos that can be listened to through headphones (as is the case at more and more secular stores); CCM apparently has its own superstars, hunks and heartbreakers, and evidently it has its own version of Weird Al Yankovic as well: I once encountered an album by one Mark Lowry, the contents of which were advertised as containing parodies of songs by other Contemporary Christian artists.

I'm sure singing in church as a child inspired all kinds of performers in all sorts of musical genres, just as the blues inspired lotsa musicians as well. Aretha Franklin's upbringing is simply an example that's handy, and hopefully such an upbringing adds to the feeling the performer is attempting to convey (sure works in Aretha's case, in my opinion).

And a recent effort in the Country and Western field (which included an infomercial hosted by Ricky Skaggs, who's never been shy about his convictions) is indicative of how the concept is continuing to evolve: The *Silent Witness* video features performances *and testimony* from a myriad of Country stars.

So the influence of religion is applicable in many genres of popular

Executive Rock

music, yet sometimes an attempt to convey a musical message may not necessarily attract those who might ought hear it. I recall a concert by a local Christian rock band in my church's multi-purpose room some years ago: (the particular denomination to which I belong is somewhat progressive in some areas) and naturally I showed up early to check out the instruments and equipment. Things took shape like any other live project: Lotsa lights and microphones were set up, along with a big mixing board out in the middle of the room. While the stage was being set up, our then-minister's wife babbled exuberantly about how the band had told her they appreciated the opportunity, "because a lot of churches wouldn't he interested in this kind of ministry."

And I can see why. When the band started playing, I only made it through a verse and a half before bee-lining it to the exit due to the excruciating decibel level (yet another comparison to secular rock, in this case). So the message didn't get heard by me (or some other folks that quickly split), although I *do* think I was able to discern one line about "look up to Heaven".

These days, it appears there are more avenues than ever regarding religious music. That one of the directions involves electric guitars, drums, and even videos is just one of the newest wrinkles in the age-old efforts of those individuals who proclaim they're out to win souls, and if they're enjoying the ride and/or successful, they have my respect, even if it's hard to "get into" their presentation, and even if I'm content with my own spiritual life.

But I'd still be more inspired if I heard songs like "I'll Fly Away" or "Amazing Grace".

P.S.: CCM has its own publications, of course, yet a while back *Bass Player* magazine showed some class by publishing articles about gospel music bassists and CCM bassists. That's not seen too often in the so-called secular press.

Genre-Mania!

"RAP MUSIC": An Oxymoron?

Malc and I were trading off oxymorons. There have been occasions where he and I will consciously attempt to improve our respective intellects by having spirited, sensible discussions, and such was the situation here. Of course, what long-term results of such one-on-one conversations have transpired over the years is quite dubious.

We'd warmed up with the simpler, more common examples that everyone knows ("jumbo shrimp", "military intelligence", etc.). Unfortunately (yet not unexpectedly), the dialogue descended into a socio-political jousting match, and as the conversation became more heated, the decibel level increased:

"'Ethical Lawyer'."
"'Right-Wing Intellectual'."
"'Liberal Realist'!"
"'Black Republican'!"
"Um.... 'WASP Democrat', I guess."
"'*Compassionate Republican*'!"
"'*NON-SANCTIMONIOUS DEMOCRAT*'!!!"
"'*RAP MUSIC*'!!!"
"Huh?"
"Gotcha."

"The first time I ever heard rap music", said the middle-aged executive, "I thought I was listening to an auction."

After I'd stopped laughing at his observation, we went on to discuss the term "middle-aged" rather than his particular spin on rap, since the executive was adamant that he was not middle-aged when it came to listening to music. "I'm forty-five", he announced, "and I'm listening the same music I listened to when I was twenty-five. What's more, when I'm sixty-five I'll *still* be listening to what I was listening to when I was twenty-five, so in that part of my existence I'll never be middle-aged *or* a senior citizen!"

That was his way of explaining that the current musical trends weren't of much interest to him, and given the advent of several types of Oldies radio formats, that seems to be the case with a plethora of Boomers these days.

I've heard rock stars as well as average music fans weighing in as to what rap is as well as what its place in the modern musical spectrum should be (GREGG ALLMAN: "'Rap' is short for 'crap'."). The thing is, rapid-fire vocals in popular songs isn't anything new. Bob Dylan's "Subterra-

Executive Rock

nean Homesick Blues" dates from the Sixties, and there was even a primeval video to go with it, MTV's lampoon of which was one of that cable network's most (intentionally) funny moments in its dubious history.

Moreover, who recalls an Country & Western ditty called "The Auctioneer"? While the title of that tune makes it obvious what the subject matter is (as well as how the middle-aged executive's opinion of rap evolved), rap itself has taken the "concept" of popular music (if rap can even be considered as music) out on a new and innovative tangent.

Yeah, it's got a beat, so you can dance to it. Yeah, it takes a lot of talent to syncopate fast vocalese with the beat. Yeah, it takes a lot of talent to work with samples lifted from other songs by other artists, yet that's the core of the debate as to whether rap even qualifies as "music", as far as many people are concerned.

And yeah, the genre has its share of unique and controversial characters. It's primarily a black entertainment phenomenon, yet there have been some reverse token artists like Robbie "Vanilla Ice" Van Winkle who seem to be knowingly embarrassing themselves; it's almost like they're doing some kind of bizarre parody (such awkward reverse tokenism has been seen before: At a Motown celebration some years ago, Adam Ant was woefully out of place; for all the wild adulation afforded to most of the other acts, which had indeed been on the Motown label, the audience *just sat there* during Ant's "performance").

Reverse tokenism aside, controversies other than whether or not rap is a legitimate music form have imbued the genre for years. The legal problems of some of its stars (Tupac Shakur, Calvin "Snoop Doggy Dogg" Broadus, etc.) have reached near-legendary proportions; Public Enemy's William "Flavor Flav" Drayton seems to have become a parody of himself.

Other rappers now fancy themselves as socio-political commentators, even if they're not performing. Tracy "Ice-T" Marrow apparently wants to revive the clenched fist salute, demonstrating such whenever I've seen him on talk shows that have an audience. And Public Enemy's Carlton "Chuck D" Ridenhour has come across at times as having a Jekyll-and-Hyde persona: For all of the positive antiviolence campaigns in which he's participated ("Self-Destruction", "Peace: Live It Or Rest In It") there's more than enough controversial (if not ludicrous) commentary in Public Enemy's performances and videos to offset the good things he's done.

Rap has its sub-genres, and considering the tabloid mentality that this country seems to have developed, the more repugnant sub-genres seem to have garnered the most attention (gangsta rap being the most obvious example). It's a sad commentary that some of the more mainstream rap performers such as Stanley "Hammer" (formerly "M.C. Hammer") Burrell

Genre-Mania!

and the aforementioned "Vanilla Ice" opted to affect gangsta facades in what were attempts to revitalize careers that were apparently flagging... but to his credit, Hammer has actually used live musicians in performance.

But does rap and its sub-genres deserve all the attention it gets? I mean, as far as I'm concerned, such facets of entertainment have been going on for decades: For all intents and purposes, Public Enemy is the Last Poets with samples; the 2 Live Crew is Rudy Ray Moore with a beat, and from a simple entertainment perspective (something which is hard to pin down in contemporary times) rap may be an "art form" that may be around for some time, which means that (like opera) it ain't for everybody, but it's got enough going for it to where it commands a measure of respect... but I predict that the gangsta rap sub-genre will choke on its own venom and bile before the entire rap phenomenon is extinct.

So whether rap is an "art form" or "music" or whatever will most likely continue to make for lively discussions, even if nothing is settled in such discussions (and perhaps that's the way it should be). I found a conversation with two former business associates to be intriguing: In discussing what rap was, one of them branded Public Enemy as "racists", while the other summed up his opinion of rap with one succinct phrase: "Maybe it's just 'entertainment'."

Well put. Oh, by the way, guess the race of the middle-aged executive mentioned at the outset of this essay, as well as the race of the two former business associates... or does it matter???

AS FUZZY AS FLANNEL

During one of those stand-up comedy specials that appears ever so often on HBO, space cadet Steven Wright (he of the monotone delivery and receding Afro) introduced a supposedly-up-and-coming comedian named Barry Crimmens. While I haven't been able to ascertain that his career went on to bigger things following his HBO appearance, Crimmens (who looks like he could be Wilford Brimley's son) had one rumination that was

103

Executive Rock

quite profound; as I recall it went something like:

"Why is it that people who work in record stores act like *they're* rock stars?... I bought an album in one store the other day and the guy behind the counter looked at it and said: 'You still listenin' to this crap?'... I said: 'Yeah; you still makin' seventy-five dollars a week, *loser?*' "

(I thought of a great follow-up line Crimmens could've said he said to the record store employee: "Now gimme my Tony Orlando & Dawn album and *leave me the hell alone!*")

Shopping in such retail establishments, for me at least, is no longer the pleasing experience it used to be. There are the usual unfortunate reasons, such as too many decibels as well as the occasional employee that fits Crimmens's stereotype. It used to be one of the few examples of when I would actually "shop" at a store; in my opinion, most men will simply "buy" items, whereas most women will "shop" before purchasing.

However, another reason I don't patronize "audio escapism stores" too much anymore is the outright *confusion* I experience when I note how "segmented" or "compartmentalized" or "genre-ized" contemporary music seems to have become. Last time I spent an extended time in a record store, it wasn't to "shop" (I didn't buy anything either, come to think of it); rather, I was attempting to note the different categories of music that the store was selling, and among the sections I saw were ones labeled "POP/ROCK", "BLUES", "RHYTHM & BLUES", "RAP", "SHOW TUNES" "HEAVY METAL", "COUNTRY", "NEW AGE", "JAZZ", "INSTRUMENTAL", "EASY LISTENING", and "ALTERNATIVE".

"Alternative" to *what*???

I'd like to know how and why some bands get "assigned" to certain genres, because I'd like to know where the hell to look if I go into a store to buy an album. EXAMPLES: I looked for Ted Nugent in "POP/ROCK" and found his slot in "HEAVY METAL"; looked for Counting Crows in "ALTERNATIVE" but found 'em in "POP/ROCK".

Younger popular music aficionados might attempt to explain that the so-called "Alternative" genre (and its subsequent separate section in a retail store) is a reaction to so-called "mainstream" music, but that doesn't seem to wash. For the life of me, I can't seem to determine where "Alternative" and "grunge" are all that different from other forms of rock music. Moreover, when the Seattle sound came barreling out of the Pacific Northwest in the early Nineties, I'd already heard a lot of similar rock songs; it seemed that maybe the mix might've been a bit denser and that's about all.

Yet I also noted that some media referred to *Nevermind* as a *punk rock* album, and it's interesting to compare the Nirvana masterpiece to something like *Never Mind The Bollocks*. While angst and anger in popular music can kiss my *** as a general rule, *Nevermind does* have some intel-

104

Genre-Mania!

ligent chord progressions, and doesn't come off like the fulminatory con that the Sex Pistols' work now seems to have been.

But as I write this, punk rock is being referred to as a separate genre once again, with the "Big Two" of this neo-punk movement being Green Day and the Offspring, but the song I heard the most by Green Day on the radio was called "When I Come Around", and it sounded more like the Spin Doctors instead of a punk rock band, but the Spin Doctors seem to defy categorization, but —

Aw, ****. Y'see how nebulous this has all gotten? Aging Boomers might like some of the riffs they hear in certain "alternative"/"grunge"/ "neo-punk"/whatever songs, but I wonder if some record store would be willing to be innovative (or regressive) enough to file any band that relies primarily on guitars and drums (and whose music has a steady beat) under just plain "ROCK". It might make for some interesting sociological observations watching Boomers and so-called Gen-Xers bump into each other as they search out their REO Speedwagon and Soundgarden albums.

Or perhaps that's the intent with the way categories are set up in record stores these days... in which case, that'd keep a consumer in his/her own favorite area, but it would also make such a policy look like customers were being treated like cattle.

The "silver lining" to all of this fuzziness concerning newer genres and sub-genres is the ongoing interest in Classic Rock; not just in radio formats, but from many younger listeners these days. I've met plenty of teenagers (I went to school with the parents of some of 'em) who've opined that they'd rather listen to the likes of the Who or C.C.R. rather than Pearl Jam. On more than one occasion, some kid has told me that the classic songs are more listenable than Madonna, rap or even Green Day. "The new stuff doesn't have anything that's really all that new", a sixteen-year old recently said.

Bless his heart. I couldn't have said it better myself.

And the other day I saw yet another new category called "Techno" in a mall music store. I don't wanna know about it.

THE ROCK & ROLL CURMUDGEON

The late Frank Zappa was arrogant, egotistical, condescending, sanctimonious, crude, obnoxious, and sardonic.

But haven't a lot of geniuses been like that?

As of this writing, Zappa's record label, Barking Pumpkin, in still in existence, and the venture's slogan is "World's Finest Optional Entertainment". As I interpret it, the phrase may be another example of Zappa's sly-but-on-target variant of condescension (or else it's completely over my head from an intellectual point of view), because when ya think about, *all* entertainment is optional, ain't it?

And another "right-there-in-front-of-you" facet of contemporary entertainment involves *sports,* because as far as I'm concerned, *sports is entertainment as well,* unless you're an active participant in the effort itself (which is particularly critical if you're in the infinitesimal minority of individuals who are actually making money from your athletic endeavors). Anybody remember what the "E" in "ESPN" stands for?

Other writers have already pontificated about how many sports have gotten to be big businesses, to the point that concepts such as sportsmanship and character development don't matter anymore. I'd take such a viewpoint a step further by opining that some sports and events have indeed become nothing but "show business", and submitted for your consideration is the following list of comparisons between the entertainment (music, cinema, etc.) and sports "fields":

1. AS NOTED PREVIOUSLY, ONLY A SMALL NUMBER OF PARTICIPANTS ARE ACTUALLY SUCCESSFUL ENOUGH TO THE

Executive Rock

POINT THAT THEY SHOULD BE CONSIDERED "PROFESSIONALS".

2. IT SEEMS LIKE A DISPROPORTIONATE NUMBER OF SPORTS AND ENTERTAINMENT FIGURES ARE NARCISSISTIC AND EGOTISTICAL. Accordingly, such behavior ought to mean that their respective intellects should be subject to scrutiny.

3. CHARLES BARKLEY'S TELEVISION COMMERCIAL NOT WITHSTANDING, SUCH INDIVIDUALS ARE ROLE MODELS *BY DEFAULT.*

4. BOTH FIELDS ARE THE SUBJECTS OF INNUMERABLE WALTER MITTY-ISH DAYDREAMS.

5. IN BOTH FIELDS, SOMETIMES THERE'S A FINE LINE BETWEEN "FAN" AND "FANATIC". The only event for which I would camp out overnight waiting on tickets would be a Cream reunion tour. One only has to look as far as the likes of John Hinckley and Mark Chapman to see to what pathetic and tragic extremes fan-dom can lead.

6. TERMS SUCH AS "PHENOM", "FLASH-IN-THE-PAN", "UP-AND-COMING", ETC. ARE EQUALLY APPLICABLE TO HYPE IN BOTH FIELDS. "One-Hit-Wonder" seems to be applicable to music only, however... but who remembers Leo Randolph? The Sherbs? Gabrielle Andersen-Schiess? The Vapors? Valeri Borzov? Bram Tchaikovsky? Ecatarina Szabo? Haisley Crawford?

7. DOMESTICALLY, THERE'S THE PERCEPTION (AND IT'S PROBABLY A FACT) THAT BOTH FIELDS CONTAIN A DISPROPORTIONATE NUMBER OF BLACK PARTICIPANTS, COMPARED TO THE GENERAL POPULATION... which, to some individuals' archaic intellects, could validate the archaic stereotype about how "they sure can sing, dance, and play baseball", which I never heard while growing up in the Deep South. (ACTIVISTS/ADVOCATES OF COLLECTIVE GUILT PLEASE NOTE: The gist of this paragraph is a "racial observation", not a "racist statement", and you know the difference, so please don't write.)

8. IN BOTH FIELDS, ALL TOO MANY PARTICIPANTS SEEM TO HANG AROUND LONGER THAN THEY SHOULD (SOMETIMES EMBARRASSING THEMSELVES).

9. ACCORDINGLY MOST "COMEBACKS" IN BOTH FIELDS USUALLY AREN'T.

And as if to add an emphatic coda and/or boldface exclamation point to this list, Jerry Garcia and Mickey Mantle died within a week of each other in August of 1995.

The Rock & Roll Curmudgeon

Yet it seemed like 1994 was a defining annum regarding how ludicrous and intertwined sports and show business had become with this country's perceived "tabloid mentality". The year began with the saga of Tonya and Nancy (neither of whom won the Olympic figure skating gold medal, lest ye forget), and media attention to the bizarre and surreal seemed to make the magnitude (and dubious importance) of further events grow like some giant amoeba; i.e., an event-driven version of the Blob. Considering the Jackson-Presley nuptials, the baseball strike, everything and everyone associated with the O.J. Simpson case, some academic's criticism of *The Lion King* as being chock fulla racist and gender-biased stereotypes, the hockey strike, a cornucopia of legal problems for certain sports and entertainment celebrities, and the huge number of acts that toured (including arthritic dinosaurs like the Rolling Stones and Pink Floyd; even the Eagles!) *plus* Lollapalooza *plus* Woodstock II (and don't forget Cobain's suicide), it seemed like 1994 was giving an exasperated and exhausted raspberry to itself when two of the final snippets that appeared in national media in late December noted Steve Tyler's daughter describing how embarrassed she was when her father groped himself onstage, and how a University of Miami football player was in hot water for some remarks he made about the upcoming Orange Bowl game. His quote went something like: "Dis is our home, youknowwhatI'msayin'? We don't take no **** offa nobody." If a viewer happened to tune into those comments without knowing the speaker was a football player, one would've thought he/she was listening to some gangsta rapper. Small wonder a veterinarian I know rightfully opined that the 'Canes make it easy to root for whoever their opponent is.

The reason this book is dedicated to my sports heroes and heroine is because in at least one point in their respective careers, these folks have shown a tremendous amount of class, which seems to be so sorely lacking in sports *and* show biz these days... and come to think of it, maybe Joe Delaney should be cited as a hero as well.

Ultimately, successful sports and entertainment figures are "fantasy people" (and some of 'em have said so themselves). They exist on a television screen for the diversion of viewers; they're *images,* but as obsessed as this nation is with imagery, it doesn't seem to be all that surprising that what ought to be diversions or casual entertainment all too often turns into escapism. What's more, I think the tendency to go overboard with optional entertainment/escapism is a problem that besets the American male more than the American female.

I realize that some folks would interpret this essay (and many of the commentaries contained in this section) as sounding, er, "Falwellian" or "Wildmon-ish", or perhaps like the rantings of a real-life Bill Needle. But

109

Executive Rock

I consider myself to be a fairly progressive individual who knows how to differentiate between "traditional values" and "traditional roles", although way too many activists with a "where's-the-camera" mentality try to equate such terms. For me, Jack Webb is a good role model when discussing such topics; i.e., my opinions are formed by considering "just the facts".

The socio-political leanings of artists noted herein are exclusively of the liberal/leftist leaning; that's because for all intents and purposes, a conservative contingent is nonexistent (or, as one of my friends said, "'Rock & Roll Republican' is an oxymoron"). So help me, the only examples I can think of are Ted Nugent and the late Lee "Backbeat" Atwater.

But that's not to say that most musicians are apolitical or aloof. Most of the players I've interviewed over the last few years have a commendable work ethic and are quite dedicated to their craft, regardless of their current status in the historical pantheon of guitar stars. I'd think such efforts would merit the admiration of any working person; unfortunately, the obnoxious and/or controversial figures in entertainment seem to garner the most attention... and can't the same thing be said for sports as well???

One thing that *won't* be done herein will be to lampoon activists who aren't particularly controversial. For example, I don't know of anything Michael "Mumbles" Stipe has done that's illegal, immoral or particularly worthy of a news item in the *National Perspirer* (nor do I feel like ferreting out such information), so he can mutter his pontifications all he wants, for all I care. That's his right, just as it's my right to ignore or dismiss such pronouncements... I could even make fun of 'em, but won't.

Another area that won't be detailed will be the legal and/or personal problems of famous musicians who are more or less *non-activist*. While I still feel like they're "role models by default" as noted earlier, supermarket tabloids can have at such folks for all I care, but that's not to say that such entertainers' lifestyles should be ignored or relegated to such publications.

I mean, let's tell it like it is: For all of the joy he's brought to millions of listeners for decades, Chuck Berry's legal problems have been so lengthy that in 1994 he was even being lampooned in *Rolling Stone*.

The Rock & Roll Curmudgeon

BRING BACK THE MELLOTRON!

"I remember", Malc was saying in a voice that somehow sounded both wistful *and* grumpy, "when a synthesizer used to sound like a synthesizer."

"What the hell are you talking about?"

"You know, all sorts of weird bleeps and squiggles, a la Keith Emerson or Rick Wakeman. Modulating tones that sounded like air raid sirens or Stuka dive bombers. Jeez, even *Hawkwind* had a recognizable sound thanks to their synthesizer sound! These days I don't know *what or even who* I'm listening to! Sampling, schmampling; it's a ripoff! How do they figure royalties?" I didn't say anything.

"So who's got a so-called signature synth sound *these* days, huh? Stevie Winwood, that's who!" Malc answered his own question before I could reply. "And his fat little riffs are done on an old Mini-Moog, I think. All this MIDI stuff is too damn confusing! It's bad enough they've got MIDI keyboards, now there's MIDI guitars! Where's it gonna end? MIDI harmonicas?!?"

I let him rave on, but he did have a point. When Walter (now Wendy) Carlos's *Switched-On Bach* came out in 1968, I never would have dreamed that electronic music would have advanced to the point that it's now tapping into the sounds of, uh, "normal" instruments.

MIDI is an acronym for Musical Instrument Digital Interface, which (as I understand it) involves the use of computer technology to make one instrument sound like another by "sampling" the sound of the instrument that is being emulated. Keyboards are (and have always been) the most convenient type of instruments to which MIDI technology has been applied, but (per Malc's tirade) there have been others as well. The possibilities for "aural plagiarism" seem endless, and such shenanigans were lampooned a while back in a song called "Sample the Dog" by Timbuk 3.

Back when a synth was still regarded as sort of a curiosity item (and like Malc says, they *sounded* like synthesizers) there were all sorts of odd releases where synthesizers would play specific genres of music; the aforementioned *Switched-On Bach* was obviously the progenitor of this idea. Even the redoubtable Mike Bloomfield put out an instrumental album of synth music called *Moogie Woogie*. A somewhat prophetic bit of dialogue and music can be found on a now out-of-print Earl Scruggs album, which is the soundtrack to a PBS special on the famed banjo player. In addition to collaborations with the Byrds and Joan "Pinko" Baez, there's one cut where Scruggs and a synth player are talking about the then-new electronic upstart keyboard, and the synth player opines that the synthesizer, at least theoretically, should be able to sound like any musical instrument in the world and like some instruments that haven't even been invented

Executive Rock

yet, whereupon he and Earl take off on one of the most unique versions of "Foggy Mountain Breakdown" ever done, with Scruggs plucking away in one channel and the synth making bizarre percolator-ish and fiddle-like noises in the other. At one point the keyboard does a verse that modulates downward and pans over to the other side, making a crashing noise into the same channel where Scruggs' banjo is. Seems like kind of an intrusion, and if I'd been Earl I'd have been p.o.'ed.

I understand that even *string players* raised all kinds of hell when the Mellotron first appeared in the late Sixties. Unlike a synthesizer, the Mellotron was a keyboard device that actually played *tapes* of other instruments playing a specific note, and the lush sound of orchestrated strings seemed to be the sound of choice. The Mellotron wasn't capable of quick changes from one chord or note to another due to its mechanics, so it was an instrument that usually served a function in fleshing out a combo's sound rather than taking a lead during a song's instrumental break.

Naturally, it was obsolete quite soon, as the first "string ensemble" synthesizers were introduced, but so help me, even Mellotrons and string ensemble synths had their own signature sounds. A definitive example of what I'm talking about occurs on the Yes' *Yessongs* triple live album *right at the outset.* A tape of Stravinsky's "Firebird Suite" is heard playing through the PA, and as it reaches its climax, Rick Wakeman's Mellotron whooshes in, doing a short segue piece prior to the entire band roaring in on "Siberian Khartru".

Other Brit progressive bands like the Strawbs and King Crimson relied heavily on Mellotrons, and outright competition between a Mellotron and a legitimate orchestra can be found on the Moody Blues' *Days of Future Passed.*

Other keyboards relegated to the technological scrap heap include Arps, Mini-Moogs, etc. What's more, thanks to MIDI some songs now feature horn charts tighter than James Brown or James Chance ever dreamed possible, so horn players have also got a reason to fume. "You Know I Love You" by that dorky techno-milquetoast Howard Jones is an example of the use of what sounds like the use of MIDI'ed horns.

Some musicians had expressed reservations that MIDI keyboards could eventually replace the instruments that they were sampling, and yet another "endangered species" might have been bass players, but according to veteran Leland Sklar (he's the guy with the long hair and beard who you've seen backing up the likes of James Taylor and Phil Collins), it ain't happened, so there does appear to be a silver lining to any ominous techo-thunderhead.

Yet three tales involving veteran British musicians seem to offer a microcosm about the use of synthesizers and MIDI: I heard that on one of his late Eighties albums, Eric Clapton used a MIDI guitar to put a sampled *saxophone* solo into the lead break of one song, and the record company

The Rock & Roll Curmudgeon

complained, saying that they wanted a *guitar* solo. Whether they knew the sax solo was sampled or not I dunno, but I understand the tune was redone per their request.

Then there was the time I cued up Dave Mason's "Something in the Heart" (from the *Two Hearts* album); "Whoziss?" I asked the Missus, as a melodic, slippery synthesizer snippet introduced the tune.

"Stevie Winwood" was her immediate (and correct) response. Thus Malc's opinion was completely corroborated from an unbiased source...

Finally, an encounter with Tony Kaye of the Yes seemed to sum up where "techno-sound" instruments have been and where they're going: While waiting backstage for an interview with bassist Chris Squire, I told Kaye that I'd been examining the stage setup, and I hadn't seen a Mellotron in his "section". Kaye's reply was that he'd actually once programmed a Mellotron sample into his MIDI.

If that ain't "time-warp technology", then tell me what is.

Ultimately, it seems like some aspects of the MIDI phenomenon are already forming *their own* technological scrap heap. One instrument manufacturer told me: "I have *scrupulously* avoided MIDI because like computers it tends to get outdated very, very quickly", yet the interviewee was a computer buff himself.

"Serves 'em right", muttered Malc when I told him about the instrument manufacturer's comments concerning MIDI getting outdated quickly. "I just hope to God I never see the likes of Jimmie Vaughan tinkering with a MIDI guitar. If I do, then I'll give up."

Ditto.

LET'S GET SANCTIMONIOUS!

"The Boomtown Rats couldn't get arrested", said Foreigner's Mick Jones, with a palpable amount of sarcasm in his voice.

It was around 1 A.M., and we were sitting in Jones's motel room following a Foreigner show (as of this writing it's still the only post-concert

Executive Rock

interview I've done), and the tired-but-congenial veteran guitarist was discussing activism by rock musicians. I'd complimented him on the band's set at the first Farm Aid, but had noted that I'd heard that Foreigner had been rebuffed by Bill Graham concerning an appearance at Live Aid (which happened a couple of months before Farm Aid I).

"We weren't rebuffed; we just weren't asked", Jones responded, going on to opine that there's an elitist group of rock stars who are always trying to save the world, and while his remark about the Boomtown Rats was edited out of the final version of the interview, his semi-caustic citing of "Your Stings, your Peter Gabriels" remained.

Here's the point: Mick Jones is a dedicated musician with an admirable work ethic who's been around since one of his bands was opening for the Beatles in the Sixties, and all Foreigner has done since its inception in the mid-Seventies is sell millions of albums worldwide.

On the other hand, the Boomtown Rats barely even qualify as a domestic One-Hit-Wonder. "I Don't Like Mondays" may have gotten a smidgen of airplay (its morbid subject matter not withstanding), but lead singer Bob Geldof's efforts concerning Live Aid elevated his status to permanent sainthood, in some folks' opinions.

And Foreigner seems to he interminably assigned by most music critics to the "faceless" and/or "arena rock" categories (Jones and I discussed this as well), along with the likes of Styx, Journey, and REO Speedwagon. What have the Boomtown Rats accomplished lately?

Live Aid ultimately inspired a plethora of Farm Aid benefits and other similar all-star efforts that did indeed seem to end up as self-righteous transmogrifications ("We care; we matter") for selective socio-political causes, and the same attitude seems to be ongoing with specific artists. Some specific examples need to be cited at this juncture:

MICHAEL "MUMBLES" STIPE: When George Bush defeated Michael Dukakis in the '88 presidential election, Stipe (of all people) was asked for his opinion (I probably saw this on MTV), and he muttered something about now it would be a time when people would take their situations into their own hands.... what the hell is *that*, a threat?

TRACY CHAPMAN: It seemed like an incredible paradox that Chapman's best selling album (on the then-still-somewhat-state-of-the-art, therefore still-innovative-and-expensive Compact Disc format) started off with a song about a revolution and how poor people were going to rise up.

PHIL COLLINS/GENESIS: Take yer choice of Genesis's video of "Land of Confusion" or Collins's video of "Just Another Day in Paradise". The former featured those hideous Spitting Image puppets; the story line showed a Reagan puppet (drowning in his sweat from a nuclear night-

114

The Rock & Roll Curmudgeon

mare) who accidentally pushed *the* red button. While many other caricatures appeared, I didn't see a Gorbachev puppet at all, and any network that shows this video since Reagan announced he has Alzheimer's ought to be ashamed of itself.

And the *But Seriously...* album by the self-described "singing Cabbage Patch Doll" was chock full of liberal guilt, according to one publication, and the aforementioned video was exemplary, flashing the dubious figure onscreen about three million homeless people in America.

It needs to be asked right here and now if these guys are U.S. citizens. If they're not, then finger-pointing such as what's seen in those videos is irrelevant. **** 'em.

YOU, TOO: "Anybody who gets lampooned by Bobcat Goldthwait probably deserves it", opined a friend of mine. He was referring to Goldthwait's devastatingly funny send-up of Paul "Bono" Hewson on some all-star comedy event. The Bobcat did indeed have Bono's sincere glare down pat as he romped through a cover of "With Or Without You", and perhaps a defining moment about U2's activism can be seen in the *Rattle & Hum* documentary (which opens with a slam-bang cover of "Helter Skelter"). Adam Clayton is shown commenting: "There are people who would say that you shouldn't mix music and politics... or sport and politics... whatever... well, I think that's kinda bull****."

Uh-huh. Well, maybe some people think that posing full-frontal nekkid on an album cover and getting engaged to a so-called "supermodel" is bull****.

MADONNA: What's the proper term for an aging bimbo? "Bimboid", perhaps? Howzabout "bimbushka"?

SINEAD O'CONNOR: Who gives a flyin' **** what a bald-headed unwed mother with a pierced nose thinks?

"SUN CITY": The problem here is that most of the artists that appeared on the song and video were either too-little-known (or in the case of "Sun City" progenitor Little Steven Van Zandt, too *ugly)* to be invited to play Sun City in the first place.

"DRUMS ACROSS AMERICA": Apparently this benefit for Native Americans was so poorly organized that the first time I heard about it was on CNN Headline News *after* the event; the news story noting that it had bombed.

Besides Goldthwait's Bono impersonation, there have been other examples of outspoken/sanctimonious/hypocritical performers who've already been satirized. Lynyrd Skynyrd's response to Neil Young is the definitive example (and one of the most enduring ones as well), but Mojo Nixon went after Don Henley ("Don Henley Must Die"), and the brilliant-but-practically unknown Tonio K. dissed Jackson Browne *real* bad. What's

Executive Rock

more, I once heard a radio tidbit making fun of "moody rocker Sting"; his paramour was being portrayed as a nagging shrew who was rasping comments like "Guess wot? I'm pregnant again, and this time, it ain't yours!"

There seemed to be a slight rebellion (for lack of a better term) that germinated in 1994 concerning the elitism of famous musicians, and the surprising-but-definitive example was a new song by the Eagles called "Get Over It" ("surprising," because it was co-written and sung by the aforementioned Don Henley; see the essay called "The Devil Goes Ice Skating"). Another interesting incident was Wynonna's pregnancy; as Country music is considered to be "heartland music" by many listeners, the harsh response by many middle-class Country music fans to a megastar of the genre having an illegitimate child (via a public pregnancy) is worthy of note. To what extent these and other '94 incidents represent possible cracks appearing in the pedestals on which show biz personalities have been placed remains to be seen, however, but it'll be interesting to stay tuned.

The Wynonna pregnancy, although associated with a Country star instead of a rock star, is perhaps its own definitive example of how some show business figures seem to think they can do as they please concerning personal responsibility, and while some of them don't concern themselves with activism, those that do seem to ignore the fact that as public figures their own personal lives are subject to scrutiny.

So do the actions of some activist musicians constitute a "best-defense-is-a-good-offense" and/or "people-in-glass-houses" line of thinking? Not necessarily, but at the very least it represents a tiresome "do-as-I-say-not-as-I-do" mentality with which most rational individuals wouldn't have much patience... but who's to say how rational and intellectual some music fans are...

Nevertheless, if the personal lives of activist show biz celebrities are tabloid fodder, such individuals are fair game. Simple as that.

The Rock & Roll Curmudgeon

FAMOUS MUSICIANS AND SINGERS I THOUGHT WOULD BE DEAD BY NOW

(Alphabetical Order)
Every member of Aerosmith
Gregg Allman
Ginger Baker
James Brown
Jack Bruce
Eric Clapton
Joe Cocker
David Crosby
Billy Ray Cyrus (assassinated)
Roky Erickson
Marianne Faithful
~~Jerry Garcia~~
Every current and former member of Guns N' Roses
Wayne Kramer
Jerry Lee Lewis
Courtney Love
Jim Morrison
James "Iggy Pop" Osterberg
Papa John Phillips
Lou Reed
Keith Richards
Grace Slick
Pete Townshend
Brian Wilson

Executive Rock

CURSE OF THE TWILIGHT CLONES

I've only ever seen one issue of *Spy* magazine for sale at newsstands or bookstores in my part of the country, but then again I haven't particularly been looking for such a periodical. The one copy I perused showed Michael Jackson on the cover dressed in a nun's habit, and among the letters to the magazine in the reader mail section was one criticizing the publication for portraying Hillary Rodham Clinton as a dominatrix in an earlier issue.

Accordingly, I formed an opinion that *Spy* is apparently some kind of smug, sarcastic periodical that's oriented towards upscalers and pseudo-intellectuals; i.e., sort of a designer *Confidential*.

But one special offering from *Spy* that gets looked at on occasion in my residence is an anthology of their celebrated "Separated at Birth?" series, which not only features every duo that ever appeared in a regular edition, but oodles of other "twins" and even *triplets*. Selections range from bland (Vicki Lawrence and Raisa Gorbachev) to spooky (former New York governor Hugh Carey and Ernest Borgnine) to bizarre (Tammy Faye Bakker and an Ewok).

Natch, there's a good number of musicians cited (U2's Bono and Robin Williams, Mick Jagger and Don Knotts), and in a few cases *both* individuals are in the music biz (Bette Midler and Twisted Sister's Dee Snider, Roy Clark and Itzhak Perlman...!!!), but I submit that *Spy* has overlooked some of the more obvious examples of "twins" in the contemporary music field. Or at least, they hadn't cited the examples that follow (to my knowledge) some years ago when I purchased the "Separated at Birth?" anthology. Submitted for your consideration (and *Spy*'s as well):

LOU REED and CHICK COREA?

GENE SIMMONS and ANDRE THE GIANT? Which would of course obliterate the theory that the "Rock and Wrestling" connection began with Cindy Lauper and Captain Lou Albano.

GEORGE THOROGOOD and TOM SCHOLZ?

ROB TYNER (Vocalist for Sixties hard rock one-shot phenoms the MC5) and HANDSOME DICK MANITOBA (Vocalist for Seventies hard rock one-shot phenoms the Dictators)? Both sure do have humungous Afros for a couple of white guys. Moreover, the Dictators' "Master Race Rock" sounds like an updated version of the MC5's "Rama Lama Fa Fa Fa" with some Ramones-ish "Let's Go" cheerleading thrown in, and both tunes occupy the same place on each group's first album (Side One, Band Four)!

RON WOOD and GEDDY LEE?

ALVIN LEE and MIKE SCORE? Score is/was (who cares?) the keyboardist/ vocalist for A Flock of Seagulls; his hairstyle has occasionally resembled a snowplow.

ALEX LIFESON and JEFF HEALEY? Both are extremely talented

The Rock & Roll Curmudgeon

lead guitarists. Both are blond. Both are Canadian. Hmmm.

PHIL SPECTOR and DUDLEY MOORE?

BOZ SCAGGS and NEIL PEART? Good grief! That takes care of the entire lineup of Rush! What does *that* tell ya?

COURTNEY LOVE and NANCY SPUNGEN?

Tiresome time-warp troubadour RICHIE HAVENS and tiresome time-warp activist DICK GREGORY?

Pink Floyd's RICK WRIGHT and BEETLEJUICE? Look at the back cover of the *The Delicate Sound of Thunder* concert video; you'll see what I mean.

Spinal Tap's DEREK SMALLS and LEMMY?

ROGER WATERS and ONE OF THOSE MYSTERIOUS, BROODING GIANT TIKI STATUES FOUND ON EASTER ISLAND? As far as I'm concerned, both have an equal amount of effervescence and charisma in their respective personalities.

SPECIAL BONUS! *TRIPLETS!* Spirit's ED CASSIDY, Lene Lovich guitarist LES CHAPPELL, and Midnight Oil vocalist/activist PETER GARRETT? Hell, they've practically got their own band... which reminds me, whatever happened to that surf band called the Pyramids? In case you're interested, Garrett lurches around onstage like one of those creatures in the Fifties sci-fi movie *Invaders From Mars*.

Maybe Dennis Miller summed it up years ago on "Saturday Night Live" when he announced that the "Separated at Birth" for that week was *Spy* magazine and *The National Enquirer*.

MATCH THAT MALEFACTION/ROLE MODEL ROULETTE!

Hey kids! Here's a fun new way to test your knowledge on current events (particularly if you're a regular reader of supermarket tabloids and other "tattletale" periodicals)!

Executive Rock

The object of this game is to match the malefactions shown in the first list with the activist and/or controversial singers, musicians, and rappers shown in the second list. Entertainers are listed in alphabetical order.

Remember, anything on the Malefactions list that anyone on the Entertainers list has done more than once counts individually. For example, any male performer who has fathered more than one illegitimate child gets one point for each child.

Not all of the Malefactions apply to all of the Entertainers listed, of course, but some performers *will* have more than one Malefaction applicable to them. Add ten extra points to your score if you correctly identify the individual who has the most *different* malefactions applicable to him/her (HINT: one person may not have *any* malefaction applicable to him/her, so don't get fooled).

First prize is one hour of free legal services from any member of the O.J. Simpson defense team. Second prize is *two* hours of free legal services from any member of the O.J. Simpson defense team. Good luck, and have fun!

MALEFACTIONS
Illegitimate children
Financial problems (I.R.S. and otherwise)
VIOLENCE: Gunplay
VIOLENCE: Against women
VIOLENCE: Other criteria
So-called "mid-life crisis"/"middle-age craziness"
Messy, public divorces/terminated relationships (includes palimony)
Multiple marriages
Alcoholism (to hell with P.C. terms like "chemical dependency" or "substance abuse")
Drug abuse (ditto)
Contributing to the delinquency of a minor
Failure to pay child support

ENTERTAINERS (Alphabetical order)
Calvin "Snoop Doggy Dogg" Broadus
Bobby Brown
Jackson Browne
Phil Collins
William "Flavor Flav" Drayton
Peter Gabriel
Don Henley
Chrissie Hynde
Kris Kristofferson

The Rock & Roll Curmudgeon

Tracy "Ice-T" Marrow
Willie Nelson
Sinead O'Connor
Tupac Shakur
Bruce Springsteen
Gordon "Sting" Sumner
Steve Tyler
Neil Young

OUTTAKES AND THROWAWAY CUTS:
An Average Consumer Gets P.O.'ed

Every once in a while one of the albums I've purchased (usually by a noted artist or group) will include some kind of bizarre, off-the-wall track on it that has no apparent relevance (musically, conceptually, whatever) to any of the other tunes. Most of the time such cuts are wacko enough to the extent that most listeners might consider them to be some sort of comic relief; however, the comparison shopper in me always feels like he's been cheated a bit if an album that I otherwise enjoy is interrupted by some dorky singalong or a few wasted minutes of apparently meaningless, abstract instrumental noodling.

Now, please understand that this, uh, "concept" isn't anything new, and when I first heard some primeval examples back in the Sixties, I did indeed consider most of them to be a sort of comic relief, but then again I'd grown into puberty listening to radio programming that included an awful lot of gimmick tunes ("Purple People Eater", "Witch Doctor", early Ray Stevens songs). The Beach Boys, for instance, had something on one of their pre-*Pet Sounds* albums that sounded like a free-for-all in a recording studio; I wasn't a fan of the BBs, but I believe the cut was called something like "Our Favorite Recording Sessions". At any rate, the snippet was neither too long nor very offensive, and of course it was immediately

Executive Rock

followed by yet another surf tune.

Another (and hopefully more widely heard) Sixties example would of course be the final cut on Cream's *Disraeli Gears* album, "Mother's Lament"; it's a boozy singalong done with only a piano for instrumentation, and the lyrics are "sung" in a hideous Cockney accent. The last thing one hears after the song lurches to a halt is someone (I think it's Jack Bruce) asking: "Do you wanna do it again?"

"Mother's Lament" is a song where I'll be a bit liberal and forgiving; at least it's at the *end* of the album, so maybe a listener is supposed to think that this tune was added as an afterthought; perhaps it was an attempt to end the album on a different, quirky note. I can handle that, and I'll even put up with a throwaway cut *at the end of Side One,* although if I was to hear such a number in the *middle* of a CD (where it would appear if the songs are arranged in the same sequence as they appear on an LP or cassette) my reaction might be different. Another "outro outtake" of note is Emerson, Lake & Palmer's "Are You Ready Eddie", a 12-bar romp that was apparently supposed to demonstrate that the English progressive juggernaut could also *ROCK AND ROLL!!!* Zzzzzz.

One of the more recent tunes that really set my teeth on edge (because it was interrupting a great album, plus it *stunk)* was "Mother", from the Police's otherwise classic *Synchronicity* album. A ridiculous raveup featuring Andy Summers' Oedipal yelp, the "song" so grated on me that I made a resolution to punch that aging blond dwarf in the nose if I ever encountered him, and I refuse to buy the CD for the same reason, in spite of the presence of a bonus track ("Murder by Numbers"). At least another, somewhat similar song on another Police album ("On Any Other Day" from *Regatta De Blanc*, which Stewart Copeland sings) is prefaced by the spoken phrase: "The others are complete bull****." Come to think of it, the album did seem to sorta go downhill after that...

So far it may seem that the only culpable combos have been English trios, but that ain't necessarily so, although it seems that a disproportionate number of offending bands have come from the British Isles. Years ago, *Mad* magazine had a feature that showed a photo gallery of certain celebrities; each was supposedly saying one thing, but he/she was thinking something quite the reverse to himself/herself (in a cloud-like "thought" balloon), and the only example I can remember was Salvador Dali in front of his abstract paintings, stating "I paint what I *feel!*", while thinking to himself: "I haven't got the talent to paint realistically!" Some artsy snobs might get offended by the following pronouncement, but I feel like it's even more of a con if I've heard brilliant music from an artist or group, but if I also have to put up with non-melodic, out-of-it filler, I get p.o.'ed, because I know the talent's there. King Crimson practically wrote the

The Rock & Roll Curmudgeon

book on this idea, from "Moonchild" on their first album to "Industry" on their '84 effort, spanning over a decade and a half. Moreover, while Pink Floyd's "Interstellar Overdrive" was I guess supposed to be considered "psychedelic" when it was released in 1967, nowadays it seems not only incredibly boring but also a fitting requiem for Syd Barrett.

"Feedback" (found on the Grateful Dead's *Live Dead*) and "Free Form Guitar" (by the late Terry Kath; from the Chicago Transit Authority debut) are exactly what the titles state, and are every bit as ludicrous as "Two Minutes' Silence" and "Baby's Heartbeat", which appear on an early John Lennon and Yoko Ono 'venture'.

Uninhibited spenders even have the opportunity to blow their bucks on *entire albums* of meaningless schlock. Usually such atrocities are jam sessions, sometimes recorded quite sloppily, but the fact that such one-offs are even marketed raises questions concerning the intent of artists and/or record companies, and to my mind the definitive example was *Jamming With Edward*, some meaningless blues jams by members of the Rolling Stones. When this came out it was rightfully excoriated by critics and consumers alike.

Rock doesn't have a monopoly on wasteful dorkism, however. The redoubtable Pat Metheny's first couple of albums were a breath of fresh air, but once he got into experimenting with guitar synthesizers, I got alienated. Such tunes as "Forward March" on the *Full Circle* album should have the same effect on most listeners as fingernails on a chalkboard.

I won't even discuss so-called "music" by so-called "performance artists".

Different strokes for different folks, I suppose, but don't expect me to sing the praises of someone's album if even a small part of it is a bit weird for the average listener.

Jeez, I just had a horrible thought. How am I supposed to know what is and isn't a throwaway cut on a *Zappa* album?!?

Executive Rock

DON'T QUIT YOUR DAY JOB: Famous Musicians, Singers, and Rappers Who Shouldn't Be Actors/Actresses (and Vice Versa, in No Particular Order)

Gordon "Sting" Sumner

Sylvester Stallone

Madonna Ciccone

Eddie Murphy

John Cougar Mellencamp

Caryn "Whoopi Goldberg" Johnson

Dan Ackroyd

Tracy "Ice-T" Marrow

Bruce Willis

Phil Collins

Bobcat Goldthwait

Huey Lewis

Val Kilmer (and everybody else in *The Doors* movie)

Patrick Swayze

O'Shea "Ice Cube" Jackson

Gene "Ol' Titan Tongue" Simmons

Glenn Frey (and every other musician who ever appeared on *Miami Vice*)

Don Johnson (tit for tat)

Philip Michael Thomas (ditto)

Joe Piscopo

L.L. Cool J

Isaac Hayes

Rodney Dangerfield

Tom Waits (the problem here is that I don't know whether Waits considers himself to be a musician or an actor)

HONORABLE MENTIONS FROM OTHER CAREER FIELDS: Shaquille O'Neal, the late Lee "Backbeat" Atwater

NOTABLE EXCEPTIONS: Sissy Spacek, Carl Perkins, Beverly D'Angelo

The Rock & Roll Curmudgeon

A COMPLETE LIST OF ADMIRABLE THINGS ABOUT MADONNA, GANGSTA RAP AND THE LATE SEVENTIES DISCO PHENOMENON

MISCELLANEOUS COLUMNS & ESSAYS

"RICKY NELSON WAS RIGHT"

There was a time in the career of the late singer/actor whose name is in the title of this essay when he was billed as "Rick Nelson" instead of "Ricky Nelson", but most people probably remember the pop star by his older and "more youthful" given name, since he grew up in front of millions of television viewers on the Ozzie & Harriet show.

With all due respect to someone who examines the lyrics of popular songs for any controversial material (subliminal, backward-masked, or up-front), I think sometimes other lyrics that *aren't* potentially worthy of a warning sticker tend to go right by an average listener's mind; i.e., he/she doesn't listen close enough to note the content and meaning (if indeed the lyrics have some intellectual value). For example, when U2's "In the Name of Love" was released, a lot of music fans I knew didn't realize that it referred to Martin Luther King; I distinctly remember repeating the lyrics about "shots ring out in the Memphis sky; free at last" to some college boy who was unaware of the song's attempted socio-political commentary/so-called "deeper meaning".

For many Boomers, one of the best-known (and most notorious) efforts at listening closely to the lyrics of a particular song would have been attempting to discern what dirty words (if any) were found in the Kingsmen's version of "Louie Louie". But it was this "I-didn't-know-the-song-meant-such-and-such" mentality that caused Ricky Nelson's name to come up at the tail end of a conversation with Rogene and Malc. We were discussing

Executive Rock

our respective music collections, and which artists had the largest representation of albums in each.

Malc is a full-blown Kinks and Rolling Stones nut, while Rogene has everything the Pink Floyd ever released (domestically, at least). Two interesting tidbits came to mind: First, all three of us had ongoing interests in veteran bands that had been *commercially successful* for years; none of us were interested in "critically acclaimed" aggregations that might have been around for the same length of time. Second, such longtime fan-dom could've been more, uh, "intense"; one of us coulda been a Deadhead...

Nevertheless, the artists that had the "thickest" sections in my CD and cassette racks caused my peers to do a bit of a double-take:

So who you got the most albums by?" asked Rogene.

"Tangerine Dream, Motorhead, and the Alan Parsons Project", I replied.

Malc practically spat out his reaction: "You gotta be ****in' kiddin'. What kinda mix is *that?*"

"Well, for one thing, I think each of 'em is probably a definitive example of their particular musical genres."

"Which are?"

"Respectively, New Age, Heavy Metal, and, uh.... High-Tech/High-Fidelity Pseudo-Intellectual Pop, I guess."

"The Motorhead portion I can understand, given your Lemmy fixation."

"Ain't no 'fixation'."

"The hell it isn't! You play a Rickenbacker bass, you raise your mike and tilt it back like Lemmy does, you do chord stuff on your Rick, you even yell out things when a song goes into a guitar break."

"You're confusing 'fixation' with 'musical influence', ya schmuck."

"Don't get pseudo-intellectual on me", growled Malc. "You've already applied that term to the Alan Parsons Project."

"True, but the fact is while I may emulate Lemmy whenever I play, there are some aspects of his lifestyle, based on what I know about it, that I'm *very* uncomfortable with, although said lifestyle is none of my business. I'd like to think that I've got enough sense to differentiate between such when it comes to rock stars."

"A lotta musicians and/or wanna-bees either can't or won't", offered Rogene, in a rare (for him) moment of profundity.

"No argument from me. But you know how Motorhead has always had some potent riffs, and how their sound has actually improved over the years, and how there's nothing pretentious about their approach; you know where they're comin' from, and you can pay attention or leave it alone. Their, er, 'evolution' has been interesting to monitor."

"Didn't you write something a while back about Tangerine Dream having been through more than one 'phase'?" asked Rogene.

128

Miscellaneous Columns & Essays

"Yeah; they started out as some electronic-psychedelic avant-garde outfit, then sorta "busted out" with that early Seventies album called *Phaedra*, then they got more into individual 'songs' on their albums instead of side-long stuff that segued from one 'movement' to another, and that's when I got alienated. About the only albums of theirs I've sampled since around the early Eighties has been the live stuff, on accounta the segues are still on those. But those Seventies albums on the Virgin label are still interesting; weird, ain't it?"

"The music or your ongoing interest in it?" Malc chortled, then changed the subject: "I don't understand the Alan Parsons Project; you know how much the critics slagged that so-called 'band' over the years."

"I don't give a **** what critics say. Quite frankly, if something appeals to rock music critics *these* days, it's almost like a red flag that I *won't* like it."

"How many Alan Parsons Project albums you got?"

"Just about everything but *Eve*."

"Did you boycott that one because the cover had been deemed by some people as being insulting to women?"

"No, I heard it, but it just wasn't as appealing to me as some of the others, before *and* after."

"Which albums on which formats?"

"What difference does it make?"

"Whether or not you're 'into' an artist enough to commit to their albums on CD, if you have or had the albums on LP or cassette."

"Okay, fair enough. I had just about everything on LP, then I started finding a buncha Alan Parsons Project cassettes in cutout racks so most of what I now have are those; they were an inexpensive way to replace records."

"I always thought the Alan Parsons Project could've been another Pink Floyd", said Rogene, throwing the conversation off track.

"How?" Malc and I said in unison.

"When *Tales of Mystery and Imagination* came out in the mid-Seventies, it was weird and psychedelic, and the Floyd wasn't too active then; *Animals* stunk. *I Robot* was unusual, too."

"Parsons wasn't and isn't the icon that the Pink Floyd was/is", I said. "But the 'mysterious' comparison might have some merit. Other than that I don't see that much in common." (or so I thought at the time...)

Malc got the conversation back on course by asking which Alan Parsons Project albums I had on Compact Disc.

"*Tales of Mystery and Imagination, I Robot, The Instrumental Works,* and *Try Anything Once.*"

"The first two albums, the instrumental anthology, and the latest one?"

129

Executive Rock

(NOTE: This conversation took place prior to the release of an Alan Parsons live album in the Summer of 1995.)

"Actually, the *Tales of Mystery and Imagination* CD is a *remixed* version, with some spoken word stuff by Orson Welles on it; I didn't know he was on there, and the first time I listened to it, the beginning scared the bejeezus out of me. *The Instrumental Works* gets a bit redundant, I'll admit. And I bought *Try Anything Once* on cassette when we were living in an apartment while our new home was being built; I got the CD when we moved in. *Try Anything Once* is credited to Alan Parsons, the individual, not the Alan Parsons *Project.*"

"And the cover looks like a Pink Floyd cover!" said Rogene, giving us an I-told-you-so smirk (turned out he was right on the money; the cover of *Try Anything Once* and the cover of the 1995 live release were designed by Storm Thorgeson, the old Hipgnosis honcho. I don't know if he did any earlier Alan Parsons Project covers; it wouldn't be surprising if he had).

"If anything like your cassette of *Vulture Culture* or *Pyramid* or even *Gaudi* tears up, you gonna replace it with a CD?"

"I don't know. I'll cross that bridge when I get to it. I may not replace it at all; I don't have as much time to listen to music these days."

"That's still an unusual trio of groups to have a lotta albums by", said Malc.

"I betcha the Alan Parsons Project has sold more albums in its history than Motorhead and Tangerine Dream combined. Parsons has certainly gotten more airplay, and would certainly be more listenable to an average consumer."

"I guess Ricky Nelson was right", offered Rogene.

"How?" Malc and I said in unison again.

"That line of his in 'Garden Party' about how ya can't please everyone so ya gotta please yourself. That song was about how he played Madison Square Garden; that's where the 'garden' in the title comes from. He tried to do some songs that were current at the time, and the audience didn't wanna hear 'em; they just wanted things like 'Hello Mary Lou'."

"Which brings up the question about whether or not veteran pop or rock stars should continue to do what made 'em famous, or branch out into something different at the risk of alienating their fan base. And you have to admit that even though Tangerine Dream *has* been through some 'phases', any album of theirs would be filed in New Age. What's more, Motorhead and Alan Parsons have pretty much stuck to their so-called roots."

"That's true", said Malc, standing up and stretching while signaling the waitress at Dimitri's for his tab, "but that's another subject for another time. I gotta go to work tomorrow."

Miscellaneous Columns & Essays

"Me too. Lemme know if you wanna borrow any of those albums we were talking about."

"I never heard that remixed *Tales of Mystery and Imagination*. Orson Welles, huh?"

"Yup. I'll drop it by your store later this week."

"I'd appreciate it. G'night."

"'Night."

IN MEMORY OF PETER GREEN

As far as I know, erstwhile British blues guitar god Peter Green is still alive as of this writing. It's not like publishing a "pre-mortem" essay (for lack of a better term) hasn't been done before; the October 1985 issue of *Spin* contained a horrifying and brilliantly-written profile entitled "The Death of David Crosby".

It's been over twenty-five years since Peter Green left the original version of Fleetwood Mac, and not much has been heard from him since. The rumors surrounding this near-mythical player from the halcyon days of British blues are the stuff from which legends are made; examples include:

(1) Green's upbringing was a real-life version of *The Jazz Singer*. His real surname is Greenbaum, and one of the reasons he got into blues (and, ultimately, one of the reasons he ended up "living the blues") was due to an strict Orthodox Jewish childhood.

(2) His erratic behavior can be blamed on ingesting some bad acid.

(3) He *did* get ahold of some too-potent drugs at one point, but he's a recluse because of his disgust and contempt for the music business.

(4) At one point he grew his fingernails several inches long so he wouldn't have to play guitar.

(5) From time to time, someone claiming to be Peter Green will surface; said individual is an imposter and has been known to give interviews... (or maybe there's been more than one phony Green).

Executive Rock

More tales regarding Green are around, but how much credence the five pronouncements listed above as well as other rumors should be accorded is debatable, since the real facts concerning Peter Green's abrupt withdrawal from public life may never be known... and perhaps that's the way it should be.

So after all this time, there probably isn't much "gray area" about Peter Green; my perception is that blues lovers worship him as a demigod in limbo, or else he's unknown to the average rock music fan, and methinks there's a lot of *Vintage Guitar* readers that fit into the former category, considering the demographics of a survey *VG* took when its 100th issue was released.

Like all too many other guitar aficionados, I became aware of Green during the latter days of his tenure with Fleetwood Mac (the latter days of his public performing career, as it turned out). I knew that the Mac was a British blues band whose lineup included former members of John Mayall's Bluesbreakers and that they'd had a minor instrumental hit called "Albatross", but their fairly straightforward approach to the playing the blues didn't seem to generate that much enthusiasm among mainstream American rock fans, and I have to admit I was among the Yanks that weren't too interested... *at the time.*

Then I heard *Then Play On* soon after it was released. Its emphasis on more volume seemed to evoke more emotional playing from the band members, *especially* Green and his remarkable-sounding Gibson Les Paul. Backtracking, I discovered gems from Green's Bluebreakers days; incredible instrumentals such as "The Supernatural" and "Greeny" hold up to this day.

But for my money, the definitive Peter Green tune was (and still is) Fleetwood Mac's cover of "Homework", from the 1969 live-in-the-studio Chicago sessions that the band recorded with some of their blues heroes. The tone that Green's guitar got on that song (with no overdubs or fancy studio effects) give me a *serious* case of "the willies", as did his plaintive singing. Eric Clapton may have had his "woman tone" back then, but I'll step out on a limb here and opine that Green's sound was even more meaningful... at least, that was the case for me. Perhaps Wishbone Ash's Ted Turner nailed it in a 1992 interview when he spoke of how Peter Green *"conveyed so much emotion with so little"*, and "Homework" may be a prime example of such.

Many tomes have been written about the debt that white rockers owe to the blues and its black founders, and while that subject could be debated ad infinitum, suffice to say that most long time Peter Green fans would probably be unanimous in their opinion that Green was one white boy to whom the blues may indeed have been a way of life. I mean, if anyone

Miscellaneous Columns & Essays

can listen to the likes of the plaintive "Jumpin' At Shadows" or the terrifying "Green Manalishi" and not feel moved by the naked emotion such songs convey, such an unresponsive listener doesn't have a soul.

Over the last few years, my own interest in Peter Green has taken on a new and revitalized sense of urgency, for reasons that I can't fully explain. I finally found *Then Play On* on Compact Disc several years ago, and I also bought some imported CD anthologies (*Like It This Way*, and a three-disc set called *The Blues Years*, which includes some of the aforementioned Chicago cuts with the studio patter edited out). Moreover, some live material by the first incarnation of the band began showing up in cassette cutout bins in record stores a while back; the two albums I found and bought were called *Greatest Hits Live* and *The Early Years*. The latter consists primarily of early rock and roll cover tunes ("Jenny, Jenny", "Keep A-Knockin' "), but the former is a tour de force performance, with great versions of "Oh Well" and "Black Magic Woman", a sixteen-minute version of "Green Manalishi" and a remarkable instrumental called "World in Harmony" that goes Wishbone Ash one better on accounta it's got *triple-harmony* guitars on it. Natch, I soon owned the Compact Disc versions of *Greatest Hits Live* and *The Early Years* once I searched 'em out...

Turns out the two live albums are culled from a series of recordings done in Boston, but I was made aware of the "Hope Diamond" of live Fleetwood Mac Phase One recordings by a *VG* reader from the Pacific Northwest. Seems that he wrote me c/o the magazine, taking exception to my listing Judas Priest's version of "Green Manalishi" in an "Executive Rock" column about cover songs. Thus began a cordial correspondence between the two of us due to our mutual admiration of Peter Green, but the other guy is much more into the subject than I am; he not only sent me items such as a photostat of a story from a British music periodical about Peter Green having been committed to a mental institution (the issue dated from the mid-Seventies), he also sent some recordings he'd dubbed off on cassette.

Among those rarities was another item from the live Boston sessions, a *monstrous* medley of songs from *Then Play On*. It starts out with "Rattlesnake Shake", works its way into a revved-up "Madge" jam, abruptly downshifts to "Underway", then slowly and inexorably chugs back up to the "Madge" riff again before exploding in a frantic, chaotic climax (Green's Les Paul is literally *screaming)* that makes any other multiple-guitar rave-up that might have attained so-called "anthem" status seem tame by comparison; nothing else even comes close. The juggernaut clocks in at around twenty-four minutes, and a listener is left feeling completely drained when it's over. Various incarnations of the Boston sessions are available on imported Compact Discs, and the medley from *Then Play On* alone makes

Executive Rock

the price of admission as well as the effort in locating such recordings worthwhile.

Another item I bought strictly due to Peter Green's playing is the recent Bacon and Day Gibson Les Paul book. That magnificent-sounding '59 Les Paul, which Green sold to Gary Moore soon after departing Fleetwood Mac, appears in the book, along with Les Pauls used by Jimmy Page, Jeff Beck, etc. Yet I find myself studying that worn Sunburst with the tight-grain top, the reversed neck pickup, mismatched knobs, and no pickguard. I've been able to view and hold such guitars as the first Fender solidbody prototype and Jeff Beck's Esquire from his Yardbirds days, and such occurrences have exciting, but if by some chance I was ever able to view and hold the Green/Moore Les Paul, I'd probably get goose bumps from the experience.

David Crosby's name is on a list I've compiled called "Famous Musicians and Singers I Thought Would Be Dead By Now"; Peter Green's name *isn't* on the list, because if someone's been out of the public eye for a quarter-century, it's hard to consider him/her "famous" anymore. I've heard Green being compared with other "pathetic icons" such as Syd Barrett, and that doesn't seem quite fair. The most recent imported Fleetwood Mac CD I purchased was *The Original Fleetwood Mac*, a sloppily-recorded-but-still-interesting live effort purported to be the band's last performance at the Fillmore West in 1970. On it, Green can be heard chatting with the audience, and he even whips out a harmonica for a solo rendition of "Oh Susanna". Sho' don't sound like no raving and drooling acid casualty to me.

So I hope Peter Green is at peace with himself, regardless of the reasons he's opted to maintain a private existence. I wonder if he realizes how many fans he still has after all these years, and how the majority of such fans would probably opine that no one has purveyed such emotional playing, before or since.

At least we've got our CDs to make sure we never forget, and to hopefully show younger players (if they'll make the effort to listen) that some rock guitarists *meant* what they were playing more than most listeners may have ever known.

But does anybody seriously think we'll ever hear the likes of "Green Manalishi", "Homework" or "Searching for Madge" again???

Miscellaneous Columns & Essays

IN PRAISE OF SNOOZE-AGE GUITARISTS AND INSTRUMENTS

There used to be a two-panel 'Hi and Lois' cartoon stuck up on our refrigerator; in the first panel, a visiting friend of the teenage son was holding a record album which had a cover that had 'Windy Hill' and 'Ambient Environment' emblazoned on its cover, and he was incredulous that another of the son's family members was apparently "into" the genre to which the album belonged. "Your dad doesn't actually listen to this boring New Age music, does he?" the visitor inquired.

"Not much", responded the son. Cut to the second panel, where Dad was shown snoring on the sofa while music notes wafted from stereo speakers. "He usually falls asleep during the first song," observed the offspring.

It's my opinion that the first so-called "New Age" album (although the term didn't exist in the early Seventies) may have been Mike Oldfield's *Tubular Bells* (for reasons that will be detailed in the "Oldfield in the Ozone"/"Boy Wonder Bounces Back" essay), although one repair guy at a local guitar store pointed out that Tangerine Dream's *Electronic Meditation* album was released in the late Sixties (at one point Oldfield and the Tangs were stablemates on the Virgin label). The guitar tech had a point, but the fact is, back then the "music" of Tangerine Dream was so abstract it was probably lumped into some kind of "experimental" or "avant-garde" categorization, and those terms have probably been utilized (perhaps as a *convenience* as much as anything else) since the first eerie howling of a theremin was recorded, or perhaps even earlier...

Hailed in the Eighties as a new, multifaceted musical genre that lent itself to individual interpretation, New Age music was also dissed by others as redundant and indeed boring, but there was apparently enough interest for New Age to get its own chart in *Billboard* magazine (SIDEBAR: It needs to be pointed out at this juncture that Disco also had its own chart in *Billboard* some time ago).

True, New Age encompasses a lot of different styles, many of which defy being pigeonholed into traditional musical categories. However, a general stereotype about New Age music is that it's lightweight, fairly melodic, ambient, airy and artsy. For my money, a good recent sampler for novice listeners is the *Polar Shift* anthology, a benefit album.

VH-l was de-programmed from my TV soon after MTV was erased in 1990, and for the same reasons: The format (like MTV) had gotten to where it was trying to be everything for everybody, and perhaps a microcosm of such attempted egalitarianism was a weekend show on VH-l called "New Visions". This program started out as a bona fide New Age video

135

Executive Rock

showcase, featuring works by Suzanne Ciani, Lanz and Speer, etc. (lotsa nature scenes and computer videography), and ultimately guest veejays began to show up; such luminaries included Ciani, steel drum player Andy Narell, the amazing Michael Hedges, and even Carlos Santana. Most of the time such hosts would play something live in the studio; one of the outstanding examples was Hedges performing a solo tune on a parlor-size guitar; he'd tentatively named the song "March", and it lived up to its (possibly temporary) title. It was quite exciting, and was exemplary of why Michael Hedges is hailed as an innovator in contemporary guitar music; he always seems to be striving to come up with something new and listenable.

And there's the rub: Y'see, unlike rock and roll, the instrument of choice in the New Age genre ain't the electric guitar; rather, keyboard instruments seem to be the dominant musical tool. From George Winston's solo piano to Yanni's orchestrations to Kitaro's redundant and boring efforts (some of his synth programs sound like a whistling teakettle), the keys outnumber the fretboards among artists found in the New Age section of a record store (ANOTHER SIDEBAR: How come both Yanni and Kitaro seem to be taking themselves so seriously in their videos? Yanni must be doing something right, on accounta his girlfriend is Linda "Forever Audra" Evans).

Another facet in the mix is of course MIDI; i.e., there's MIDI keyboards that can sound like guitars, and there's MIDI guitars that can sound like keyboards, so instrumentation may sometimes be as nebulous as categorizing the music itself. A guitarist named David Torn once hosted a "New Visions" show, and his rig was so complex that when he performed his in-the-studio solo piece, what came out didn't sound like a guitar at all; the effort sounded like a hamster dribbling a billiard ball on a marble floor, and it seemed appropriate that Torn was playing a headless Steinberger instrument.

The overrated Windham Hill label actually released a couple of guitar anthologies a while back; the first was primarily acoustic while the second featured artists like the aforementioned Hedges and Torn, plus Michael Manring, who may be the most talented bass player on the planet (an electronic keyboard anthology from Windham Hill had the neat title of *Soul of the Machine*). But when you think about it, who besides Hedges has exhibited any durability as a guitarist in the New Age category? Alex DeGrassi, maybe? Who else???

As noted in the "LISTS" section, one cutout cassette that I'll buy if I ever encounter it on Compact Disc is *Into the Rainbow* by Max Lasser, who was/is a peer of electro-harpist Andreas Vollenweider (and many people consider Vollenweider to be a progenitor of the New Age phenomenon). Indeed, there are times when Lasser's guitar and Vollenweider's harp sound quite similar, but I like this earlier effort of Lasser's much

136

Miscellaneous Columns & Essays

better than his later major-label albums, because Lasser (like Vollenweider) apparently got hung up on producing recordings that concentrated too much on artistry and arrangement; i.e., they ended up sounding somewhat pretentious. What's more, the reed solos on such Lasser albums as *Earthwalk* and *Timejump* sound out of place and annoying.

And that's why the recent efforts of none other than Craig Chaquico are so refreshing. The former Jefferson Starship guitarist has crossed over to New Age in admirable fashion, and his playing represents the direction in which Lasser should have gone. Both *Acoustic Highway* and *Acoustic Planet* were Grammy-nominated, and the latter album actually bumped Yanni's grandiose-but-listenable *Live at the Acropolis* from the top of the *Billboard* chart a while back. Chaquico deftly walks the fine line between New Age and simple, melodic guitar music, and the popularity of his efforts speaks for itself. Cynics might dis Chaquico's playing as treading somewhat close to the dreaded "L.A. Happy Jazz" pigeonhole (especially since he covers Starship's "Find Your Way Back" on *Acoustic Planet*), but it sounds like Chaquico is having the time of his life on his instrumental albums, and while ya can't sing along with the tunes, you'll probably find yourself *humming* along with the majority of 'em.

Ultimately, I haven't kept many New Age albums in my collection. It's difficult to listen to lower-volume recordings while riding in an automobile, due to the road noise, so the likes of Chaquico, Lasser, etc. usually get listened to around the household early in the morning or during "winddown" time in the evening.

And with all due respect to the cartoon noted at the outset of this essay, it turns out the so-called soporific effects of New Age music were actually *marketed.* I once encountered a cassette (in the cutout section, natch) called *SLEEPER: Soundtrack to a Dream* by a musician named Michael Lee Thomas; the album was supposed to help a listener take a nap then awaken him/her in a refreshed state of being, and it even came with a warning that a listener should not be driving an automobile or operating machinery while playing the cassette! That kinda hype is like a high-tech audio equivalent of some of the stunts that director William Castle used to stage for his horror flicks back in the Fifties and Sixties ("*$1000 IF YOU DIE BY FRIGHT!*").

Yet it also seems to me that the New Age genre may have gotten so muddled that like Disco, its days as a separately-noted category may be numbered (I've noticed that some record stores no longer have a separate New Age section; for the most part, New Age albums are now found in the Jazz or Instrumental sections of such stores).

I think that's what ultimately happened to "New Visions" on VH-1, for that matter. It got to where there were separate "New Visions" shows

Executive Rock

appearing each night of the week, concentrating on Jazz one night, so-called World Music the next, etc., and such shows were usually hosted by the redoubtable Nile Rodgers (on some occasions he'd sit in with some of the guests; many times he was playing an old 3/4 scale Gibson ES-140 guitar). Perhaps a telling moment about how "New Visions" had gotten too diverse and/or multi-cultural for its britches was seen in an advertisement for the show. Some musician I'd never heard of named Jovon was shown, and Rodgers was seen enthusing to the camera: "This guy plays strong stuff, and you're *definitely* not gonna hear it on the radio!"

Uh, maybe there's a reason for that, Nile...

But what about the instruments themselves? It seems like there are some unique stringed instruments that are sometimes seen and heard within the New Age genre, and it might be appropriate to cite some of those as well. One might think that the title of this essay should have said "...AND FRETTED INSTRUMENTS", but the fact is more than one traditional-looking guitar or bass we'll note is indeed fretless, as we'll soon see.

An obvious starting point would the electric harp of Andreas Vollenweider, since, as noted earlier, Vollenweider is probably considered by many New Age aficionados to be one of the cornerstones of the genre. Indeed, some of the guitarists cited earlier (Craig Chaquico, Max Lasser) purvey tones that often sound a lot like Vollenweider's expressive efforts.

More than one electric *harp guitar* has been seen (and heard) in the New Age genre. Michael Hedges was toting one on the cover of the October 1990 issue of *Guitar Player*, and an almost-unknown player named Timothy Donahue performed a solo piece called "Watching A Movie" on his handmade harp guitar on VH-1's "New Visions" program some years ago. The guitar portion of Donahue's instrument was a solidbody electric with a *fretless* neck; it had a "meow"-like tone as Donahue played the melody on the neck with his left hand while accompanying himself on the harp strings with his right hand. It was a brilliant, innovative work, made all the more enthralling because it was a solo effort. Donahue released an album called *The Fifth Season* some years ago; while some solo pieces are on there in addition to songs performed with other musicians, "Watching A Movie" isn't included. I once saw a magazine article on Donahue that featured photos of some of his other handmade instruments, including a fretless flat-top acoustic(!).

Then there's Michael Manring's exotic Zon Hyperbass (also fretless). As of this writing, Manring's done three solo albums that fit into the New Age category (*Unusual Weather*, *Toward the Center of Night*, and *Drastic*

Miscellaneous Columns & Essays

Measures), a rock album with the improbable title of *Thonk*, plus a couple of albums with a band called Montreaux (while *Thonk* features guitar players like Steve Morse and Alex Skolnick, invariably it seems to end up in the New Age section of most stores I've frequented).

The Hyperbass even *looks* imposing; not only is it fretless, it has an unusual shape and de-tuner levers for every string. Supposedly Manring always wows 'em at NAMM shows with his solo demonstrations (during which he changes the tuning of the Hyperbass without missing a beat). And that's one reason his solo pieces on his New Age recordings are so intriguing. Some of his group efforts seem to concentrate too much on bleating woodwinds, but when Manring proffers ambitious solo efforts like "Red Light Returning" and a cover of "Purple Haze"(!) it's easy to see why his bass playing is so highly regarded by other musicians (if not by a large segment of average music fans).

The redoubtable Electric Stick, an invention of one Emmett Chapman, is an obvious choice for a list such as this. It's been around for a couple of decades, from what I can determine, and in essence it's a ten-stringed plank that is played with both hands (somewhat like a piano; bass lines with the left hand, melody lines with the right hand). There's also a recent "upgrade" model known as the Grand Stick, which has *twelve* strings.

I've written about the Stick before and won't get too redundant here; the previous essay featured a conversation with Stick player Trey Gunn, who at the time was playing with longtime cutting edge guitarist Robert Fripp in a band called Sunday All Over the World. Since then, Fripp and Gunn have continued their musical relationship in yet another incarnation of King Crimson.

However, the previous *VG* column about the Stick prompted some correspondence between a player from the Phoenix area named Mike Kollwitz and me; Kollwitz sent me some of his recordings, including one recorded live in concert at a local park with a drummer accompanying him. While the Stick is capable of holding its own in almost any musical genre, I'll have to say that some of the most intriguing passages of music produced by Stick players are solo pieces (which would probably be stereotyped as New Age-ish), and most of the unaccompanied tunes Kollwitz sent me simply reinforce such an opinion.

It's interesting that the instruments cited herein are played with *both* hands by their respective players. Whether they're tapping or plucking, the likes of Vollenweider, Donahue, Manring and Kollwitz are true artisans, and while their recordings may not be in the platinum sales level, they should command the respect of almost any person (especially other musicians) for their efforts in creating new sounds on unique stringed instruments.

139

Executive Rock

Players like these folks (and some of the guitarists cited earlier) could really figure into a discussion about whether a player is a "musician", artist", or "entertainer" (or combinations of the terms). And goodness knows what kind of response I'd get if I posed that sort of question to the aforementioned Robert Fripp.

LEMMY OUTTA HERE! Seventeen Reasons (in No Particular Order) Why Kilmister is Cool

1. Has one of the ugliest mugs in rock and roll, and could care less. I bet if Lemmy ever encountered the likes of Duran Duran he'd punch their collective lights out.

2. Whomps a Rickenbacker bass, and it's about the only one seen in Heavy Metal. What's more, his unique playing style as well as the inherent tonal properties of the Rick have helped distinguish Motorhead's sound from other bands.

3. Is hardly ever seen (on TV *or* in videos or photos) not wearing black leather.

4. Motorhead's "no frills" approach is also apparently applicable to their videos. The most dramatic "concept" I've seen in a Motorhead video showed Lemmy playing cards with the "Pinhead" character from the "Hellraiser" movies; all the other Motorhead videos I've seen were either live cuts or pantomimed performance clips (Again, it needs to be noted here that I de-programmed MTV from my TV on 15 APR 90, so maybe I've missed a couple of more complex Motorhead videos. B.F.D.).

5. Writes antidrug songs. After one particular verse of "White Line Fever" on the *What's Words Worth* live album, Lemmy throws in an ad-lib, rasping: *"Issa slow death!"*

6. Reason #1 is reinforced by the fact that an earlier incarnation of his teeth resembled a vandalized cemetery (I think he got a new set of choppers). The original dental aesthetics rivaled those of Joe Strummer, "singer"

140

Miscellaneous Columns & Essays

for the late, unlamented Clash. "Just call me Snaggletooth", indeed...

7. Older than I am and still going strong.

8. Songs by Motorhead are among the most memorable in Heavy Metal, usually due to the thunderous riffs and choppy lyrics. When their live *No Sleep At All* album came out in the late Eighties, a sticker was found on the cover proclaiming the contents to be "A Different Kettle of Metal", and such a pronouncement was pretty much on the mark.

9. I cringed in the mid-Eighties when I read that Motorhead had hooked up with producer Bill Laswell; Laswell had produced dance/pop artists and was also playing in an oddball jazz/rock combo called Material. However, the resulting album, *Orgasmatron*, was a sonic masterpiece; the drums on the first tune, "Deaf Forever" (wotta title!), sounded like *cannons*. I only heard the cassette, so for all I know the Compact Disc version might literally knock a listener over backwards.

10. Some years ago, when I read his comments about why he raises his microphone I decided to try it myself, and so help me, *it works*. Not only do I have a lot more lung power, but it's also easier to sing since my throat isn't being compressed by having to sing into a mike that's at mouth level or lower. Sure, it looks a bit awkward (in fact, it was downright unsettling to one club owner for whom my band was auditioning), but I've used this setup ever since I first tried it, and the credit goes to Kilmister.

11. Reason #2 is reinforced by the fact that many Motorhead tunes have a roaring, throbbing intro that uninitiated listeners might think is a guitar, when it's actually Lemmy's *bass*. Examples include "Ace of Spades", "Nothin' Up My Sleeve", and "Back at the Funny Farm", which also has the classic line: "I really like this jacket, but the sleeves are much too long!"

12. It takes, uh, "stones" to record a duet of "Stand By Your Man" with ex-Plasmatics "singer" Wendy O. Williams (NOTE: Williams' initials spelled upside-down equals "MOM").

13. Didn't ask to see a preliminary copy of his interview before it was published in *Vintage Guitar*.

14. Only guy I've every heard that pronounces the second 'b' in the word "bomber".

15. Whatcha see (and hear) is whatcha get: No hype, no bull****, and as the title of one of many Motorhead anthologies states, no remorse. Take it or leave it.

16. Blatantly copped the signature riff from Ray Charles' "What'd I Say" and got away with it ("Boogieman" on the *Rock and Roll* album).

17. Last but not least, if I ever wrote anything negative, I'd be afraid of getting beat up if I ever ran into him.... eh, wot?

141

Executive Rock

THIS MONTH'S CONTEST: Name That Gobber!

One of the most intense scenes I've ever witnessed in rock video can be found on the "Police Around the World" videotape, which is a documentary of the Bottle Blonds' fabled 1980-81 world tour. In addition to performance footage and sight-seeing in such exotic locations as Bombay and Hong Kong, there's a disturbing incident that happened when the band was onstage in France.

The group has just begun playing "De Do Do Do, De Da Da Da" (Sting is utilizing a fretless Precision; Andy Summers has his trusty battered Telecaster Custom), and as they start the first chorus, suddenly the redoubtable Mr. Sumner gets doused by a fusillade of spit from stage right!

As might be expected, Sting responds by shrieking obscenities at his assailant, but trouper that he is, he nevertheless storms through the remainder of the song, all the while glaring daggers and muttering threats. You can practically *see* the malevolence gushing from his pores, but he never misses a beat.

As the band meanders into the instrumental passage that winds up the tune, Sting *dances* out to the front of the stage, and hocks a *monster* wad back at his tormentor in the audience. He must've been saving up for the whole song, on accounta in slow motion it looks like some kind of *hideous, flying oyster!*

The question is, who was the person in the crowd that went spitooey? Paul Simenon? Jaco Pastorius?... How 'bout Frank Herbert?

142

Miscellaneous Columns & Essays

THIS MONTH'S CONTEST: Name The World's Ugliest Rock & Roll Trio!

Rock trios have always represented "bare bones" music (supposedly), and have usually consisted of guitar, bass, and drums. If the total number of musicians is just three, that leaves fewer faces to have to look at, and if said faces are homely enough to make a train take a dirt road, it's a wonder some of the acts are successful at all, since all too often a band's looks seems to take precedent over their music (a trend that particularly seemed to come into vogue in the Eighties).

This venture spans the entire history of rock music, so groups don't have to be in existence anymore. I nominate the following (in no particular order):

CREAM: Strictly because of Ginger Baker's teeth.

BUDDY HOLLY & THE CRICKETS: Role models for *Revenge of the Nerds*, one of the worst movies ever made.

MOTORHEAD: A voter has several incarnations to choose from with this band. I wonder what you'd come up with if you ever held down Lemmy and played "connect-the-dots" with his moles, using a tattoo stylus? (Lemmy's moles were also the subject of the only Beavis & Butthead gag that I thought was funny.)

STRAY CATS: Speaking of tattoos, the illustrations on these reprobates look like rejects from an Ed "Big Daddy" Roth t-shirt catalog, circa 1964 (remember the "Rat Fink" and "Mother's Worry"?).

RONNIE JAMES DIO & ANY TWO OTHER MUSICIANS OF YOUR CHOICE: Even Simon LeBon and Nick Rhodes...

Executive Rock

RANDOM RUMINATIONS, UPDATES, VERITIES AND BALDERDASH

...Roy Orbison's death shook me up more than Elvis's did, not simply because it happened twelve years after the King's bathroom croak, but also because Orbison had endured so much personal tragedy, yet always seemed so down to earth. His passing was even more sad since he died while on the verge of a major comeback, due primarily to the Traveling Wilburys concept (which I bet was a lot of fun for the participants). From where I stand, his legacy is much more laudable for the average person than Presley's.

...Another alienating aspect of MTV that caused it to be ultimately deprogrammed in my home was the growing tendency of many videos to jump around so much it aggravated the Missus's astigmatism. Primeval examples included Rush's "Time Stand Still", the Alan Parsons Project's "Stereotomy", and Huey Lewis & The News' "Hip To Be Square". Anytime I happen to encounter MTV elsewhere these days, I've seen no evidence that the trend has abated.

...Speaking of Rush, what's techno-wuss Howard Jones doing on the cover of their *Power Windows* album?

...The latter part of the title of this essay is also the title of an album by the late Harry Chapin, who admitted when it was released that "verities and balderdash" could be freely translated as "truth and bull****". Too few people remember Chapin's pioneering efforts to help alleviate world hunger, *years* before Live Aid. What's more, his "storytelling" songwriting style is also sorely missed by a lot of my peers.

...Despite the efforts of the likes of Linda Ronstadt and Eric Clapton, reggae music has never really caught on in the U.S., and most likely never will.

...Rudy Sarzo's nickname should be "Mr. Sell-Out" or at least "Mr. Endorsement", on accounta I know of at least *three* brands of bass guitars to which he's lent his moniker.

...Pop/rock bands from the Continent usually stink, other than the one hit that they might have on U.S. radio. Examples go all the way back to Shocking Blue ("Venus"), and even though Golden Earring has hung in there, their *Moontan* album not only included the hit "Radar Love", but every gawdawful rock music cliché *ever* in one convenient package. Focus ("Hocus Pocus") gets an exemption because of erstwhile guitar god Jan Akkerman, and who remembers Diesel ("Sausalito Summer Night")? Sho' sounds like the Steve Miller Band to me.

...The "bimbos on parade" trend in music videos took a dramatic (and hilarious) turn in late 1989. Michelle Shocked's "On the Greener Side" not only saw her disposing of her, um, "tomboy" image (at least tempo-

144

Miscellaneous Columns & Essays

rarily) by strutting around in a miniskirt, but the video also featured a gaggle of *male* bimbos (I suppose female viewers would call such individuals "hunks") who were posing in bathing suits, in an extremely funny gender reversal of the, er, Robert Palmer "concept". As for Palmer himself, a telling segment of the "Simply Irresistible" video occurs at the outset, when the camera shows him standing in front of all those models; watch for the split-second "it's-a-tough-job-but-somebody's-gotta-do-it" look of resignation.

...Stereotypically, many musicians aren't very good business people. Does that mean that accordingly, many business people probably aren't very good musicians?

...Ever notice how most solo efforts by members of platinum-selling combos usually bomb or stink (or both)? Mick Ralphs nailed it in a 1994 interview: "I think it's obvious in this business that a band is bigger than any of the solo projects its members might do."

...Rush's *Exit Stage Left* would be an excellent live album if its production wasn't so murky. Same goes for Blue Oyster Cult's *On Your Feet or On Your Knees*, but both bands subsequently released better live efforts.

...Why do Michael Bolton's performances attempt to leave a listener with the impression that it's physically painful for him to sing?

...Death to "power ballads"!

...The longer one stays away from keeping up with contemporary music, the more difficult it could become to ascertain which is the *band moniker* and which is the *album title* on certain releases, particularly in the Alternative/Grunge/Punk/whatever "genre(s)". Examples include Tool/Undertow, Throwing Copper/Live, and my personal favorite mystery, Dookie/Green Day.

. . . In some respects, the marketing of "anthology" albums seems to be getting out of hand these days. In particular, some of the cassettes and CDs that turn up in the likes of K-Mart and Wal-Mart are improbable assemblages: In late '94, I encountered an album called *Arena Rock* with *exactly* the bands on it you'd expect to find (Loverboy, etc.). Then there was *There Is Love: The Wedding Songs*, which is a nice idea, but unfortunately there's an alternative anthology (not the Alternative "genre", which shows how damn confusing the use of that term can be) called *There Was Love: The Divorce Songs*, the cover of which shows a chain saw plowing through a heart-shaped box of chocolates. Yeesh.

...Another improbable discount store anthology was called *Biker Rock*, which included "Born to Be Wild" (natch), "Iron Butterfly Theme" (awright!), and Sailcat's "Motorcycle Mama" (huh?).

...The best/definitive REO Speedwagon album is *T.W.O.* It still has a fresh, vibrant, and aggressive feel to it, and it's chock fulla power chords and potent vocals. It was recorded *years* before the band got into its "arena

145

Executive Rock

rock"/"power ballad" phase, and in a 1992 interview, guitarist Gary Richrath (who departed circa 1989 after eighteen years) hinted that *T.W.O.* might be his all-time favorite REO album as well. However, the lyrics to "Golden Country" still sound banal and pretentious.

...One of many classic movie moments in *Animal House* happens so fast it's almost subliminal, so use the pause control on your VCR if you ever want to examine it. It involves "Sink Night" at the Delta house, where the brothers are examining photos of incoming freshman projected on a basement wall; they're considering candidates for pledges. It's obvious that Bluto (John Belushi) is more than half-drunk; he exudes a fuzzy, semi-sour demeanor that's vaguely menacing as well. But when the photo of Kent Dorfman (Steven Furst) flashes in front of the fraternity, the reaction of Bluto is a nanosecond ahead of everyone else, and it's a gut-level yelp of abject loathing and terror; nothing but a primeval response to a stimulus. The point is, I had the same type of reaction when (1) I found out Blue Cheer's *Vincebus Eruptum* was available on Compact Disc, (2) I walked into a convenience store and saw a cover of *People* magazine trumpeting the "comeback" of David and Shaun Cassidy, and (3) I found out Blue Cheer's *Outsideinside* was available on Compact Disc.

...One song that should have been a hit but wasn't was Christopher Cross's "Words of Wisdom", from the *Another Page* album. It has a rolling guitar line a la the zillion-selling "Sailing", a gorgeous string arrangement, a lead guitar that sounds somewhat like Larry Carlton, and a nice piano. For some reason it ended up as the B-side of another single.

...Yet another "mini-art film" (a black and white video) that showed up on MTV after I de-programmed it was Tears for Fears' "Woman in Chains".

...If a preview for an upcoming movie flashes a list of the musical artists that appear on its soundtrack, doesn't that kinda give you the feeling that the movie itself might be a clunker?

...It always galls me whenever I happen to be listening to a live cut on an album, and the tune fades out rather than coming to a cohesive end followed by applause (I bet a lot of full-time and part-time musicians feel this way). Examples of what I'm talking about include "Telegraph Road" on Dire Straits' greatest hits anthology, and more than one B.B. King tune. I'd even include flexi-disc magazine inserts in this "category", and an example of *that* format is a collaboration on a song called "Phone Booth" by Robert Cray and Eric Clapton.

...Speaking of B.B. King, his terrific set at the festival noted in the "A Few Moments with The Master" essay was the *antithesis* of the performance by another legendary musician who headlined the previous year; said headliner threatened to stop his performance if a video camera wasn't turned off. He'll remain nameless here on accounta I'm a nice guy, but I'll give you a

Miscellaneous Columns & Essays

hint: He had a succession of similarly-titled albums, and I've thought of a disparaging title for yet another album in the "series", if he ever records anything again (B.B. King was/is more successful than this performer).

...The best rock & roll documentary ever was *The Kids Are Alright.* Runner-up: *Gimme Shelter.*

...I DON'T GET IT: Talking Heads, Ween, Patti Smith, Green Jelly, Thrill Kill Kult, almost anything by Brian Eno, Laurie Anderson.

...I've heard stand-up comedians being called "the rock musicians of the Eighties" and "the rock musicians of the Nineties". So which is it?

...I bet Chris Duarte is already tiring of being compared to Stevie Ray Vaughan, but if he's not the heir apparent (while still sounding somewhat distinctive), I'd like to know who is.

...Is that Adrian Belew singing lead vocal on "Neal and Jack and Me" (found on King Crimson's *Beat* album) or is it actually *Steve Miller?* I played the tune backwards (a friend of mine still has the LP) and could've sworn I heard the line "Somebody gimme a *cheeseburger!*"

...The Divinyls showed up on TV again; this time it was on ABC's new version of *In Concert*, and apparently Christina Amphlett got censored again (this time I think it was because of her shenanigans with the microphone stand). She scares me even more than Lemmy or Henry Rollins.

...And speaking of Henry Rollins, it goes without saying that the Rollins Band's "Liar" one-ups any Nirvana tune in the "schizophrenic song" category.

...Another song that should have been a hit but wasn't: Billy Joel's remarkable "Miami 2017 (Seen The Lights Go Out On Broadway)". The live version of this on *Songs In The Attic* is incredible, except for Liberty DeVito's over-the-top drumming.

...What's the big deal about the Black Crowes? Another guitar writer I know once observed: "If I want to hear music like that I'll dig out my old Faces albums", and his opinion seems to be pretty much on the mark. On the other hand, I think the band showed a tremendous amount of class by postponing an Oklahoma City concert following the bombing of the federal building in April of 1995, and I read that they were donating part of the receipts from the rescheduled performance, and for that they have my respect.

...Billy Idol's *Cyberpunk* album cover was changed pretty quickly after its release. I bet it was on accounta on the first version, Idol was sporting a hairstyle that looked like either an automobile distributor cap or a buncha stalagmites.

...It occurs to me that sometimes certain columnists (Larry King in *USA Today*, f'rinstance) may temporarily run out of decent topics to address at length, so instead they come up with a buncha short, "sound bite" type comments, all unrelated to each other except in a very general way...

SLOG ON, YOU TARNISHED AND/ OR OUT-OF-HOCK DIAMOND

The letter, dated September 14, 1993, was forwarded to me from the *Vintage Guitar* home office. Its writer was simply letting me know that he enjoyed the interviews I did for the magazine, yet his final comment had me scratching my head when I read it: "It must be fascinating meeting all the has-been musicians you interview."

I didn't know whether he was being serious or sardonic.

Malc read the letter, and inquired: "You mean to tell me that a lot of the so-called 'veteran musicians' you interview *shouldn't* be considered as 'has-beens'?"

"Not if they're still putting forth what would probably be perceived as an honest effort, even if they're relegated to 'journeyman' status, and even if they're now playing on some 'package' tour; several bands appearing at one concert... which, come to think of it, is probably how a lot of 'em started out, decades ago. There's a big difference between that and blatant nostalgia exploitation, and there may be a fine line in the hype between a 'legend', a 'journeyman' and a 'has-been'."

149

Executive Rock

"So how do you tell the difference?"

"I'm not sure. Depends on how much of a fan you are of the individual or band, I suppose."

"But what about your *personal* concept of what defines a so-called "has-been"?"

"Guys I've interviewed that acted burned out. In a couple of instances, I sent 'em CD and cassette covers to be autographed and they didn't return 'em."

"Did their interviews end up getting published?"

"One was; one wasn't. The point is, that's only two interviewees, and most of the other 'journeyman' players have given eloquent and detailed interviews. Guys like Steppenwolf's John Kay and the Classic Rock All-Stars' Mike Pinera seem to be content with their current status, and my perception is that they've settled into their current performing situations and are determined to do the best they can with what they've got. Sometimes it might tread into the 'nostalgia exploitation' area, and I'm sure a lot of people *would* use the 'has-been' term, but I think for the vast majority of veteran players, that 'Ricky Nelson was right' philosophy is applicable if they're still making a decent living."

Yet long hair and crow's feet *does* seem like a bit of a paradox, doesn't it? Sometimes it seems that some performers have gotten to the point (or will arrive at the point in the not-too-distant future) where they're the rock and roll equivalent of a bad lounge singer with an ill-fitting toupee and a stained cumberbund on a worn and frayed tuxedo.

On the other hand, many of the bands we were listening to in high school are still out there, and some are still capable of chart-topping recordings. Who'da thunk the likes of the Rolling Stones or Pink Floyd would have been capable of not only releasing successful albums in 1994, but mounting large-scale tours as well, lampooning by Letterman's Top Ten List ("I Can't Get No Metamucil") not withstanding?

Take Bad Company, for instance. The original mid-Seventies foursome came out of legendary British bands like Free (vocalist Paul Rodgers, drummer Simon Kirke), Mott the Hoople (guitarist Mick Ralphs) and King Crimson (bass player Boz Burrell), and recorded six albums, the last of which was released in 1980. The band went into hiatus for several years until they regrouped with an alternate lead singer circa 1985.

However, Burrell only lasted about six months with the reunited Bad Company, and ultimately veteran (there's that word again) bassist Rick Wills (who spent well over a decade in Foreigner) joined the band, and a

Slog On, You Tarnished And/Or Out-Of-Hock Diamond

supplemental guitarist, Dave "Bucket" Colwell, was also added.

Following the band's first-ever live album, released in 1993, the lead vocalist slot changed again. Robert Hart was brought on board, and while he *does* sound like Paul Rodgers at times, his singing is still distinctive and expressive.

So it was the lineup of Kirke, Ralphs, Wills, Colwell and Hart with whom I got to hang out with for a short time prior to a Spring 1995 concert. They were on a double-bill tour with Ted Nugent, in support of their new album, *Company of Strangers*, and the band was in an ebullient mood because they'd just been notified by their publicist that the album's first single, "Down and Dirty", was the number one song added to A.O.R. playlists in the U.S. that week.

(Actually, I'd been talking with Mick Ralphs a bit earlier in the dining area, and had gotten him to sign the cover of the Mott the Hoople *Backsliding Fearlessly* CD I'd bought some months earlier. Ralphs had heard the anthology was out but hadn't seen it, so he took off with the cover to show to his bandmates. Thus I ended up in the band's dressing room looking for Ralphs, who introduced me to other band members I hadn't met.)

The point is, this wasn't some bunch of louts who were tearing up furniture or ingesting mind-altering substances in celebration of the playlist success of "Down and Dirty". Things were loose but quiet as the band waited their turn onstage.

And I didn't even recognize Simon Kirke at first. With his short hair and tortoise-shell-frame glasses, I'd have thought I was looking at someone like the band's *accountant,* fer cryin' out loud. Later, Nugent's lead singer, Derek St. Holmes, rightfully proclaimed Kirke to be "a master of holding back"; i.e., a drummer who keeps impeccable timing with a minimum of flash (which made his drum solo on the aforementioned live album a surprise and a delight).

So the affable bunch of blokes that comprise the successful rock band known as Bad Company continue, as of this writing, to enjoy the success that they've earned through decades of dedication and hard work. You'd never know they were rock stars from talking with 'em, however. It's just their job, y'know?

The, um, "guidelines" for this section are somewhat personal, I guess. In general, the performers to be cited herein have been in the public eye for a minimum of two decades, and are still active. In many cases, the personnel of some bands has changed (and that will be addressed in more than one essay), and in *many* cases, the bands may indeed be in the afore-

Executive Rock

mentioned "journeyman" status, but they apparently still have enough fans to merit a continued effort at being professional musicians.

And what's "personal" about this facet is that I happen to be a fan of each band that has its own essay, and I probably own more than one album by every combo mentioned in the "listing" articles, but I'm not "into" such bands as much as I'm into the likes of Wishbone Ash or Emerson, Lake & Palmer.

The point is, anyone who's a fan of popular music would probably have a different list of bands that he/she is really "into". As noted earlier, this book (nor this segment of it) ain't no "history of rock & roll" dissertation; that's already been done so many times in both the print and electronic media that a new version would be tiresome and predictable, in my opinion.

While the contributions of the Beatles, Springsteen, U2, etc. to the evolution of popular music are acknowledged, they won't be examined here; lotsa other tomes are around to consult... and believe me, I know plenty of *fans* of the Beatles, Springsteen and U2, but I'm not really among 'em. I don't *dislike* what they've done (I think Side Two of *Abbey Road* is timeless); there are simply other aggregations that I listen to more often.

And the same can be said for *any* music fan. A list of favorite performers for each person would probably be as individual as the person himself/herself. So some of the groups noted in this section may not be too familiar to some folks, but maybe such bands should've been heard more (and they may yet be heard, as more classic material becomes available on Compact Disc).

So even the Cream and the Police won't be discussed herein, on accounta they ain't together anymore. Naturally, I have everything that either group ever released on Compact Disc, from *Fresh Cream* to the 1995 *Police Live* album.

Admittedly, more than one of the bands cited might've taken a long time between "active phases" (Emerson, Lake & Palmer and Lynyrd Skynyrd were each in limbo for about a decade, and the Eagles probably have the record with around fourteen years of inactivity, but who's to say how long the current active phase for the Eagles will endure). But as of this writing, every group noted herein is still making music, and if they're treating their particular facet of entertainment in a businesslike manner, I'm even more of a fan, and such a band has my respect, even if I don't have all of their albums.

Depending on the band or artist, many veterans are continuing to hone their craft by maintaining an interest in state-of-the-art equipment, which these days includes MIDI, Fairlights, and other computer doo-dads. That's another admirable facet of still-active musicians, and the flip side of such is how many players are advocates of vintage guitars and amplifiers to evoke legendary tones, which is also admirable.

Yet it's also gotten to the point where some performers now seem to be parodying themselves. Vincent "Alice Cooper" Furnier is a handy example, and while some critics would cite the Rolling Stones as convenient

Slog On, You Tarnished And/Or Out-Of-Hock Diamond

targets as well, their 1994 release, *Voodoo Lounge*, was hailed by most critics as the best album the Stones had done in years.

That's not to say that all of the successful veteran rock bands noted in this section will march on until they reach retirement age, although I bet a lot of 'em will make the attempt. An inspirational figure for bands and fans alike is blues icon B.B. King, who turned seventy on 16 SEP 95; he noted in an interview that ran in *Vintage Guitar* in honor of his birthday that he'd never retire. Nevertheless, as this book was being prepared, there were ominous signs regarding the longevity of at least one aggregation cited herein, and I'm not going into details.

Yet any phenomenon that merits commentary from Tom Bodett in one of his Motel 6 commercials deserve a bit more examination and reflection, eh? I mean, even *Blue Cheer* recorded a "comeback" album around two decades after *Vincebus Eruptum* was released. Its title was *The Beast Is Back*, and one weisenheimer I know (who shall remain nameless) opined that the title was incomplete; that the phrase "And Toothless" should've been added.

So what follows in an appraisal of ongoing musical ventures that may be decades old, yet the bands noted are still out there, and by now many of 'em may have fans that are in more than one generation. While I still listen to most of the artists noted herein, hopefully I'll never end up as dedicated/ obsessed as the Deadhead character portrayed by Charles Martin Smith on one of the last episodes of *L.A. Law*. The story line was funny, and right on the money until Patti D'Arbanville "reverted" too... God help me if I ever get like that again, whether it's the Grateful Dead or any other band.

I been there before.

DARK SIDE OF THE SUN/PUNK FREUD

"He's so *old*-looking," observed the Missus.

And the thing is, she was talking about Rick Wright's appearance in the "Learning to Fly" video; i.e., her comment was made in the *late Eighties*,

Executive Rock

when the resurrected Pink Floyd released its first video from *A Momentary Lapse of Reason*, its first album sans Roger Waters following a prolonged and well-publicized legal battle between Waters and the other band members over the rights to the name and goodness knows what else (or maybe the litigation was still going on at the time).

Wright had been on, er, hiatus for years, and was apparently brought back on board (on a salary, one source reported at the time) in an effort to bolster the case of guitarist David Gilmour and drummer Nick Mason in their efforts to keep the British behemoth going as a legitimate musical entity.

The protracted litigation and enmity was only one facet in the saga of a band that sprang from the "anything goes" mentality of the late Sixties British music scene, and since the Grateful Dead always seemed to function more as a collective venture, the lyric about "what a long, strange trip it's been" seems in many ways like it might be more applicable to the Floyd instead of the late Jerry Garcia and associates.

The psychedelic hook of "See Emily Play" was irresistible when it wafted out of radio speakers in the U.S. during the first half of 1968. Granted, it wasn't exactly Top 40 material, considering the eerie, modulating intro (which was apparently a primitive synth or some studio trick), the "doom-boom" of the two notes that introduced each verse, and the revved-up portion where it sounded like someone had turned the turntable speed from 45 up to 78.

But that initial single apparently turned a lot of heads, because as of this writing (Summer 1995), the Pink Floyd is still one of the biggest, most successful acts in rock music history, and they're still high on the charts (a live double album from their 1994 tour).

The history of the Floyd has been well documented in several tomes, and the best of the lot is the late Nicholas Schaffner's *A Saucerful of Secrets*. It's an excellent, enjoyable read, and the 1990 photograph of mad genius/icon/basket case Syd Barrett is worth the price alone; the overweight, balding individual that's shown ambling down a Cambridge street could easily be mistaken for a plumber or some other blue-collar-occupation individual.

Yet Barrett (sporting a Fender Telecaster with mirrors stuck all over its body) was the focal point of the initial lineup of Pink Floyd; bassist Waters, keyboardist Wright, and Mason seemed to be along for the ride, which was quite bumpy due to Barrett's legendary chemical excursions. It seemed like all too many early Pink Floyd concerts were "improvisational" in that

Slog On, You Tarnished And/Or Out-Of-Hock Diamond

it was uncertain as to how coherent the singer/guitarist would be. Nevertheless, *The Piper at the Gates of Dawn* was perfectly suited for the Age of Acid, even if nowadays it sounds a bit pretentious. Barrett contributed somewhat to the Floyd's sophomore album, *A Saucerful of Secrets*, before consigning himself to his own little personal oblivion (subsequent solo efforts not withstanding).

The business-like David Gilmour was eased in as Barrett was gradually being eased out of the band, and subsequent albums around the dawn of the Seventies (*Ummagumma, Atom Heart Mother*, etc.) were faithful to the Floyd's psychedelic roots (such as they were), but somewhat unsatisfying. Things seemed to get more accessible (i.e., less abstract, spaced-out noise-fests) with *Meddle*, however. A throbbing bass guitar rave-up called "One of These Days" (which is still a concert staple) introduced the album (the song's title comes from its only "lyric", a spoken-word, guttural snarl that rumbles: "One of these days I'm going to cut you into little pieces"). There's a couple of weird Side One tracks that seem more off-the-wall instead of "psychedelic" ("Fearless" melds into a scene from a soccer stadium where the fans are singing "You'll Never Walk Alone"; "Seamus" is an acoustic blues tune with a dog yowling in accompaniment). But the magnificent "Echoes" (all of Side Two) is one of the best extended rock tracks ever (and as previously noted, contains an unsettling middle part). Thus *Meddle* served as a harbinger of what many popular music fans consider to have been the ultimate rock album of all time, *Sgt. Pepper* not withstanding.

Around this time, a documentary which showed the Pink Floyd performing (for no audience) in the ruins of the amphitheater at Pompeii was filmed; other portions of the flick showed the band playing in less historical/exotic surroundings, and footage from the recording sessions for *Dark Side of the Moon* was also featured. Of note was David Gilmour's experimentation with some guitar gizmo, as well as unadorned versions of "One of These Days" and "Echoes" from the amphitheater. The movie is available on video, and while it seems a bit primitive (since it preceded MTV by about a decade), it's still historically interesting.

Nearly a quarter-century after the release of *Dark Side of the Moon*, the album was still on Billboard's Top 200 chart. The first time I heard it, I smashed a pair of cheap headphones; a local college station played the album in its entirety, and when those alarm clocks went off, I slapped my headphones off with both hands in a purely reflexive action. But *Dark Side of the Moon* did indeed set a standard (chart time and otherwise), with its incredible fidelity and memorable hooks, as well as its pulsating VCS3 synths and by-now-a-staple-of-every-Pink-Floyd-album use of sound effects ("On the Run" seems to be nothing more than a synth-fest accom-

Executive Rock

panied by a high-hat cymbal and the sounds of a heartbeat, someone running, and an out-of-control airplane; the "song" is still quite listenable). The album is as viable now is it was when it was released in 1973.

One of the more intriguing aspects of the Pink Floyd saga (as well as one of the most marketable) was the evolution of their album covers, and the mid-Seventies album *Wish You Were Here* has to be considered one of the high points, since it showed up in record racks with what appeared to be a plain, navy blue cover with no writing whatsoever on it. However, the *shrink-wrap plastic* was blue, and tearing off the protective material revealed a photograph of two men standing in a movie studio lot shaking hands... and one of the individuals was enveloped in flames.

Wish You Were Here wasn't a musical triumph like *Dark Side of the Moon*, however. An extended work in several parts called "Shine On You Crazy Diamond" was a wistful toast to Syd Barrett, and other tracks such as the sardonic "Have A Cigar" are passable, but *Wish You Were Here* didn't break any new ground.

And the old "try-to-figure-out-what-this-picture-means" game that also became a staple of Floyd albums was in fine form on their next offering, *Animals;* the cover showed the Battersea power station in England with a giant inflatable pig hovering over it. Unfortunately, the cover photo was about the best thing the album had going for it; the contents were uninspired, and some songs that the band had already been performing were given alternate titles to fit the "format" of the presentation. The "vocals" on one song ended up getting Vocoder-ized to the point of being indecipherable, and the fact that a portion of that tune was a parody of the Twenty-Third Psalm also provided plenty of fodder to televangelists about subliminal lyrics.

Yet another fodder facet was the fact that *Animals* was released during the glory days of the British punk rock movement, and John "Johnny Rotten" Lydon was seen sporting a Pink Floyd t-shirt with the words "I Hate" scrawled above the band's moniker. It was almost as if the Floyd was intentionally allowing itself to become the subject of ridicule, considering how insipid *Animals* was. One poll by a Floyd fanzine indicated that *The Final Cut* was the least favorite Pink Floyd album of respondents, but non-fanzine subscribers (like me) would probably give *Animals* a hefty amount of scorn as one of the low points in the band's history.

It needs to be pointed out at this juncture that Gilmour, Waters, Wright and Mason have all put out solo or non-Floyd collaborations over the years (and of course, Waters is now exclusively solo), and Gilmour's moniker-titled 1978 album is among the best of the lot... probably because it sounds a lot like a good Pink Floyd album. Among the musicians on *David Gilmour* was a pre-Floyd bandmate named Rick Wills, who went on to play bass

Slog On, You Tarnished And/Or Out-Of-Hock Diamond

with Foreigner and Bad Company, as noted previously.

While an average rock music fan might consider *Dark Side of the Moon* be a watershed for popular music (since it's held up for so long), in many ways 1979's *The Wall* is the Pink Floyd's masterwork. It's almost without peer as a concept album, and many of the songs can (and did) stand on their own. However, as noted in the desert-island-Top-Ten column, it's so depressing that Roger Waters ultimately comes off looking like a embittered, malevolent *******. To what extent such an excellent effort is laudable due to its "downer" theme could probably be discussed ad infinitum. And how in the hell did "Another Brick in the Wall (Part Two)" get to be a hit single? What's more, the movie version added to the morbidity of Waters's "vision".

It was obvious that things were really in a tailspin for the Floyd (conceptually *and* for the band's personnel) once *The Final Cut* was released in the early Eighties. More and more, hired studio guns were taking the place of band members on certain tracks (Rick Wright had departed by then), and the anti-Falklands diatribe on the album was once again morbid and alienating. It was almost as if Waters was determined to choke to death on his own regurgitated ranting. No wonder the fanzine respondents cited the album as their least favorite. By the middle of the decade, it appeared that all of the cracks in the facade of the mighty Floyd had finally caused the band to self-destruct by collapsing in on itself. But any obituaries citing the band's death by implosion were premature.

It was curious that a cryptically-titled instrumental, "Signs of Life", introduced the first post-Waters Pink Floyd album, *A Momentary Lapse of Reason*, which was probably an acquired taste to many longtime Floyd listeners and fans. It was gratifying that there wasn't a negative, sociopolitical concept to the album, but on the other hand it seemed like the band was parodying itself a bit; i.e., recycling some psychedelia and sound effects. The lyrics to the songs were nebulous enough that nobody would have been offended by 'em, and there were some good individual songs on the album such as "Learning to Fly" and "On the Turning Away". On the other hand, *A Momentary Lapse of Reason* just didn't seem to be as *powerful* as other Pink Floyd albums had been. It was competent, but it just didn't grab your attention and hold it on the first listening as almost every album since (and including) *Meddle* had done. There was almost a palpable yin-and-yang subliminal message floating around that seemed to indicate that to get a potent album from Pink Floyd, one had to tolerate the leftist pap of Roger Waters in its contents. Had he really been that much of a cornerstone?

David Gilmour had stated in an interview during the tour supporting his *About Face* solo album that playing guitar "is what I do for a living and

157

Executive Rock

I'm not ready to retire", and he repeated that line several years later as he readied the Floyd for a major, extended tour. Supported by several other musicians and backing vocalists, Gilmour, Mason and the newly-reinstated Wright presented a light-and-sound extravaganza that was highly successful, but the live album that was culled from the tour, *The Delicate Sound of Thunder*, seemed to be a perfunctory, by-the-book workout, as noted in "The Lost Art of Audience Participation", and the concert video only fared slightly better. By this time, many Floydophiles were probably resigned to expecting that further efforts by the band would probably be "dependable", for lack of a better term... and there could he positive and negative connotations to such a term; we just had to take a "wait and see" attitude.

Hauptman Steinhaus is as much of a Pink Floyd fan as Rogene, and he told me about how a store in Louisville, Kentucky, promoted the release of Pink Floyd's 1994 album *The Derivative Bell* (Whoops! Freudian Slip!... make that *The Division Bell*) by giving away all sorts of paraphernalia and putting the album out for sale at *midnight* on its release date (and he was there). Further discussions with him revealed that we were on the same wavelength about our ambivalence concerning the Floyd's latest offering.

Y'see, *The Division Bell* is overall a better presentation than was *A Momentary Lapse of Reason* (one reason may have been that this second effort by the post-Waters Pink Floyd was a bit more coherent, and this time, listeners had a better idea what to expect), but a lot of the songs seemed to sound familiar, even at the first listen. I submit for your consideration the following tunes from *The Division Bell* and other songs to which they might be compared:

"What Do You Want From Me": "Have A Cigar" (*Wish You Were Here*).
"Take It Back": Any number of U2 songs.
"Lost for Words": "Wish You Were Here" (*Wish You Were Here*).
"Keep Talking": "Round and Round" (*A Momentary Lapse of Reason*... the previous album!).

Other examples that seemed vaguely redundant included "Marooned", an instrumental that sounded like the last part of "A Saucerful of Secrets" with a guitar added, and "Poles Apart", which has an endless echo as heard on the *Animals* album. However, *The Division Bell*'s production, which is impeccable, ultimately makes it a winner.

"Who's this?", I asked the Missus, cueing up the lush guitar intro to "Coming Back to Life" (one of the album's strongest cuts, despite a wood block effect that's too far up front in the mix).

"Dire Straits" came the reply from the kitchen. An excellent guess.

Slog On, You Tarnished And/Or Out-Of-Hock Diamond

Der Hauptman also grumbled that the introductory instrumental, "Cluster One", was too long. At least there was a bit of throwback guitar gimmickry; Gilmour utilized one of those "golden throat" gizmos on one track (more popular examples include what's heard on songs like "Rocky Mountain Way" by Joe Walsh & Barnstorm, Peter Frampton's "Show Me The Way", and Bon Jovi's "Living On A Prayer").

Nevertheless, *The Division Bell* seemed to hold together better as an album, but the next-to-last and last songs should've been swapped; i.e., it seemed like "Lost for Words" would have made a better final tune than "High Hopes" (which is *not* the ant-moving-a-rubber-tree-plant ditty). For all our mutual agreement on *The Division Bell*'s positive and negative facets, Steinhaus and I both seemed to be satisfied with it, and maybe that's the mark of a real diehard fan, to forgive and forget... or maybe that's the mark of a real chump, depending on the band in question.

And it shouldn't have come as any surprise that the Floyd cranked up another gargantuan show, but this tour was considerably shorter than the one that supported *A Momentary Lapse of Reason*. There were reports that it took *days* to set up the elaborate staging; the veterinarian noted earlier saw the show in Clemson, South Carolina, and reported that it was incredibly professional. He said that the percussionist was actually hammering a giant bell on "High Hopes".

Interestingly, there was more than one opportunity to hear a Pink Floyd 1994 tour concert on software. An unauthorized recording from Europe was available some months before the *P.U.L.S.E..* album was released. The bootleg is supposedly a soundboard recording (sho' sounds like one) and could've caused immeasurable dread among the fans who might have heard it before *P.U.L.S.E.* because the bootleg performance began with "Shine On You Crazy Diamond" and "Learning to Fly," *just like The Delicate Sound of Thunder did!*

Turns out the bootleg is somewhat of an "audio precursor/harbinger". It's a performance recorded in London on 20 OCT 94, which was later released as a *legitimate* concert video!

But the performance that was purveyed on the bootleg was awesome: The songs from *The Division Bell* translated better in concert than songs from *A Momentary Lapse of Reason* did during the late Eighties tour ("High Hopes" and "Coming Back to Life" were standouts) and there was an astounding performance of the entire *Dark Side of the Moon* album ("On the Run"'s electronic noodling was extended somewhat, which added to the proceedings). Overall, the musicianship sounded *much* more loose and confident than what had been heard on *The Delicate Sound of Thunder* in the late Eighties. Perhaps one reason was the fact that many of the players (guitarist Tim Renwick, keyboardist Jon Carin, percussionist Gary

Executive Rock

Wallis, and bassist Guy Pratt) as well as one of the backing vocalists (Durga McBroom) had been on the late Eighties tour as well, and it was obvious that things had matured for the touring company.

And Storm Thorgerson (of Hipgnosis fame) struck again (assisted by Jon Crossland and Finlay Cowan) with the cover design for *P.U.L.S.E.*, the "legitimate" live album released in mid-1995. Y'see, the double CD set comes in a small hardback book which contains tour photos, credits, etc.) that's packed into a rigid cardboard/fibre box. That might be expected, but what was probably unexpected (but ultimately not surprising) was the blinking red LED on the end panel of the box. It's powered by a couple of AA batteries, and the circuitry adds a bit to the weight, but it's another example of the unusual cover concepts (and unique marketing) that has always distinguished Pink Floyd albums (even if the contents have been unsatisfactory).

But *P.U.L.S.E.* triumphs over *The Delicate Sound of Thunder* in spades, as far as over-the-counter live Floyd product goes. It *does* open with "Shine On You Crazy Diamond", but for the second track the band reaches way back into the vault to resurrect the Syd Barrett-penned "Astronomy Domine", and its modern interpretation is exhilarating. Again, the tunes from *The Division Bell* are noteworthy, and there's the presentation of *Dark Side of the Moon* here as well. Even if someone had been able to hear the unauthorized recording of the '94 tour prior to hearing *P.U.L.S.E.*, the official release is still impressive.

And it's interesting that the last line on the first page of the *P.U.L.S.E.* booklet states: "This is an analogue recording."

So once again, three English rock veterans and their musical associates are currently ensconced in the upper echelon of popular music. It's gotten to the point where, as is the case with the Rolling Stones, a Pink Floyd album and tour isn't just a new musical offering, it's an *event,* but the participants have always indeed been "faceless" (see Mick Jones's comments in the essay about the Alan Parsons Project) when compared to Jagger & company, and that'll probably always be the case, but so what?

And David Gilmour, for many fans, has ultimately become the Steve Cropper of rock guitar; i.e., he could hit *one note* and you'd know who it was (DEFINITIVE EXAMPLE: The first guitar lick on "Shine On You Crazy Diamond"). That's yet another reason for the Floyd's ongoing success, and his commitment to his craft does indeed exemplify that he's not ready to retire... and it's been over a decade since I first heard him make that statement.

In the epilogue to *A Saucerful of Secrets*, Rick Wright observes that he could see the Pink Floyd continuing as a musical entity until the members were in their seventies. As players from earlier genres did such (Count Basie, Duke Ellington, etc.), the Pink Floyd seems to be one of the aggregations that will be most likely to end up in the improbable position of septuagenarian rock musicians.

It's now been several months since I purchased *P.U.L.S.E.*, and the CD box still sits on my bookshelf. Its LED continues to flash around two times per second, and it gives no indication whatsoever that its batteries are worn out or that its circuitry is about to shut down, perhaps permanently.

"Shine on", indeed.

"........THE SHOW THAT NEVER ENDS"

...or "The Band That Wouldn't Die", according to the title of one review of a single-disc live album that closed out Phase One of the Emerson, Lake and Palmer saga, circa 1980.

Critically slagged since its inception, the ELP triad ruled the so-called progressive rock/art rock category/genre during the Seventies. While the trio had more talent than most bands with *five or more* members, there may have been a fine line for the average consumer when it came to differentiating between some amazing chops and music that became so overblown it metamorphosized into nothing more than a pretentious format to allow the band members to show off.

2/3 of the band had previously taken up residence in the aforementioned progressive rock category. Keith Emerson had already established himself as a major talent in an underrated combo called the Nice, which started out as a quartet but ended up as a trio (the departing guitarist wasn't replaced; such was the breadth of Emerson's ability). Greg Lake had grown up with Robert Fripp (they both had the same guitar teacher); both were founding members of King Crimson. Lake played bass and sang on the debut album, *In the Court of the Crimson King*, and just sang on the second album, *In the Wake of Poseidon*. Drummer Carl Palmer had played with the Crazy World of Arthur Brown and Atomic Rooster (the former

Executive Rock

band had was a One-Hit-Wonder in the U.S. with the bizarre "Fire"; the latter band was virtually unknown Stateside).

The new trio hit the ground running in 1970, performing at the Isle of Wight Pop Festival. Its self-titled debut album opened with an unusual but accessible instrumental called "The Barbarian", which featured unique tempo changes and a fuzz-drenched bass guitar, so a listener's attention was grabbed right at the outset. Other songs showed off each member's abilities, and there were two tunes that became staples on FM radio ("Knife Edge" and "Lucky Man").

The sophomore effort, *Tarkus*, had more of a conceptual feel to Side One; Side Two's tunes were a bit more, uh, mainstream. The live third album, *Pictures at an Exhibition*, had actually been recorded before *Tarkus* was released, and it would be interesting to determine how many rock fans had never heard the classical work by Mussorgsky prior to ELP's interpretation. The encore number, a cover of "Nutrocker", was appropriate and fun. One might've thought that the CD version of *Pictures at an Exhibition* would have been remastered to where the effort was nonstop (a la the first three sides of the first *Live Dead* album) but that wasn't the case; the psychedelic thrash-fest that closed out Side One on the record fades out on the CD, too.

Trilogy clicked for ELP as well, and one track, "From the Beginning", is a definitive example of Greg Lake's talent; he's not only one of the finest bass guitarists/vocalists that British rock has ever produced, he's a helluva guitar player as well. Curiously, another fine English bassist/vocalist, John Wetton, is from the same part of the country as Fripp and Lake; Wetton ended up in King Crimson Phase Two. There's a sharp cover of Aaron Copland's "Hoedown" on *Trilogy* as well.

By the time *Brain Salad Surgery* rolled around, however, Emerson, Lake and Palmer were starting to get a bit too far out on the cutting edge for a lotta folks; the too-long "Karn Evil 9" was a bit much (yet it's the work from which "Welcome back my friends, to the show that never ends" comes). A subsequent triple-LP live offering seemed to add credibility to the rock critics, and *Works* (volumes 1 and 2) seemed to be nothing more than show-off albums, period. One bright spot was a cover of Copland's "Fanfare for the Common Man", featuring Greg Lake's remarkable-sounding eight-string Alembic bass, but the pretentiousness was really starting to pile up.

Love Beach stunk.

ELP had already cashed in the chips when the live album noted at the outset of this essay was released; it had an abbreviated version of the "Pictures at an Exhibition" suite performed with a symphony orchestra, and the only memorable song was "Peter Gunn", on which the eight-string bass was heard again.

The saga of the erstwhile band members during the Eighties was some-

Slog On, You Tarnished And/Or Out-Of-Hock Diamond

what bizarre ("It was like musical chairs", said Lake in a 1994 interview). Palmer re-emerged rather quickly with ex-Yes guitarist Steve Howe, former Yes and Buggles keyboardist Geoff Downes and the aforementioned John Wetton in a band called Asia (reviving the so-called "supergroup" concept/hype), then after two albums Wetton left just as the band had been booked to do a live concert on MTV at the Budokan in Tokyo (natch, it was promoted as "Asia in Asia"). Carl Palmer called on Greg Lake to fill in, and Lake did so in a confident and professional manner. Critics dissed Asia in the Eighties as much as they did ELP in the Seventies, but the Budokan concert went off quite well.

However, that's the only project Lake ever did with Asia; that band was headed in more of a pop direction, which Lake wanted to avoid. Asia went through its own tribulations for the balance of the decade; John Wetton returned, Steve Howe left, and the band put out a third album called *Astra* (a tune called "Go" from this album was the most radio-ready song Asia ever did). Yet another change in the guitarist chair led to a not-so-hot live album recorded in Moscow. The last I heard about Asia, another album called *Aqua* was released, and the group that toured in support of it was composed of Downes, Howe, and a bass player and drummer that nobody had heard of. So much for the "supergroup" idea, and it showed how second-generation bands could be just as fragmented as their predecessors.

Anyways, another ELP showed up in the mid-Eighties, hut this one was called Emerson, Lake and *Powell.* Drummer Cozy Powell has been in the Jeff Beck Group and Ritchie Blackmore's Rainbow, and was more of a "boomer" percussionist (whereas Palmer was more of a technician). Cozy had actually had an instrumental hit of his own in 1974 (a drum solo-oriented rave-up called "Dance with the Devil").

The only album Emerson, Lake and Powell proffered was an stunning surprise to cynics that might have expected a return to the bombast of yore. *Emerson, Lake and Powell* was loud and lyrical, and "Touch and Go", while too slow to be danceable, nevertheless probably had many a listener bobbing his/her head in time to the music and/or playing air instruments. The token classical cover on the album was an exciting version of Holst's "Mars, the Bringer of War".

But that lineup lasted for all of one album, and the next project to showcase former members of Emerson, Lake and *Palmer* was something called the 3, which had Emerson and Palmer in it, but an alternate bass player/vocalist named Robert Berry. The 3's only album ended up in cutout bins fairly quickly, but for what it's worth, they *did* play the Atlantic Records 40th Anniversary concert.

Ultimately, a record company executive managed to convince the original ELP to reunite to do a movie soundtrack, which never got accomplished

163

Executive Rock

since the band's recording efforts morphed into a full-blown, brand new Emerson, Lake and Palmer album at the dawn of the Nineties. *Black Moon* may have been an acquired taste to longtime fans; the title track starts off like Queen's "We Will Rock You", and its toned-down middle part sounds like a lower-volume version of the instrumental break on McCartney's "Live and Let Die". Weird references, but that's what "Black Moon" seems to be crediting... the token classical cover on *Black Moon* was Prokofiev's "Romeo and Juliet", and the album seemed to be an assertive statement that the veteran progressive trio was still capable of competent, potent music.

And what better way to reinforce such an assertion than another live album? A Royal Albert Hall concert was a tour-de-force excursion, especially since it even pulled out material from the *Tarkus* album as well as "Rondo" from Emerson's days with the Nice. Ol' Gregory's pipes ain't quite what they used to be, but this was the most listenable ELP live album ever.

An unusual mid-Nineties marketing effort for ELP was something called *Return of the Manticore*, a four-CD boxed retrospective that included new versions of songs made famous by the bands each member had been in *prior* to the formation of Emerson, Lake and Palmer in 1970. "Fire" and "21st Century Schizoid Man" were just so-so, but "Hang On to a Dream" was commendable. Another new recording was a first-ever *studio* (but abbreviated) version of "Pictures at an Exhibition", recorded in Dolby Surround Sound. Yet even without the new material, this boxed set was better than a lot of others. *Return of the Manticore* was hyped during an appearance by ELP on the now-defunct *Arsenio* show.

Greg Lake had opined in the aforementioned 1994 interview that the next Emerson, Lake and Palmer album would probably be something quite unique for the band, and in some respects, his prognostication was correct. For one thing, 1994's *In the Hot Seat* doesn't have a token classical cover on it, and there's no individual song that "grabs" a listener the way songs like "Knife Edge" or "The Barbarian" did a quarter-century ago. In other words, this album takes longer to "get into", but there's still a lot of capable musicianship and writing to be found in *In the Hot Seat*.

One song on *In the Hot Seat* is notable for unusual circumstances. "Daddy" has some of the most banal lyrics that Greg Lake has ever written, but the *subject matter* is quite serious, so maybe Lake was trying to address such subject matter head-on. Y'see, the song's about a little girl who's kidnapped and murdered, and Lake was moved to write it by news reports of a real-life incident such as the one he describes from a father's viewpoint in the song. In a classy move, ELP donated royalties earned from "Daddy" to a nonprofit foundation for missing and kidnapped children.

The CD version of *In the Hot Seat* also contains the aforementioned studio version of "Pictures at an Exhibition".

Slog On, You Tarnished And/Or Out-Of-Hock Diamond

So as of this writing the critically-dissed progressive rock juggernaut known as Emerson, Lake and Palmer is still cranking out chops-a-plenty, and still touring. I doubt we'll see the likes of the flying piano again (a one-off stage trick performed at the California Jam in '74) but for some reason I get the feeling that Keith Emerson, Greg Lake, and Carl Palmer will always be striving to improve their individual musicianship, even if (who knows?) the future portends another dissolution of the band that bears their surnames.

THE ULTIMATE "FACELESS" BAND

Another intriguing facet of the interview with Foreigner's Mick Jones was his observation concerning the application of terms such as "arena rock" and "faceless" to hugely successful rock bands, of which Foreigner was an oft-cited example in the rock press. I advised Jones that in an interview with former REO Speedwagon guitarist Gary Richrath, it was agreed that those terms weren't always complimentary, and that Richrath had opined that the "Big Four" that were usually noted were REO, Styx, Journey, and Foreigner.

Jones's response was: "I think it needs to be noted that I was from the 'English school' when it comes to the use of the word 'faceless', the way Pink Floyd was a 'faceless' band, for example. The American use of the term seemed to mean 'bland', so I resented that term a little bit if it was used in the American context. My idea was to keep us private, and to let the music do the talking. Looking back, I can see we've matured and I'm proud of what we've done, just as I'm sure someone like Dave Gilmour is proud of what he's done."

Well-stated, but if the concept of so-called "faceless" bands is examined even further, it could bring about a blunt and unique question: Had the Alan Parsons Project ever even done a live concert?

I would accidentally stumble on the answer in August of 1995, two weeks before the deadline for this book, and some nineteen years after the Alan Parsons Project released its first album.

Executive Rock

Maybe Rogene's rumination about how "the Alan Parsons Project could've been another Pink Floyd" has more merit than one might think. Alan Parsons engineered *Dark Side of the Moon*, for one thing, but perhaps a more important event is the fact that *Tales of Mystery and Imagination* (based on stories by Edgar Allan Poe) was released in 1976, between Pink Floyd's *Wish You Were Here* and *Animals*, which aren't considered by some folks to have been among the Floyd's finest efforts.

Yet that first release by the Alan Parsons Project was capable of standing on its own merits, Pink Floyd comparisons not withstanding. It was heavily orchestrated (the nearly-side-long "The Fall of the House of Usher" would just about qualify as a symphonic work), and it succeeded as a concept album due in no small part to its macabre subject matter. With the advent of *I Robot*, from which sprang the first A.P.P. hit single (albeit minor), "I Wouldn't Want To Be Like You", Parsons seemed to already be making a gradual shift away from inordinate amounts of orchestration to more reliance on, er, "traditional pop/rock instrumentation" (*I Robot*'s instrumental title track is anchored by a squiggly synthesizer riff, for example).

When the A.P.P.'s third album (*Pyramid*) was released in 1978, its "concept" was even looser, and by then Parsons was firmly ensconced in his practice of utilizing various vocalists throughout his albums. Ex-Zombie Colin Blunstone appeared on *Pyramid*, and semi-famous singer John Miles was on *Tales of Mystery and Imagination* and other A.P.P. albums.

(Another reason Rogene might have compared the A.P.P. to the Pink Floyd was obvious, but I never asked him about it: The pyramid as an icon is featured prominently in the "goodies" packed in every *Dark Side of the Moon* LP, and the A.P.P.'s *Pyramid* LP contained a bizarre poster that would have been equally at home inside the *Dark Side of the Moon* album jacket.)

Alan Parsons Project albums were churned out on a regular basis in the late Seventies through the mid-Eighties; any so-called concepts on 'em were so nebulous that an average listener probably wouldn't have recognized an overall theme on an album like *Ammonia Avenue* or *Eye in the Sky*. Such efforts up to and including *Stereotomy* were simply well-produced, slick-sounding collections of pop/rock songs with a token instrumental or two found on each album. Some songs such as "Eye in the Sky", "Time", and "Prime Time" garnered a moderate amount of airplay, and the Project began releasing videos on MTV as well.

And another thing that could be counted on while the Alan Parson Project was in its most active phase was critical lambasting from the music media.

Slog On, You Tarnished And/Or Out-Of-Hock Diamond

I'm not sure if any writer or publication ever advocated a boycott of *Eve* due to its so-called gender-insulting cover photo, but one reviewer *did* state that the only thing *Eve* had going for it was its high-quality fidelity; the comment was something like "*Eve* would make a great demo record in a hi-fi shop." (Ouch)

But in 1987, Alan Parsons put on the brakes (in more ways than one) with *Gaudi*. He abruptly reverted to the concept album concept, and the results were so highbrow that the average fan would probably have considered *Gaudi* to be pseudo-intellectual, therefore unappealing.

Get a load of the liner notes (anytime an explanation of an album's contents has to be written, that's a dangerous signal): "This album was inspired by the life and works of Antonio Gaudi (1852-1926), a Catalan architect whose grand conception, the Sagrada Familia Cathedral in Barcelona, involves a construction timetable which will run for hundreds of years. He is buried in the crypt of his unfinished masterpiece."

Uh, right. While Parsons also resurrected a nominal amount of orchestral arrangements on *Gaudi*, the results were downright unsavory. The Missus rightfully opined that the leadoff song (a dirge-like effort in a minor key) was "depressing", and the same could be said for the entire album, with the exception of a radio-ready track called "Higher Ground".

The other way Parsons put on the brakes was to apparently suspend his own recording efforts for about seven years; I didn't see any new product until 1994.

And as noted in "Ricky Nelson Was Right" essay, 1994's *Try Anything Once* was by Alan Parsons, not the Alan Parsons Project. I'm not sure why Parsons made such a minor marketing move after so many projects with the word "Project" following his name, but the results are, well, somewhat ambivalent (as the attitude of longtime listeners would probably be).

Astoundingly, the aforementioned backhanded critical observation about *Eve*'s outstanding fidelity may have (subliminally?) inspired whoever was chosen to market/hype *Try Anything Once*, on accounta there was a sticker on every album proclaiming the contents to be "Sixty Minutes of Music to Test The Limits of Your Stereo".

What's more, *Try Anything Once* provides more fodder for Rogene's Pink Floyd comparisons. Examples include the fact that the Floyd's last studio album prior to 1994's *The Division Bell* was 1987's *A Momentary Lapse of Reason*, and the same years marked the releases of *Try Anything Once* and *Gaudi*. The Floyd *did* release a live album in 1988, and the remixed *Tales of Mystery and Imagination* also dates from 1987; *The In-*

Executive Rock

strumental Works was released in the interim.

As was the case with *The Division Bell*, the contents of *Try Anything Once* might sound somewhat derivative, but they're listenable. So as was the case in the Pink Floyd dissertation, here's a list of certain tunes on *Try Anything Once* and the previous Alan Parsons Project efforts that such songs recall:

"WINE FROM THE WATER": "Money Talks" (*Gaudi*).

"BREAKAWAY": "I Robot" (*I Robot*) There's also a grinding saxophone that can be found on several other A.P.P. instrumentals.

"JIGUE": A smattering of "Paseo De Gracia" (*Gaudi*), what with the castanets 'n such.

"SIREN SONG": "To One in Paradise" (*Tales of Mystery and Imagination*).

The *feel* (for lack of a better term) of other songs found on *Try Anything Once* remind a listener of previous Parsons efforts, and what's more, the lush "Dreamscape" sounds a *lot* like the introduction to Pink Floyd's "Coming Back to Life" on *The Division Bell* (you readin' this, Rogene?).

I can't discern that there's supposed to be any concept to *Try Anything Once*, unless it's the aforementioned "hi-fi hype". Yet another common and "irregular" thread to previous A.P.P. albums are some of the lyrics, which are as banal as anything this side of Boston (the band, not the city).

Nevertheless, *Try Anything Once* is an enjoyable listen from time to time. It is indeed sonically spectacular (sounds great through headphones), and if the songs aren't so innovative, that should mean they're easily accessible to an average listener.

The 1995 live album is another matter, however.

A longtime Alan Parsons listener/fan might not have known what to expect musically *and* sonically from a live effort by such a studio whiz, and if and when the Alan Parsons Project ever did a concert or tour prior to the 1994 European tour from which these tunes are culled, I never heard about it.

The selections for the live album are interesting, to say the least. Five and a half of the twelve live tracks are from *Eye in the Sky* ("Mammagamma" appears in a medley with *Eve*'s "Lucifer"), and there's not the first song from *Try Anything Once* (one would've thought that a nominal amount would've been featured, since one would've thought this was a tour that was supporting that album).

As for the performance, it's... well, perfunctory. There's very little stretching out (put this on the same list as Pink Floyd's *The Delicate Sound of Thunder* and Rush's *A Show of Hands*, cited earlier in the essay titled "The Lost Art of Audience Participation"), and the fidelity is passable but not what Parsons aficionados would have expected. In particular, the drums are quite vanilla-sounding. About the only track that seems to fare better

Slog On, You Tarnished And/Or Out-Of-Hock Diamond

than its studio version is "Limelight". There are also three new studio tracks included. Ultimately this may not be a requisite addition to a collection of Alan Parsons (Project) recordings.

I'm unsure what Alan Parsons's next musical move will be (or how long it will be in coming), but he apparently took his time following *Gaudi*, and perhaps for good reason. Regardless of how bad the critics slag any Alan Parsons album, such works are well-produced and a simple diversion for anyone who has a relatively decent audio system.

But I doubt that I could listen to *Try Anything Once* and King Crimson's *THRAK* back to back, y'know?

GOD RE-EXAMINED

The bottom line is that Eric Clapton isn't someone who should be envied.

Most likely, many rock fans who are now in their mid-forties first heard Clapton on Cream's immortal "Sunshine of Your Love", from their second album, *Disraeli Gears* (released in 1967). The oozing snarl of the guitar (which Clapton dubbed as the "woman tone") turned a lot of heads; it was a previously-unheard sound that may have inspired other guitarists (Spirit's Randy California, Ted Nugent of the Amboy Dukes, Randy Bachman on the Guess Who's "American Woman"), but to many players, the original is still the greatest. That tone was all over *Disraeli Gears*, and it probably came as a surprise to fans who did further research to discover that Clapton had been the guitar player for the Yardbirds in their earlier days.

Likewise, the first image of Eric Clapton that aging Boomers could recall would probably be the photograph of a guitar player sporting an Afro, aviator sunglasses, and a psychedelic-painted Gibson SG/Les Paul (last I heard, Todd Rundgren owned that guitar). And who knows how many budding guitar players were inspired to dig back into British guitar history a few years to check out Clapton's efforts with not only the Yardbirds, but with John Mayall's Bluesbreakers, and on Cream's first album (*Fresh Cream*) as well.

169

Executive Rock

Yet many aspiring teenage musicians in the Sixties would probably cite *Disraeli Gears* as a defining moment of their own respective quests for influences. Not only did Clapton's woman tone grab a listener's ear, but the rock-steady drumming of Ginger Baker ("player's player" Jeff Berlin, who's been a bass player on all sorts of recording projects, once accurately described Baker as having "perfect disco timing"), and Jack Bruce's plaintive singing and innovative bass guitar efforts were also evidence that the band's moniker wasn't just a borderline exercise in egomaniacal arrogance.

And the *Wheels of Fire* double set (one studio record, one live) only strengthened the trio's position (then *and* now) as one of the most important rock bands of all time. The studio LP experimented with some unusual instrumentation and effects on a few tunes, but three out of the four songs on the live disc were blues-based workouts that were stunning. In particular, the notion that Willie Dixon's chugging "Spoonful" could have its tempo revved up in mid-song to become an all-out, every-man-for-himself jam session seemed preposterous at first, but Cream's cover is now considered a cornerstone of improvisational rock. And "Spoonful" also marked the first time I heard Clapton pull off a unique guitar trick that sounded like an old Warner Brothers cartoon sound effect ("*Beeeeeeee-yoop!*"); it's heard twice on the over-sixteen-minute jam.

The *Goodbye* album was a bit less palatable; the studio tracks are passable but the live cuts are somewhat thinner-sounding than the Fillmore tracks on *Wheels of Fire*. Two subsequent live albums fared better, with terrific extended versions of songs like "N.S.U." and "Sunshine of Your Love" (on the latter song, the band simply stretches out the "A" chord that ends the tune).

After Cream's demise, Clapton and Baker turned right around with what may have been the ultimate exercise in futility for a so-called "supergroup". Teaming with Stevie Winwood and former Family bassist Rick Grech, the quartet known as Blind Faith lasted for all of one uninspired album. The 1969 issue of *Newsweek* that covered the first moon landing also contained an article about the band's American concert debut; it opens with: "Blind Faith is what they're called and blind faith is what they've got". What the band *didn't* have was any memorable material.

Apparently out of frustration, Clapton retreated to the role of sideman with Delaney & Bonnie and Friends, a relatively unknown band that had been the warm-up group for the Blind Faith tour, and from that aggregation sprang what was probably the most star-crossed band in rock history (considering what happened to its members), Derek & the Dominoes. The 1970 solo album by Clapton had heralded his switch from the primary use of Gibson electric guitars to the thinner-sounding Fender Stratocaster, which may have alienated some guitar tone freaks, but it also seemed to put somewhat of a

Slog On, You Tarnished And/Or Out-Of-Hock Diamond

damper on his fiery playing. Yet the subsequent use of a Strat with the Dominoes still evoked some passionate licks (particularly on the live album).

And speaking of passion, "Layla" is perhaps the most heartfelt rock song ever written about unrequited love. I don't know to what extent Eric Clapton's then-unfulfilled quest for the love of Patti Harrison was responsible for his seeking solace with various and sundry addictions, but it was around this time that he really plummeted into the abyss, becoming a reclusive junkie for about three years. He emerged only to do George Harrison's Concert for Bangla Desh plus an awful gig at the Rainbow Theatre in London, which had been organized by some friends of his who were trying to pull Clapton out of the netherworld into which he'd withdrawn (pun intended).

The '74 "comeback" album, *461 Ocean Boulevard*, started out in an upbeat manner with a rollicking cover of "Motherless Children", but "Mainline Florida" was about the only other tune that had any kind of an uptempo groove; the balance of the album was lightweight, reggae-oriented material ("I Shot The Sheriff" was a hit). Thus began a too-long series of solo albums that were laid-back and tepid (one music publication cattily suggested that the title for an album called *Backless* should instead be *Spineless*). In spite of the presence of commendable musical associates such as Albert Lee, and an occasional hit ("Wonderful Tonight", a cover of "Cocaine"), Ol' Slowhand seemed to be content to go at his own pace, which, while commendable, probably left a lot of his longtime fans somewhat dissatisfied. There were also rumors that he was also bouncing back and forth between bouts with drugs and alcohol again, and rumors that he was bouncing back and forth between flirtations with religion, which made the erstwhile guitar god with the fiery tone look like some kind of emotional ping pong ball. But who really knew?

Patti and Eric had finally married in 1979, but the union would prove to be stormy and unstable for its duration. Musically, however, the 1985 concert tour seemed to indicate that Clapton was in fine form; there was a hit single called "Forever Man", and the concert preserved on video (*Live Now*) shows E.C. in peak condition (see "Rating the MTV Concerts").

Through the rest of the Eighties, Clapton seemed to be experimenting with his albums and producers; some efforts were worthwhile, some were uninspiring. As a single, "Bad Love" seemed to get closer to the Sixties woman tone than anything else by Clapton since *Disraeli Gears*.

Clapton's participation in a variety of benevolent and/or socio-political projects was noteworthy during the same decade. There was the ARMS benefit, Live Aid, the Prince's Trust, and the Free Nelson Mandela concert. He also delved into the role of sideman on occasion (Roger Waters's *Pros and Cons of Hitch Hiking* tour), and took part in efforts honoring veteran rockers like Carl Perkins and Chuck Berry. Then there were his

Executive Rock

own humungous multi-night Royal Albert Hall projects that began in the latter part of the Eighties.

But cynics would opine that the real-life coda to "Layla" ended on a dissonant note. Eric and Patti split as Clapton fathered a child by an "actress/model" (Clapton himself was illegitimate). A few years later, the child fell to his death from a skyscraper window, adding even more angst to Eric Clapton's existence.

Which is why it wouldn't have been surprising to pick up the paper not long after the death of Clapton's son to read about the death of Clapton himself. I can't imagine what losing a child would do to my psyche, and it would have been easy to imagine that such an incident would have pushed Clapton right over the emotional edge, considering how tortured his life seems to have been.

Yet the opposite seems to have occurred. Eric Clapton is still active and erudite, giving eloquent interviews and recording albums that still garner a moderate amount of praise. His mid-Nineties effort, a straight-blues album called *From the Cradle*, was accompanied by a PBS special featuring performance clips, where it appeared that Clapton was favoring a large Gibson Byrdland electric guitar.

And in early 1993, Cream was inducted into the Rock & Roll Hall of Fame, and Clapton, Bruce and Baker whipped out an enthralling set. The Doors were inducted during the same ceremony, and guitarist Robby Krieger noted in an early 1994 interview that while it was a treat to get together with John Densmore and Ray Manzarek again (Pearl Jam's Eddie Vedder sang in lieu of Jim Morrison), the highlight of the evening as far as Kreiger was concerned was getting to see the Cream perform.

I know it smacks of hypocrisy to omit Eric Clapton from certain lists in the "The Rock & Roll Curmudgeon", but his participation in socio-political events seems to have been somewhat perfunctory and restrained, almost as if he's going along with everybody else. And yes, most of his problems have been self-inflicted, and an average music fan would having difficulty relating to a rock star who's been "living the blues" as long as Clapton has. Anybody wanna debate that such an opinion is out of line???

So if Eric Clapton's main accomplishment in popular music has been to simply *survive,* it's in some ways a tribute to one of the most evocative guitar players in the history of rock, and anytime an Eric Clapton song comes on the radio, it usually commands the attention of anyone who's listening. He's still a guitar hero to a lot of folks, including yours truly.

But I wouldn't want to have been what Eric Clapton's been through. It ain't worth it.

Slog On, You Tarnished And/Or Out-Of-Hock Diamond

"OLDFIELD IN THE OZONE"/"BOY WONDER BOUNCES BACK"

The two contradictory titles of this essay are indicative of how ambivalent I felt when I first heard Mike Oldfield's *Tubular Bells* in 1992. I didn't even know that such a release was even available until a entertainment writer for the local newspaper noted the new album in his column.

The original *Tubular Bells* came along around the time I graduated from college; ultimately I think it was the first so-called "New Age" album, although the term itself didn't really evolve until over a decade later. But think about it: Had anyone ever recorded anything like *Tubular Bells* previously? Oh sure, there were avant-garde albums, experimental albums, whatever; yet this effort by a British teenager was both innovative and melodic, in a style that could appeal to an average popular music listener as well as a serious student of music. But ya damn sho' couldn't boogie to it, eh?

Starting with a simple, repetitive piano figure, the "song" went through several seques on Side One that were difficult (at the time) to categorize; the final passage on that side was a dramatic buildup of quite a few instruments doing a particular progression over the bass guitar riff that anchored the segment. Master of ceremonies Viv Stanshall introduced each one, from "grand piano" through several types of guitars to glockenspiel to the final "tubular bells". Side Two wasn't quite as nifty as the first side; the latter half had its moments, but it was interrupted during one passage by a growling, howling werewolf. Yet the second side managed to redeem itself at the close with a rapid-fire version of "Sailor's Hornpipe", of all things (PERSONAL HISTORICAL FOOTNOTE: One of the bass players in a band I played in back then had been injured in a construction accident before I knew him; he was confined for weeks with a broken back. While he was hospitalized he got his mom to bring him his bass; he honed his chops so well he could play a verbatim version of "Sailor's Hornpipe"... wow!).

Admittedly the sales of the original *Tubular Bells* were bolstered by the fact that the first part of the work was heard in the soundtrack of *The Exorcist* (as far as movies of that particular genre go, the original was the greatest, in my opinion). Yet I'd heard *Tubular Bells* quite some time before that movie came out, and I had been immediately hooked by its listenability.

Another former band-mate of mine had never heard *Tubular Bells* until a sorta live version of it was staged on "Don Kirschner's Rock Concert" one night; my acquaintance had just done some, uh, "mushrooms" when he turned on the show. He reported that he felt like he was melting right into his vinyl chair as he watched the circle of musicians play Side One; a

Executive Rock

player would occasionally stand up and walk over to an alternate instrument and begin playing it, jumping right back in where he was supposed to be. See why such a first listening under the influence of mind-altering substances might cause a brain fry.

Oldfield followed *Tubular Bells* with *Hergest Ridge*, which beget *Ommadawn*. Both of those albums were similar in concept to *Tubular Bells*, but were more orchestrated and lush (it was reported that one passage on Side Two of *Hergest Ridge* has *several dozen* guitars playing on it at one time; talk about overdubs!). By the time *Ommadawn* rolled around, Oldfield seemed to be experimenting with so-called "world music" (again, the term didn't come into existence until the Eighties); *Ommadawn* featured appearances by some African drummers and the redoubtable Paddy Moloney of the Chieftains. Yet some of the guitar licks in the middle of all of it were astounding: Oldfield pulls off some down-the-scale riffs in the middle of Side One that to this day can knock Yngwie Malmsteen's pick in the dirt, as far as I'm concerned... or was it some kind of fancy studio effect?

Ommadawn was released in 1975, and by then I was such an Oldfield fan that a short time later I even bought a four-LP set called *Boxed*, which featured all three Oldfield albums up to that point (*Tubular Bell*s and *Hergest Ridqe* were remixed), plus a fourth record containing odd recordings. As far as new material, Mighty Mike wasn't heard from again until late 1978, when an imported double set called *Incantations* was released, and it was at this juncture that things began to get alienating.

Incantations is competent, of course, but its repetitive, orchestrated portions treads dangerously close Phillip Glass-type redundancy, and while Maddy Prior's vocals on a musical version of Longfellow's "Hiawatha" were interesting, the album just didn't hold on to one's attention from the outset as the other albums had done. A minor exception was the very end on Side Four, in which some instrument that sounds sorta like a xylophone is doing a repeating riff, accompanied by handclaps, jingle bells, and a loping bass guitar. It's interesting to try to figure out where the hell the rhythm is going, especially when the guitar and Prior's singing cut back in, but the last five minutes of a work that's four sides long don't necessarily salvage it. I remember grousing to myself: "I waited over three years for *this*???"

I decided to refrain from purchasing any further releases by Mike Oldfield without hearing at least part a new album before buying it; yet I knew this guideline was for all intents and purposes not practical, and I contradicted myself in 1981 when I bought an imported live album called *Exposed* immediately upon spying it in a record rack. This two record set temporarily assuaged my alienation in a big way; it's a brilliantly-executed example of why Mike Oldfield was such a dynamic musician. Consisting of an appropriately abbreviated version of "Incantations" and a rearranged

Slog On, You Tarnished And/Or Out-Of-Hock Diamond

version of "Tubular Bells" (plus a final dance tune called "Guilty"), this album (as previously noted in these pages) would be one of my Desert Island Top Ten picks. In case you're interested, Oldfield is seen playing a Gibson L6-S Deluxe in the concert photos on the cover.

However, subsequent Oldfield releases such as *Airborne* (which contained segments of the live version of "Tubular Bells" plus new studio material) and *Q.E. 2* were so uninspiring I pretty much gave up on the erstwhile Boy Wonder of progressive rock music. Some years ago, I saw that he'd done the soundtrack to *The Killing Fields*, but I didn't make an effort to hear it because I just wasn't interested.

As noted at the outset of this essay, two decades after the original *Tubular Bells* was released, I was made aware of a *Tubular Bells 2* by a blurb in the local paper. Curiosity got the better of me, and I bought the cassette; I noted with an ironic smirk that it was the first time I'd ever seen the word "sequel" in an album's liner notes.

I found it more difficult to get into the so-called "sequel" than the original work, probably because I halfway knew what to expect at certain points in the proceedings, but there was enough difference in the arrangement and the fidelity (considering how audio technology has progressed in twenty years) to make *Tubular Bells 2* a worthy successor to the original version. The different passages now have titles ("Sentinel", "Red Dawn", etc.), and the multi-instrument buildup at the end of Side One now features riffs by "digital sound processor" and "the Venetian Effect"(?); curiously, the individual who introduces each riff is identified in the liner notes only as "A Strolling Player" (I don't think it's Stanshall again).

There are some segments on *Tubular Bells 2* that evoke an image of songs like "Bicycle Built for Two" or "In the Good Old Summertime", what with the banjos and multiple mandolins, while another passage sounds like a snippet from a Giorgio Moroder soundtrack. Bagpipes appear on Side Two; unfortunately that damn werewolf does a reprise as well. Instead of "Sailor's Hornpipe" as the finale, a buckdancin' ditty called "Moonshine" finishes things up; it's every bit as refreshing and lively as "Sailor's Hornpipe" was on the original.

Ultimately I've decided that *Tubular Bells 2* is an idea that works, at least from a conceptual standpoint; as I no longer subscribe to contemporary music periodicals, I don't know how well the album did on the charts (if it charted at all), but I *did* see an ad for a Mike Oldfield concert in the L.A. area when I was in Pomona for one of the 1993 guitar shows.

So most likely I'd be safe in stating that if you liked the original *Tubular Bells* , you'll find the sequel satisfying as well. However, I can't honestly say I'll buy the next release by Mike Oldfield; I still don't know what to expect from him. However, if the next release is called *Hergest Ridge*

Executive Rock

2, I'll reach for my wallet immediately upon spying it in the CD rack.

(NOTE: Some of Oldfield's early albums, which were most likely imports only, have now been released on Compact Disc. Among them are the aforementioned *Ommadawn* and *Exposed*, and a so-so album called *Platinum*; I believe the studio cuts found on *Airborne* originally appeared on *Platinum*, which I never saw in domestic release).

WISHBONE ASTERISK

"What kind of bull**** hype is *this*?"

Such was probably the reaction of many *Rolling Stone* readers in the summer of 1972 upon reading an ad touting "The World's Greatest Twin Lead Guitar Band" (or words to that effect). The combo was named Wishbone Ash, and two guitarists, Andy Powell and Ted Turner, were pictured; they were playing a Gibson Flying V and a Fender Stratocaster, respectively.

"That was one of Miles's entrepreneurial moves", said Powell in a 1992 interview (referring to the redoubtable Miles Copeland, who went on to work with the Police; he also founded I.R.S. Records). "I was embarrassed by it; it wasn't where we were coming from at all. I cringed when I saw that ad, but it probably was responsible for people taking notice. Miles was aware of what it could do for us from a business standpoint, but it wasn't our style at all."

Another initial reaction back then by *guitar players* who weren't familiar with Wishbone Ash might have been to opine that such an ad being placed not-so-long after the death of Allman Brothers Band bassist Berry Oakley was a bit pretentious as well as coldly calculating. Duane Allman had died the previous year, and the Allmans had released a half-studio, half-live double album called *Eat A Peach* earlier in '72.

Nevertheless, Copeland's so-called "entrepreneurial move" was apparently successful, since the album being proffered by the ad, *Argus*, is probably considered to be the band's "breakthrough" album, at least in the U.S. The Ash (as longtime fans have come to nickname the aggregation)

176

Slog On, You Tarnished And/Or Out-Of-Hock Diamond

had two previous albums (a self-titled debut and a follow-up called *Pilgrimage*) under their belt, but the third time was the charm.

And one reason may have been *Argus*'s enigmatic cover, which, perhaps not surprisingly, was conceived and photographed by Hipgnosis, the outfit that has been associated with many Pink Floyd album cover projects over the years (and covers for the likes of Led Zeppelin and Paul McCartney as well). The mysterious cover photograph found on *Argus* showed what appeared to be a medieval warrior gazing across a misty landscape on the front of the album; the rear of the jacket was a continuation of the same photo... with a U.F.O. hovering in midair.

The contents of *Argus* ably demonstrated why the celebrated/notorious *Rolling Stone* ad was conceived, and that the hype wasn't hollow. Powell and Turner put on an amazing demonstration of soaring, ethereal harmony guitars that were in no way similar to stylings of Duane Allman and Dickie Betts. A tight rhythm section, composed of bassist Martin Turner and drummer Steve Upton, made for a unique listening experience.

"We *did* create that sound; and it's considered our 'identity'," said Ted Turner (also in a 1992 interview). "In some ways we were even sort of folk-oriented but our sound reflected the personalities of the band. Culturally, where we came from, we weren't like the Allman Brothers Band and their 'Southern boogie' style. I also think that when you get two guitars in a band, you have to compromise, and that cleans up the sound a bit."

Argus may well have been the definitive Wishbone Ash album; songs like "The King Will Come", "Time Was" and "Warrior" are classics (and are still concert favorites). The band's next effort, *Wishbone Four*, was a bit mellower, but tunes such as "Sorrel" featured intricate and astounding harmony guitars.

Following a murky-sounding live double album (*Live Dates*), Ted Turner departed the Ash, and was replaced by one Laurie Wisefield. While competent on guitar (if not vocally blessed), Wisefield's addition seemed to herald a passage of sorts; it seemed like *There's the Rub* signaled the metamorphosis of Wishbone Ash into a "journeyman" combo; i.e., a band that would continue to record and release product for a core of fans that was apparently large enough to continue supporting such a musical effort (NOTE: *There's The Rub*'s feature track is an extended instrumental with the cutesy acronym title of "F.U.B.B.").

The Ash maintained the lineup of Powell, M. Turner, Upton and Wisefield for about a decade, releasing albums such as *Just Testing*, *Front Page News*, and *New England*. The stand-out album from that era was the live *Hot Ash*, which was the domestic version of the larger *Live Dates II*. Production-wise, it beat the first *Live Dates* in spades, and any Wishbone fan who might have fallen by the wayside would have probably opined some-

Executive Rock

thing like "Now that's more like it!" upon hearing *Hot Ash*, which contains better versions of older Ash material as well snappy tunes from the "Wisefield era".

Then Wisefield got an offer to join Tina Turner, and the band went through a succession of guitarists; ultimately Martin Turner departed the band as well. Apparently Powell and Upton continued to trudge along, but most folks probably didn't hear much about 'em.

Ultimately, the original foursome of Wishbone Ash regrouped in the late Eighties, at the behest of Miles Copeland, who was attempting an instrumental series called "No Speak" on his I.R.S. Records venture. The first four releases were by William Orbit, former Police drummer Stewart Copeland (let's hear it for nepotism... but Stewart Copeland is a phenomenally talented musician and composer), Pete Haycock (formerly of the Climax Blues Band) and the Ash, whose effort was titled *Noveau Calls*. I'm embarrassed to admit that it was over two years after I'd bought the album that I realized the pun in its title.

But *Noveau Calls*, while demonstrating that all of the musicians still had considerable chops, probably left a lot of longtime Wishbone Ash fans a bit disappointed due to the noticeable absence of the band's trademark harmony leads; persons who'd been "into" the band since the *Argus* days had every right to expect such. While the idea of an instrumental album was appealing to the band, Ted Turner noted: "I had problems getting out of the country at the time, so I got involved with things really late. In fact, it was like 'meet the guys after fifteen years and go into the studio the next day'."

The follow-up effort, *Here to Hear*, also lacked a plethora of harmony guitars (but had vocals), and Martin Turner's bass had a "beefy" or "upfront" sound on the album ("That's because he mixed it!" laughed Andy Powell). Ted Turner described both *Noveau Calls* and *Here to Hear* as representing "a transitional phase for the band". Another release, *Strange Affair*, was released worldwide except for the U.S., and by the early Nineties Martin Turner had departed again, and Steve Upton left to manage a mansion in France.

Supplanted with Andy Pyle and Ray Weston, the Ash released their third live album in 1993; it's a "concert club" effort that a lot of "journeyman" rock musicians seem to have been recording and releasing as they've gotten on the other side of forty. Some of the tracks on *The Ash Live in Chicago* sound a bit "hesitant" (for lack of a better term), but others, such as "Standing in the Rain" and "Strange Affair" are as potent as anything the band has ever done (and those two tunes are helped immensely by harmony guitar breaks, of course).

1993 also saw the release of an excellent anthology called *Time Was/ The Wishbone Ash Collection*. It's a two-disc, twenty-three song package

Slog On, You Tarnished And/Or Out-Of-Hock Diamond

that borrows primarily from the Ash's first four albums; even though Laurie Wisefield's tenure lasted more than twice as long as Ted Turner's initial membership, only six songs on the anthology date from the decade or so that Wisefield was in the band.

Of particular note on the anthology are the tunes culled from *Argus*. Turns out they've been remixed by Martin Turner, and while as expected his bass is more up-front in the mix, those five tunes sound great.

1994 was *not* a good annum for Ted Turner. He opted to leave the band once again early that year, and soon afterwards his son was killed by an hit-and-run driver. Kipp and Ted Turner were walking home from a video store in the Phoenix area (where Turner resides), and an out-of-control automobile struck the younger Turner, killing him instantly. A driver was arrested and charged the next day.

Ultimately, Ted Turner's efforts following the death of his son resulted in a new and stricter law concerning hit-and-run automobile accidents being signed by the Arizona governor (the date of the signing was the first anniversary of Kipp Turner's death), and as this book was going to press, a longtime Ash fan from Idaho told me that Turner's wife was pregnant.

So now it's just Andy Powell as the lone original member (as noted in "Sole Survivors or Time Warp Bandits?"). Wishbone Ash has been touring Europe as of late, and the new lineup has been concentrating on harmony vocals as well as harmony guitars. The other guitarist is Roger Filgate, who at one time was the band's guitar tech (seems like a logical step up, eh?), and Powell still relies heavily on his '66 Flying V, which has probably attained icon status among-knowledgeable guitarists; other examples would include instruments such as Duane Eddy's Gretsch 6120, Eric Clapton's psychedelic-painted SG/Les Paul from the *Disraeli Gears* days, etc.

It remains to be seen what the current incarnation of the Ash will accomplish, but as is the case with many bands, they're still out there pluggin' away.

In the meantime, the most popular classic Ash material is available on Compact Disc; do yourself a favor and check out *Argus*, and if you like what you hear, the aforementioned anthology is a worthwhile investment (and don't forget the *Argus* cuts on it are remixed, so technically there's no absolute redundancy). About the only thing Wishbone Ash might ever get cited for in some "encyclopedia of rock" would be their trademark harmony leads, but their unique, vibrant and melodic music holds up to this day, and they were/are a definitive example of a "player's band".

But be forewarned about the cover of the *Argus* CD: For some reason (perhaps the photo had to be cropped), the U.F.O. is missing on the back. I wonder if Hipgnosis meant for that to happen?

Yet another enigma...

179

Executive Rock

THE HOWARD COSELL OF HARD ROCK

A viewer would probably suspect that Ted Nugent's instructional video (on Star Licks) is going to be different when the opening sequence shows the guitarist stalking what he terms "the enemy" on his own property in Michigan. Ultimately he "discovers" an electronic keyboard instrument in the woods, and vowing to "make the world safe for electric guitar players", blows the keyboard to smithereens with his shotgun.

"I think I got him", observes Da Nuge, as he treads carefully towards the debris. Then he freezes. "Oh my God", he chortles, "You're not gonna believe this! It was *pregnant!* It was a female, and it had a baby!" Whereupon Nugent reaches down and pulls up one of those dinky white plastic battery-powered keyboards that's about fifteen inches long. "Oh, no!", yells the hunter, "A little mutant!" Then he pulls out a handgun and obliterates that gizmo as well.

Nugent's then exhales loudly and says to the camera (while sporting that semi-maniacal grin of his): "I don't know about you, but I'm feeling much better already!"

One person who saw this portion of the instructional video for the first time immediately opined: "He's *crazy!*"

My immediate retort: "Yeah, like a *fox.*"

The "Detroit sound" that emanated from the Motor City in the late Sixties was poles apart from the "Motown sound" (which was also in full bloom around that time). Ultimately, Motown was the more durable and memorable style *by far,* but the loud Detroit rock purveyed by the likes of the MC5, the Stooges, the Rationals and SRC brought forth some memorable sounds and personalities, not the least of which was a teenaged guitarist for the Amboy Dukes named Ted Nugent.

The Amboy Dukes were essentially a One-Hit-Wonder that charted with a song called "Journey to the Center of the Mind"; the title and subject matter now seem dated but the tune still holds up, due to the lyrical licks and "oozing" tone purveyed by Nugent, who, when discussing such times, has averred that "there was a real 'competition' factor among Detroit bands; it was a 'race' and led to a very aggressive sound; everybody was really into live club bands. The competition between individual musicians and all of the bands was unprecedented and was very volatile. A lot of people mistakenly equated the intensity of Detroit rock and roll with the 'industrial' element of Michigan, but that wasn't the case." Nugent, in one of his rapid-fire commentary modes, has described the Detroit rock sound as

Slog On, You Tarnished And/Or Out-Of-Hock Diamond

having "a lot of attitude, a lot of spirit, a lot of rhythm & blues, a lot of guts, a lot of honesty, a lot of edge, a lot of tension, a lot of flow."

Come to think of it, "Journey to the Center of the Mind" was probably one of the few Detroit rock songs that got any respectable amount of chart action and/or airplay back then (off the top of my head, the only other example I can think of would be "Ramblin' Gamblin' Man" by the Bob Seger System... and who remembers the hidden images on the front and back cover of *that* band's first album???).

As the Amboy Dukes put out more albums, the group's moniker changed to Ted Nugent & the Amboy Dukes. Whenever a band puts the name of one of its members out in front in mid-career, the initial interpretation by an average music fan would be that it was an egotistical move, but considering how Nugent's, um, "unique and assertive" personality (both on-stage and off) were developing, such a move now seems logical, as was his ultimate self-monikered musical career.

Such "developments" included Nugent's no-holds-barred concerts, which featured the star performing in nothing but a loin cloth and demonstrating his bowhunting prowess onstage. Then there was his penchant for the Gibson Byrdland electric guitar, a large, hollow-body model that looks like it would be better suited for a jazz guitarist. The Byrdland is one reason Nugent's unique tone transpired; in an early 1995 interview, he said: "What motivated me was a desire to play on the edge of volume and the edge of tone, where it can get out of your hands. I also attribute it to the use of a Gibson Byrdland; I'm the only guy on the planet who can grab a Byrdland and do what I do with it." Nugent still favors that model even today, and is still looking for 'em; he wants spruce-top Byrdlands rather than maple-top variants.

However, the one thing for which Ted Nugent has been noted more than anything else in his public life has been his outspoken, against-the-grain lifestyle as a purveyor of loud rock and roll. Examples include the fact that Nugent is probably the only rock musician who's an acknowledged member *(lifetime,* for that matter) of the National Rifle Association, and the fact that his bowhunting enterprise (headquartered out of Jackson, Michigan) is an enormously successful venture, with a bimonthly magazine, a plethora of events for bowhunters (including hunting trips conducted by Nugent himself) and an extensive line of catalog items.

And get this: A second improbable occurrence on Nugent's videotape was the blatant and hilarious way he hawked his hunting products, which had nothing to with learning how to play rock guitar. He even showed off his wife's exercise video, as the toll-free phone number (1-800-434-HUNT) flashed across the bottom of the screen.

Another facet of Da Nuge's uniqueness is his vehement antidrug stance;

181

Executive Rock

he's been espousing a "drugs suck" attitude since at least 1970, when he held forth about such in an issue of *Creem* magazine (which was still in newsprint tabloid format back then). And he hasn't let up (see "Bullfrog Blues/In Terms of Two").

Nugent *has* participated in a group project since the days of the Amboy Dukes; he got together with ex-Styx guitarist Tommy Shaw, former Night Ranger bassist Jack Blades, and drummer Michael Cartellone to form a band called Damn Yankees; while their albums sold well, as of this writing the band is "on hiatus". Nugent released a solo album in early 1995 called *Spirit of the Wild*, and Shaw and Blades came out with a duo album.

Spirit of the Wild is a typical Nugent stomp-fest, replete with song titles like "Thighraceous", "I Shoot Back", and "Lovejacker". The interestingly-titled "Kiss My Ass" has a list of organizations and individuals on the lyric sheet to whom the song is, uh, dedicated.

The front cover shows Da Nuge rockin' out with a Byrdland (bassist/producer Michael Lutz, who was with Brownsville Station, is visible at the edge of the photo). Nugent's sporting a bona fide Indian (READ: "Native American") ceremonial headdress in the front cover photo, and the back cover picture shows the belly of a stuffed armadillo which Nugent killed with a bow and arrow ("I'm the only rock guitarist in the world who has his own taxidermist", he advised).

As for the headdress, Nugent waxed serious and explained that it was made by a Lakota brave; "I got a letter from the chief of the Strongheart Society, which is an organization of the Lakota Sioux, Arapaho, and Cheyenne nations. I'm the only white man who's ever been made a brave in the Strongheart Society; it's a Cheyenne warrior tribe established by Chief Sitting Bull and a couple of other famous chiefs. It's an organization of the red man, to return their people to the land and return their land to the people, and return to that 'connection' with family, tribe, and nature." Nugent had appeared in a public television special, and said that it represented "a white guy living the Native Americans' bow-hunting lifestyle heritage better than the red people themselves are." The guitarist averred that he was more honored with the Strongheart Society membership than having been named to the Board of Directors of the N.R.A.

Ted Nugent is definitely a one-of-a-kind personality, and rock music could use more folks like him. But for some reason, Da Nuge gives off the perception that the niche of popular music from which he has operated for years, and the attitude that goes with it, are *his and his alone;* it's almost like he's hunkered down in his own exclusive little facet (armed with God only knows what kind of firepower), *daring* anyone to try and get in the same foxhole with him.

So like the late Howard Cosell, Ted Nugent knows full well that his, er,

Slog On, You Tarnished And/Or Out-Of-Hock Diamond

"forthrightness" is one of the main reasons for his success, and he's exploited it well. Nugent could quit playing loud rock and roll *tomorrow* and would still have an admirable business empire. Either ignore him or get the hell outta the way.

And did I mention that Nugent also has a radio show? When does the man *sleep*???

Readers interested in Nugent's bow-hunting magazine and products can contact:

Ted Nugent World Bowhunters
4133 W. Michigan Ave.
Jackson, Michigan 49202
ph. (517) 750-9060.

Hey, capitalism's contagious, y'know?

THE DEVIL GOES ICE SKATING

"A hundred and eighty degrees," observed the CPA.

He was referring to a song called "Get Over It", one of several new studio tracks on the Eagles' mid-Nineties album with the self-depreciating title of *Hell Freezes Over*. "Get Over It" is a snarling anti-victimization tune, of all things, with cutesy sardonic lyrics such as "I'd like to find your inner child and kick its little ass", and the reason the CPA was using an opposite-direction analogy to describe the song was due to the fact that it was sung and co-written by Don Henley, who's dabbled in sanctimonious activism (of a liberal bent, natch) on more than one occasion.

The CPA used to sing and play guitar in a successful circuit band, and his outfit used to do a plethora of Eagles songs, from "Take It Easy" on the 1972 debut album to tunes found on *Hotel California*, which many fans consider to be the band's definitive album.

Another appropriate analogy the CPA cited during the course of our conversation was to describe the live tracks that comprise the bulk of *Hell*

Executive Rock

Freezes Over as being "like fine wine" (the CPA is a bit more erudite than me, and we're constantly trying to one-up each other in our conversations by using what the Missus calls "ten dollar words"). And adding to the irony about "Get Over It" was the fact that the CPA and I had each first heard it on Rush Limbaugh's radio show...

Three hits singles from a debut album is an auspicious accomplishment, and in all probability "Witchy Woman", "Peaceful Easy Feeling" and the rollicking anthem "Take It Easy" still fetch a considerable amount of airplay on Classic Rock radio stations these days compared to other songs from the same era. But there really wasn't a "throwaway cut" on the Eagles' first album, and other songs had hooks that were just as potent as the ones that charted. In particular, "Chug All Night" was a roaring, sing-along hellraiser that would have been at home at any fraternity party.

"Earlybird" was powered by Bernie Leadon's banjo (the other members of the original quartet were Don Henley, Glenn Frey and former Poco member Randy Meisner, who has one of the greatest high-pitched voices in the history of rock), and in an "In Concert" performance not long after the release of their first album, the Eagles cut loose with an extended, revved-up version of "Earlybird" that was classic; the image of Leadon hollering "C'mon, boy!" at Glenn Frey (who was playing slide guitar) is still memorable (somebody oughta dig into ABC's vaults and resurrect and remaster those shows and release 'em on home video or CD. There were some other great songs on "In Concert" from time to time, such as Joe Walsh & Barnstorm's "Turn to Stone" and Rory Gallagher's "Hands Off").

Successful concept albums in rock music have been around since the Who's *Tommy*, but the Eagles' second effort, *Desperado*, doesn't normally get cited as one. And it wasn't until 1994 that I rediscovered how powerful the album and its theme were; I hadn't heard *Desperado* in its entirety since the mid-Seventies, and ordered it as a last selection from a CD club to complete my obligation. The first time I popped it into the CD player was late at night; I was staying up to assemble some dealer catalogs for future distribution and had donned the headphones.

But when the opening song, "Doolin-Dalton", got to the line about how "the towns lay out across the dusty plains, like graveyards filled with tombstones waitin' for the names," I stopped what I was doing. Somehow I realized (or recalled) that this wasn't an album that could be listened to casually or as background/ambient music. I sat back, closed my eyes, and paid attention. Nobody was hearing this but me.

Slog On, You Tarnished And/Or Out-Of-Hock Diamond

By the time the final track, a reprise medley of "Doolin-Dalton" and "Desperado" began to fade out, I was in tears. *Desperado* is nothing less than a classic example of conceptual American rock about a quintessential part of American history; both the album and its subject matter are timeless, and I'm ashamed that I forgot to consider *Desperado* when I was conjuring up that desert-island-top-ten-album-list for Malc's perusal. I'm not sure Henley's ever sounded better; the album is, quite simply, indispensable.

On the Border and *One of These Nights* were not so much letdowns as they were simply albums of well-crafted songs (with several hits in 'em), and by this time personnel changes had begun to take place. Another guitarist, Don Felder, was added, and Leadon departed, to be replaced by the redoubtable Joe "Ol' Putty Face" Walsh.

Then *Hotel California* put the Eagles back into prominence as an important American band with a vengeance. Even songs that *weren't* hits could've been; "Wasted Time" and "The Last Resort" are brilliantly executed, even if the "concept" of *Hotel California* is a bit more nebulous.

But trouble was apparently brewing within the ranks. Meisner departed, to be replaced by Timothy B. Schmit (no better choice, in my opinion). The one studio album on which Schmit appeared, *The Long Run*, was somewhat of a bona fide disappointment since it followed *Hotel California*, and it was reported that one of the reasons the band broke up as the decade ended was due to dissatisfaction with *The Long Run*. The Eagles sold more records in the Seventies than any other American band.

And the post-mortem live album was more of a fitting tribute to the Eagles than ELP's *Emerson, Lake and Palmer In Concert* was to *that* particular band (the latter live release seemed more like an afterthought). It's interesting that both combos split around the same time, considering how different their music was.

Naturally, all of the ex-members of the Eagles attempted solo careers; Walsh, of course, already had access to that particular parachute. Henley was the most successful, and for all of the times he's alienated an average listener like me with his public stances and pronouncements, I'm sure I'll buy his solo greatest hits album eventually.

"For the record, we never broke up; we just took a fourteen-year vacation."

That particular remark opens the live portion of *Hell Freezes Over*, and I surprised myself by not buying the album immediately following its release (there was no real reason or excuse why I didn't). As noted at the

Executive Rock

outset, I heard "Get Over It" on the Rush Limbaugh show and an occasional live track on the local Classic Rock format radio station, but I just didn't think about making the effort to purchase a new release by a legendary band.

There was a concert video as well, and I didn't see it until the early Spring of 1995, while we were participating in the Great American Ritual of taking a family vacation to Disney World.

Channel-surfing through the TV set in a motel room on the Disney World grounds reveals a lotta mouse ear-oriented stations, and Nickelodeon's missing, for obvious reasons. However, the local PBS affiliate was among the "outside" channels that were available, and just as we were about to conk out, the Eagles concert came on (PBS was in the middle of one of its fund-raising campaigns, which is when a viewer is more likely to see such fare).

And I sat there mesmerized, just as I had been about a year earlier when I heard *Desperado* in its entirety for the first time in almost two decades.

There *are* some differences in the live part of the *Hell Freezes Over* album and the concert video. The latter starts out stronger with Don Felder's amazing fingerpicking intro to a unique "unplugged" arrangement of "Hotel California", which shows up *second* on the album, following "Tequila Sunrise". The video also features more of the members' solo material, including Henley's "Forgiveness" and a terrific version of Walsh's "Help Me Through the Night". Schmit pulls off "Love Will Keep Us Alive" in concert with ease (the studio version of it is on the *Hell Freezes Over* album).

The Eagles' 1995 concert tour featured ticket prices that were probably surpassed only by the Streisand tour of '94. I'm unsure how much further cooperation will ensue between the "California rock" veterans (the term is taken from *Hell Freezes Over*'s liner notes), but the mid-Nineties album, video and tour by this perhaps irreplaceable American band was a dynamic moment in rock history. Perhaps they oughta be made aware of Mick Ralphs's comment regarding solo albums

186

Slog On, You Tarnished And/Or Out-Of-Hock Diamond

2/3 OF A DREAM......
OKAY, MAKE IT 90% OF A DREAM

Because to completely ignore Gary Moore's contribution to the music of a trio known as BBM would be insulting (the other two players are Jack Bruce and Ginger Baker). It's interesting, however, that every reference I've seen to the band uses *just its initials;* there's nothing about a combo called "Bruce, Baker and Moore" or "Baker, Bruce, and Moore", and that's probably exactly how the "hyping" of BBM was intended.

It was noted at the outset of this section that the Cream wouldn't be discussed, but since that aggregation represented a musical milestone in the history of rock to many people, it seems only fair to do a bit of follow-up on Jack Bruce and Ginger Baker, since Eric Clapton was cited earlier.

After Cream split, Bruce embarked on a solo career (his first release was called *Songs for a Tailor*), sat in with the Tony Williams Lifetime, and more or less took Felix Pappalardi's place in Mountain (which was renamed West, Bruce and Laing) in the mid-Seventies. Since then it's probably fair to say that he languished in relative obscurity (compared to Clapton), but he did release some solo projects from time to time, and E.C. *did* help him out on a couple of tunes for an anthology.

Ginger Baker took everyone from Blind Faith *except* Clapton into some gargantuan project called Ginger Baker's Air Force, and also seemed to flounder in the pop music world's offstage netherworld for the next couple of decades, surfacing on occasion with bands like the Baker-Gurvitz Army ("Mad Jack" featured the same poetry-reading-on-top-of-a-beat concept that "Pressed Rat and Warthog" did), or some almost-New Age or World Music collaborations with the likes of L. Shankar; while the latter fare wouldn't have been palatable to most rock fans, nevertheless these later projects indicated that Baker had cleaned up and was playing better than ever.

Cream's 1993 induction into the Rock and Roll Hall of Fame set off speculation (for the umpteenth time) that the trio would record and tour again, and post-Hall of Fame ceremony comments by all three players found on a videotape called *Fresh Live Cream* merely fueled the hype; the videotape also dates from 1993 and more or less leaves a viewer hanging as to the resolution (much as the old Saturday morning movie serials like "Flash Gordon" or "The Purple Martian" used to do).

Well, apparently Bruce and Baker got tired of waiting, because BBM's *Around the Next Dream* was released in 1994; I wouldn't have known about it if another *Vintage Guitar* writer hadn't mentioned it almost in passing.

187

Executive Rock

Guitarist Gary Moore is probably the best choice Bruce and Baker could have made (if such was the case) for a venture like this, just as Tim Schmit was probably the best choice to replace Randy Meisner in the Eagles. Moore's been a "player's player" for some time, and had spent a while in Thin Lizzy. He's got a respectable catalog of albums to his credit, and is an advocate of tone-oriented guitar playing. While some of his efforts on *Around the Next Dream* tread close to Clapton's "woman tone" (any closer would probably be considered blasphemy), his playing is expressive and distinctive, and it fits in with Bruce and Baker just fine.

Yet any comparisons to Cream (BBM *had* to expect such) are further validated by some of the riffs or *entire songs* found on *Around the Next Dream*. Examples include:

"WAITING IN THE WINGS": "White Room" (there's even a wah-wah pedal!).

"CITY OF GOLD": "Crossroads".

"WHERE IN THE WORLD": The strings sound sorta like what was heard on "Passing the Time".

"HIGH COST OF LOVING": "Born Under a Bad Sign" and/or "Strange Brew".

"GLORY DAYS": "Those Were the Days".

"WHY DOES LOVE (HAVE TO GO WRONG)": "We're Going Wrong".

And the last song, "Wrong Side of Town", is a lament that sounds a lot like Sting's "Moon Over Bourbon Street".

So there's a lot of time-warp self-plagiarism on BBM's album, but so what? This is a well-produced modern effort by some longtime veterans who have still got the chops, and if they figured that their potential listeners/customers would want something that gave a nod to a momentous musical effort almost thirty years ago, then that's sensible marketing... ain't it?

I'm unsure what the status of BBM is these days; the one article I read about 'em in a guitar magazine alluded to fractious on-stage behavior, so the volatility that ultimately doomed Cream may figure into the ongoing survival and/or success of BBM as well.

Yet for all of those Cream fans who've hoped for a reunion tour, this may be as close as we'll ever get.

Slog On, You Tarnished And/Or Out-Of-Hock Diamond

YES: A Definite Maybe

"This is *real* Yes music", Jon Anderson announced from the stage.

While some concertgoers may have thought his remark introducing a song called "Endless Dream" (which clocks in at over a quarter-hour in length) was cryptic or perhaps even cynical, my interpretation was that he was referring to the fact that the opus was exemplary of the kind of extended work that longtime Yes fans know and love: Like "Close to the Edge", "Starship Trooper" and perhaps even "Machine Messiah", "Endless Dream" effortlessly jumps back and forth from frantic, complex tempos to lush, orchestrated passages featuring brilliant vocal harmonies to roaring power chords without ever alienating a listener.

The thing is, unlike the other Yes gems cited in the previous paragraph, "Endless Dream" isn't fifteen or twenty years old. It's the final 'song' on the Yes' 1994 album, *Talk*.

The Yes' cover of Richie Havens's "No Opportunity Necessary, No Experience Needed" could easily be cited in previous essays titled "The First Cut is the Deepest" and "The Cover Story". The reason this song is so memorable is due to its "internal medley" with some orchestrated passages from the soundtrack to a sprawling Fifties Western called *The Big Country*. Tony Kaye's grinding organ introduces a racing string section, and once the band storms into their version of the Havens tune, there were other snippets from the soundtrack, including Peter Banks performing one of the signature, uh, "riffs" from *The Big Country* on guitar. It's a very exciting tune that probably got a lot of listeners' attention in the early Seventies.

(PERSONAL HISTORICAL NOTE: My father's favorite sequence from *The Big Country* was the one where the patriarch of a rough-and-tumble frontier family, played by Burl Ives, had sent for his ne'er-do-well son, portrayed by a scruffy-looking Chuck Connors. When the son lurched into the house, muttering "You want me, Pa?", the father paused a moment to size up his offspring before grousing: "Before ya was born I did.")

"No Opportunity Necessary, No Experience Needed" was the leadoff track on the Yes' second album, *Time And A Word*; their debut was self-titled. Back when they first began to be noticed in the U.S. market, they were of course lumped in with other British progressive rock/art rock aggregations like King Crimson and Emerson, Lake and Palmer. But this quintet seemed to have a few different sonic aspects going for it, some of which may have been an acquired taste: The singer had a high-pitched, almost effeminate voice, and the bass sounded *quite* different from other

Executive Rock

bottom-end areas in other rock bands. Chris Squire's rapid-fire riffing was beefy, bright, and *way* up front in the mix.

The original material may have also been an acquired taste, but the unique cover songs on the first two albums (including the Beatles' "Every Little Thing" and the Buffalo Springfield's "Everydays") most likely hooked a listener long enough to get him/her used to the band's own compositions as well. That's shrewd, and while the Yes did acknowledge the influence of the Vanilla Fudge during those times, they actually went the Fudge one better on accounta their original material from the first album and *Time and A Word* has stood the test of time better than the Fudge's original songs.

Banks was out by the time *Time And A Word* rolled out; he was replaced by the remarkable Steve Howe, whose almost-bebop guitar licks meshed perfectly with the increasingly complex arrangements the band was forging. Songs from the third effort, *The Yes Album,* included some of the most memorable in the band's history; tunes like "Yours Is No Disgrace", "Your Move", and "Starship Trooper" (with its fascinating third section that builds on a simple E-C-A chord progression) can still be heard on Classic Rock format radio.

But *Fragile* is probably the definitive Yes album to a lot of folks, since it heralds the first association of another remarkable musician, Rick Wakeman, with the band (he replaced Kaye). *Fragile* also contains the so-called "signature song" for the Yes, "Roundabout". The fifth album, *Close to the Edge*, featured all of three tunes ("Siberian Khartru", "And You and I" and the multiple-part title track) but it was an adventurous effort which sold well.

The three-LP live album (*Yessongs*) would, as noted earlier, be a personal choice for a desert-island-top-ten list. But by then drummer Bill Bruford had departed to join the second version of King Crimson (he's heard on some of *Yessongs*'s tracks, however, including the one that has a drum solo). Alan White has been manning the percussion ever since then.

No offense to Patrick Moraz, but it seemed like around the time he replaced Rick Wakeman, the Yes started getting so complex with works like *Tales from Topographic Oceans* (Wakeman was still around) and *Relayer* (Moraz on board) that it was quite difficult for even a longtime fan to get a handle on such efforts.

Eventually, Wakeman returned for a couple of albums (*Going for the One, Tormato*); there was also a second live effort called *Yesshows*, then it appeared that entire Yes enterprise would implode as Wakeman left for a second time, and Jon Anderson departed as well.

But the addition of Trevor Horn and Geoff Downes (who'd been the Buggles, of "Video Killed the Radio Star" fame) resulted in a not-too-shabby effort called *Drama*. Curiously, an authorized history of the Yes

190

Slog On, You Tarnished And/Or Out-Of-Hock Diamond

was released around this time, and it's ironic that the book refers to that lineup of the band in the present tense, on accounta said lineup only lasted for that one album.

Following *Drama*, things once again looked ominous for the band's survival. Chris Squire and Alan White actually recorded some songs with Led Zeppelin's Jimmy Page following the death of Zep drummer John Bonham; the tentative moniker for this band that never materialized was the XYZ Band (for "Ex-Yes and Zeppelin").

Quite possibly, the Yes could also be cited in the "Phase Three Bands" essay, but the Phase Two variant didn't sound all that different from the various aggregations that made up Phase One (and as just noted, Phase Two only recorded one album), yet Phase Three marked a noticeable shift by the band to a more pop-oriented sound.

After the XYZ Band had failed to get past recording a few songs, Squire and White began another unit with the working moniker of Cinema. Tony Kaye, of all people, was brought onboard as keyboard player, and the guitar player was former South African pop star (now a U.S. citizen) Trevor Rabin. Ultimately Jon Anderson came back around, and the resulting album, *90125*, was the Yes' biggest-selling effort in its history. Most listeners would probably have opined if asked that Rabin's blazing, melodic guitar playing was the main reason that *90125* and *Big Generator* (with radio-ready tunes like "Owner of a Lonely Heart", "Rhythm of Love" and ""Love Will Find A Way") meant a more accessible Yes.

And as if to prove such, Jon Anderson departed again after *Big Generator* to hook up with three other members of the "classic Yes" lineup in something called Anderson Bruford Wakeman Howe. The resulting album and a video for "Brother of Mine" were awful.

Then when the Yes's *Union* album was released, son-of-a-gun if it wasn't a combined effort of the "Eighties" Yes and ABWH; i.e., *eight* band members. However, Chris Squire noted in his *Vintage Guitar* interview that there's no song on the album that had all eight guys on it; the album is essentially Jon Anderson bouncing back and forth between two bands ("Can't tell the players without a program," grumbled Malc). It shouldn't come as any surprise that this "concept" lasted all of one album, yet "Lift Me Up" is a great song that almost salvages the entire *Union* effort. The band even toured as an octet.

It might come as a surprise to some readers that I don't attend concerts on a regular basis. In fact, a Yes performance during their *Talk* tour was the first show I'd been to in around *seven years*. In 1987, the Missus and I went to a

Executive Rock

Huey Lewis & the News concert (the opening act was Robert Cray); she was somewhat astounded when I walked out of the concert hall to hang around the lobby for a while because the proceedings had gotten too loud for me.

Many of the interviews I've done have been at concert venues or hotels prior to a show, and I've usually been invited to the concert, but I've always declined for various reasons, not the least of which is a bit of potential guilt that could have been possible if I was hanging out at a loud rock & roll show while the Missus and Princess were at home; I stay gone enough anyway, so my usual style is to get the interview done and head back to the house. The one *post*-concert interview I've done (Foreigner's Mick Jones) saw me showing up backstage about twenty minutes before the show was over; the Princess was already in bed before I left the house. All of the previous "concert interviews" had been within a one hundred mile radius of my home; if I wasn't on the road so much anyway, I might've stayed around for more concerts. Someday I may regret such actions, but I haven't lost any sleep....

Yet the offer from the Yes' public relations firm made for a slightly different scenario. For one thing, the concert venue was a hundred and seventy-five miles from home; another factor was my (scheduled) major surgery that was coming up about two weeks after the show, and there were a lot of unknowns about the medical event (length of recuperation, prognosis, etc.).

So after consultation on the home front and with the *Vintage Guitar* home office, a decision was made to go. I purchased a cassette of the band's new album, *Talk* (by now, the personnel was back to the lineup of Squire, Rabin, Anderson, White and Kaye), so I could discuss this latest release with Squire and/or Rabin (I was uncertain who I'd be interviewing, and wouldn't find out until I got to the venue).

And ya know something? *Talk* is such a good album, it would've gotten a lot of playing time in my cassette player even if an interview with one or more of the players *hadn't* been pending. It was recorded using some kind of new computer technology that doesn't sound sterile (as a lot of digital recordings are wont to do), and there's not a bad song on the album. I found myself listening to *Talk* more often than any Yes album I'd had in years, which of course added to the expectation that I'd get a good interview or interviews.

Getting backstage at the concert venue to check in with the tour personnel, I was able to watch how things were taking shape for that evening's show. A multitude of people were scurrying around tending their assigned tasks, which ranged from operating computers in the temporary office to assembling the giant lighting system (a massive rig that looked somewhat like a triangular space station hovered above the stage as its centerpiece).

After receiving a gold "Band Guest" pass, I went to the hotel as directed

Slog On, You Tarnished And/Or Out-Of-Hock Diamond

by a tour official. I happened to encounter Alan White and Tony Kaye at the entrance, and I flashed a copy of *Vintage Guitar* at them, saying "I'm sorry; you don't fit the format of the publication." That got a couple of nonplussed looks from the drummer and keyboard player (I was to encounter Kaye again later, when he made that backstage remark about a Mellotron sample). Following several conversations on the house phone with the tour manager, and a couple of false starts, I was finally able to do a rapid-fire but cordial interview with Chris Squire about an hour before showtime.

Soon after that, I was escorted to the side of the stage and dismissed into the floor level seating area by a member of the local promoter's security folks, who took his job a bit too seriously, in my opinion (it was the only example of what might be construed as discourtesy I experienced while I was there; everyone else was very businesslike and polite). I settled into an aisle seat about twenty rows back.

I don't know about you, but whenever I hear the word "critic" it tends to take on a negative connotation, which is understandable since most of the words in the same area of a dictionary as "critic" ("critical", "criticize", et. al.) have a *first* definition that refers to something like "an act of judging or judgement", followed by a *second* definition that uses terms like "harsh" and "finding fault".

The point is, I've said before that I'm no critic (and sometimes I question the credentials one has to attain to be considered a critic), but I find myself observing performances (even on T.V.) with a somewhat different perspective than many popular music fans might have, since I'm a player (albeit a limited talent, and it ain't my livelihood), but I bet a lot of frustrated musicians like me are the same way. I'll try to enjoy a performance, but at the same time I'll be noting certain licks, stage moves, etc. Hopefully such a "casual analytical" attitude won't overpower being able to actually *enjoy* a concert, but I suppose it depends on the individual.

So what I both "observed" *and* "enjoyed" was over two-and-a-half hours of music by a quintet of veteran progressive rock musicians (augmented by a sixth player) that was competent, tight, and yet loose enough to where one could tell the band members were enjoying themselves, just as the audience members were.

When the house lights dimmed, a lot of smoke under ultraviolet light filled the stage (okay, so call it a "purple haze"; the pun is irresistible); this was the first concert I'd ever attended that had staging that included ramps and hidden amplifiers. A throbbing, New Age-type electronic ditty filled the arena (which had been rigged with a quadrophonic sound system); strobes began flashing under various portions of the staging, and eventually the quartet of Trevor Rabin, Tony Kaye, Chris Squire, and Alan White walked down the center to their respective instruments; support musician

193

Executive Rock

Billy Sherwood was barely visible as he took up his station in a remote portion of the set. So where was Jon Anderson?

It was surprising (and a real treat) to hear Rabin kick off the proceedings with the two distinctive guitar chords that introduce "Perpetual Change". The band roared through several minutes of the extended instrumental introduction of that song before Jon Anderson finally came ambling down the center ramp, toting an acoustic guitar. Dressed in a white tunic tied with a white sash, Anderson looked like either a quasi-religious figure or a neophyte karate student. The band segued easily into an acappella introduction to the new album's leadoff track, "The Calling" (For what my opinion's worth, one of the strongest facets of the post-*90125* Yes incarnation is the astounding vocal harmony that permeates many of their songs).

Not surprisingly, the vast majority of songs in the program were from *90125*, *Big Generator*, and *Talk*; all of the tunes from that current album were performed save "State of Play". The pre-*90125* selections included "Heart of the Sunrise", "And You and I", and "Your Move", which had an in-through-the-side-door introduction featuring Alan White on maracas. No song from *Union* was performed.

I need to eat a bit of crow concerning Jon Anderson's singing voice. I've referred to it before as "effeminate"; well, I guess there's a difference between that term and whatever adjective applies to Anderson; while his voice was high-pitched, it was *incredibly* strong, cutting through the mix with ease. On the other hand, some of his comments between songs were a bit, uh, "cosmic"...

The crowd was enthusiastic but well-behaved (i.e., there wasn't a mosh pit). Some of the newer songs such as "Walls" and the aforementioned "The Calling" sounded downright "anthem-ish" (or should that be "anthemic"?) and had the audience clapping their hands and pumping their fists; crowd calisthenics like that would have been almost unheard of at a Yes concert in the Seventies.

My perception was that a few times during the concert, the light show wasn't quite coordinated with the music. Again, it's the first time I've been to a performance with such elaborate visuals, and that's an example of where I might have been scrutinizing things a bit more closely than other concert-goers, who didn't seem to notice such apparent split-second faux pas a bit.

Each band member (as well as Sherwood) tended to his chore with a relaxed manner, handling solos and intricate portions with aplomb. The "Endless Dream" suite cited at the beginning of this essay was the final number, but they encored with "Roundabout" (natch) which had an extended ending that lurched into a few bars of "Purple Haze", of all things. All in all, it was a thoroughly professional and enjoyable gig.

Slog On, You Tarnished And/Or Out-Of-Hock Diamond

In the boisterous world of popular music public relations, I bet it's possible to experience an enormous amount of overkill about how some veteran band is "revitalized and ready for the next century" or whatever. In a lot of cases it's a buncha psychobabble, but as far as the Yes goes, it ain't no hype. I feel like *Talk* is the best album they've done in years; it captures some of their distinctive, art rock sound, yet it sounds fresh as well. A guy who works at a local music store caught the Yes in concert the very next night in Atlanta, and he's seen them in concert many, many times. He's in complete accord with me regarding the *Talk* album and the *Talk* tour. When rock musicians who have been around as long as the Yes can still write, record, and perform as well as what I experienced in Pensacola, Florida, one realizes that some aging rockers truly are trying to "keep on keepin' on", instead of rolling out some gargantuan tour every few years (with stratospheric ticket prices) like some arthritic exercise in brontosaurus nostalgia.... and I ain't namin' names.

And I wonder if I'll still be wanting to go to another Yes concert circa 2030, when the band members will most likely be performing in wheelchairs, promoting a new album they've just released.

"THE LIL' OL' CONGLOMERATE FROM TEXAS"

The title of this essay is in quote marks on accounta it represents a slight transmogrification of a remark concerning ZZ TOP that appeared in some music periodical some time ago (I think it was during the *RECYCLER* tour, if not an earlier tour), opining that the erstwhile "Lil' Ol' Band From Texas" was now a large conglomerate (or perhaps some other business term was used; at any rate, my interpretation of the comment was that it was written in an unflattering context).

The title of ZZ TOP'S first album was just that; *ZZ TOP'S FIRST ALBUM*. It had a sorta sepia-tinted front cover photo (the layout included a Les Paul guitar), and the back cover was what appeared to be a water color

Executive Rock

portrait of three musicians. One of 'em had a beard and small wire glasses; anyone who perused the back of the album might've thought he was Amish. The band members' names were Billy Gibbons (guitar), Dusty Hill (bass) and Frank Beard (drums).

The musical contents of *ZZ TOP'S FIRST ALBUM* was a blues-based melange served up in a no-frills and listenable way; there seemed to be an emphasis on guitar tones (and obviously that would be the tendency of every ZZ TOP album thereafter) yet the overall production was a bit "murky", for lack of a better term (but it didn't put off a potential listener).

At this point it needs to be noted that an unauthorized history of ZZ TOP called *Sharp Dressed Men* (written by the band's former lighting director) was released in 1994. It's a behind-the-scenes look that doesn't take an "exposé" point of view; it's simply a history of the many incidents and personalities who have contributed to the success of ZZ TOP during the band's quarter-century of public life. Some of the anecdotes might be somewhat controversial, while others will have a reader laughing out loud, and among the author's assertions is his contention that the first two ZZ TOP albums (the second being *RIO GRANDE MUD*) were *intentionally* recorded with a "dark" tonal mix.

"Just Got Paid", with its howling slide guitar, garnered a minor amount of FM airplay in my neck of the woods, but it's probably fair to say that the third effort, *TRES HOMBRES*, was really the breakthrough album for Messrs. Gibbons, Hill and Beard. "Beer Drinkers and Hell Raisers" was

FANDANGO FASHION! The Sartorial splendor of the mystery tramp (left) was created by Mr. Billy of Houston (right)

Slog On, You Tarnished And/Or Out-Of-Hock Diamond

another modest FM success, but "La Grange", a toast to the Chicken Shack whorehouse, is *still* a staple of umpteen Classic Rock stations. By this time the band was carefully cultivating a memorable Texas aesthetic, which included Nudie suits and ten-gallon hats. The inside photo of *TRES HOMBRES* showed off a humungous Mexican food spread.

Ultimately, other *TRES HOMBRES* tunes such as "Waitin' On The Bus" (which segued into "Jesus Just Left Chicago") became FM staples as well. ZZ TOP exuded some of the tightest interplay ever heard from a rock trio, and the studio side of *FANDANGO!* simply backed up such a presentation. "Heard It on the X" is a definitive example of a guitar-bass-drums setup at its finest. The live side of *FANDANGO!* was a rip-roaring party recorded in New Orleans (and as of this writing that's the only live material the band's ever released, although Gibbons has advised that there's plenty in the vaults).

TEJAS was a tad mellower, but still chock fulla rude tones such as the in-your-face guitar on "Arrested For Driving While Blind". It was also around this time that ZZ TOP mounted an ambitious and ultimately leg-endary world tour that featured live animals on the concert stage.

Following that Herculean venture in the mid-Seventies, the band went into virtual seclusion for about three years, but as hard as the trio (and all of their associates) had worked for about seven years, the hiatus seemed to be well-deserved.

When ZZ TOP emerged with a new album, *DEGUELLO*, the aesthetic had gotten a bit more, um, "unique"; Gibbons and Hill were sporting Rip Van Winkle beards that made them look like rejects from a Smith Brothers Cough Drop box. There were also "unique" moments in the music on *DEGUELLO* and its follow-up, *EL LOCO*; weird voice-overs on songs like "Manic Mechanic" and "Heaven, Hell or Houston" probably made more than one longtime fan go "Huh?" Yet there were also plenty of memorable tunes such as "Tube Snake Boogie" and "I'm Bad, I'm Na-tionwide", so the masses had plenty to pacify them.

Then in the early Eighties, ZZ TOP shifted gears, in more ways than one.

Can anyone name another veteran combo that was an established major act *before* the advent of MTV that has managed to forge an even more successful career (utilizing the now-mandatory music video concept) any better than ZZ TOP has done? I mean, just think of all of the images that are now indelible whenever the topic of ZZ TOP comes up. The beards and cheap sunglasses preceded MTV, but were fully exposed and exploited when ZZ TOP began to make videos. Then there's the Eliminator auto-mobile, the lightning bolt/double-Z keychain, the trio of drop-dead mod-els, a plethora of unusual custom-made guitars and basses, and the hand signals.... Intelligent marketing is always an important facet of the busi-ness practices of a successful conglomerate, ain't it???

Executive Rock

The *ELIMINATOR* album also seemed to herald a switch by the band to a slightly-more straightforward sound. There were more songs with a predictable rock & roll beat; fewer with tight riffing between the band members. Some of the tones sounded a bit more mainstream as well.

But the old adage about a half-empty cup versus a half-full cup must've figured into the mix somehow, on accounta what may have had the potential of alienating some longtime fans probably attracted more new fans than ever, what with the success of the hits (and the videos) from *ELIMINATOR* as well as *AFTERBURNER*. At the dawn of the Nineties, *RECYCLER* didn't sell as well as the two albums that preceded it, but a couple of folks I know who saw one of the concerts during the *RECYCLER* tour raved about the music and the special effects that were presented.

A reissue of note for ZZ TOP was a three-CD set or six albums, the first five plus *EL LOCO* (*DEGUELLO* had preceded *EL LOCO*, but was already out on Compact Disc as a single album). Some of the tunes were remixed; the drums on "La Grange" now had a bit of digital reverb added to 'em, for example. The six-pack is an excellent value in multiple-CD sets.

Billy Gibbons is considered by most knowledgeable guitar collectors and enthusiasts to be one of the pre-eminent rock stars who are also guitar collectors themselves. While his most legendary instrument is his late Fifties Gibson Les Paul known as "Pearly Gates" (the song "Apologies to Pearly" is so named on accounta Gibbons used a Fender Stratocaster on the track), ZZ TOP's lead guitarist/vocalist has a plethora of old guitars and amplifiers. He's incredibly meticulous about getting just the right sound for a particular song, and relies almost exclusively on the bridge/treble pickup of his guitars of choice. The man is a consummate tone freak, and fully admits such with considerable pride.

And the tones on ZZ TOP's *ANTENNA* were astounding; the band seemed to be taking a retro-vibe approach to this 1994 effort. I'd been in touch with Gibbons since 1991 about doing an interview for *Vintage Guitar*; he'd touch base from time to time, promising that it would ultimately come about, and he'd send in gift subscriptions for other individuals on a regular basis.

It turned out that Rev. Gibbons and I began recording his interview around the time of my surgery (it would be presented as a three-partner; there was *that many* questions). The first two parts were done via phone while the band was on the road in support of *ANTENNA*, and I was invited to an upcoming concert to record Part Three in person.

As long as it had been since I'd attended a concert prior to going to a Yes show in early August of 1994, here I was showing up backstage again

Slog On, You Tarnished And/Or Out-Of-Hock Diamond

at a large arena for another interview with a member of a major act about two months later. And it almost goes without saying that one probably couldn't come up with two veteran rock acts that are more opposite; the Yes' ethereal art rock is the antithesis of the raucous, hot-sauce drenched blues-rock served up by Rev. Gibbons, Dusty Hill and Frank Beard.

Yet both bands have been around for a quarter-century, and both were actively promoting new releases during extended tours in 1994. So while there might be a lot of differences in musical styles, I happened to be a longtime fan of both bands, which meant that in both cases the possibility of attending a concert was all the more exciting.

Musical differences aside, my observations backstage about how such concerts are staged left me quite impressed with how such acts rely on literally dozens of individuals to do their respective assignments in an efficient and timely manner. As I was backstage longer at the venue where ZZ TOP performed, I was able to observe more, and every person was going about his/her task before, during and after the concert to the best of his/her ability, from what I could tell. I saw no evidence of alcohol or other (illicit) mind-altering substances.... come to think of it, I don't remember seeing anyone smoking.

The Production Office was the temporary nerve center of the show, and it was there that I received my all-powerful "All Access" pass; in an apparently subliminal Walter Mitty-ish fantasy, I stuck it front and center on my shirt where it couldn't be missed. A bit pretentious, perhaps, but I figured I'd be moving around a good bit while I was at the venue, so I suppose I was wanting to pass from one area to another with a minimum of hassle.

Gibbons and I settled into a dressing room to converse "on the record", and I was introduced to Dusty Hill when the bearded bassist walked in. Part Three of Rev. Gibbons' interview was completed prior to showtime, and I was ultimately dismissed (temporarily) from certain areas backstage, as were all other non-tour personnel. Unlike the Yes concert, however, I was allowed to remain in other backstage areas to observe the show, and I also signed up to be in the photo pit when ZZ TOP took the stage, which meant I had to report to the Production Office twenty minutes prior to ZZ TOP's starting time. The venue was filled with tens of thousands of excited fans as the house lights dimmed, right on time.

Also unlike the Yes concert, there was an opening act, a hair band of the poser metal variety called Jackyl. While some of their guitar tones weren't as shrill as what is stereotypically heard in such a genre (both guitar players used Les Pauls; I didn't see or hear a whammy bar/idiot stick at all during their set), the *attitude* was predictable, particularly when it came to the lead singer. At one point he revved up a chain saw and demolished a bar stool (to his credit, at full r.p.m. the drone of the chain saw harmonized

Executive Rock

with the guitars). The drummer's gear was decked out with a blower and chrome exhaust pipes, as seen on a rail job dragster. I went about three-quarters of the way back into the floor seat section, and even that far back the volume was *incredibly* loud; I could feel the decibels physically pounding me. I'm sure a band such as Jackyl being booked as an opening act for a veteran band such as ZZ TOP probably represents an egalitarian move designed to appeal to younger listeners, but a guitar salesman at a local music store (he's in his twenties) opined that bands such as Jackyl "have gotten to the point to where it's almost like they're parodying themselves", as I recall his comment on the day after the concert. He didn't go to the show, but my observations seemed to add credibility to his opinion.

Following Jackyl's set, their equipment was rapidly dismantled, and a black curtain behind their stage area was lowered to reveal yet another visual barrier, a giant canvas-like sheet with the *ANTENNA* logo on it, including the words "Tone, Taste, Tenacity". Portions of the elaborate set were already visible; mock-ups of electrical line towers and wires were arranged on and above the stage. When the aforementioned canvas-like curtain dropped abruptly, the stage setup was revealed as the "guts" of a giant, old-fashioned radio, including humungous vacuum tubes and a monstrous dial numbered with AM designations. At that moment, the sound of radio static was heard, and many gizmos on the stage began to glow with an eery orange light, as did the wires suspended above the stage; sparks spat from the "electrical towers", and the collective roar of the audience was deafening (by now I was stationed in the photo pit, front and center). Laser images danced on large opaque circles in the rear of the set, as the buildup tweaked the crowd even more.

The trio emerged from an elevated area in the upper rear portion of the set. Frank Beard settled into his drum kit, which was also located in the elevated stage area, and the band cranked off the proceedings with "World of Swirl" from *ANTENNA*. Surprisingly, that tune is one on which Dusty Hill handles lead vocals; the bulk of ZZ TOP's singing is done by Billy Gibbons. Brandishing matching black Fender Custom Shop instruments, the bearded 2/3 of the band remained parallel to the drum kit for the duration of the first song before walking down to the front of the stage. The second song was "Pincushion" (also from *ANTENNA*); the proximity of Gibbons and Hill to the photo pit made it obvious that they were concentrating intently on their task but having a great time.

Security personnel escorted the shutterbugs from the photo pit following "Pincushion", which in some ways was unfortunate, since the next song ("Breakaway") featured the first, uh, "special effect" of the evening. The aforementioned opaque circles were illuminated from behind to reveal shapely feminine shadows accompanying the band on various per-

200

Slog On, You Tarnished And/Or Out-Of-Hock Diamond

cussion instruments; this "shadow play" was greeted enthusiastically by the audience, and was a harbinger of things to come.

ZZ TOP tore through all of their hits from previous albums and a commendable helping of *ANTENNA* as well in a ferocious yet competent manner. I was over off of Stage Right (closer to Gibbons), and was able to observe him exchanging guitars (Custom Shop Esquires exclusively, except for a fur-trimmed Explorer used on one song late in the performance). His guitar tech was busy monitoring all facets of the performance; three Marshall heads were only part of an intricate performance system. I wasn't able to make it over to Stage Left near Dusty Hill's rig; suffice to say that he too stuck with Custom Shop Fender basses except for using a fur-trimmed Explorer-shaped bass.... and this time, those instruments even had fur on the *tuning keys*!

The mix of Gibbons' and Hill's instrument tones was quite interesting. I walked out to where I'd been when Jackyl was performing, and while ZZ TOP's performance was loud, it sounded much "clearer" (for lack of a better term). Hill's bass was bright and resonant, and Rev. Gibbons was evoking all sorts of sounds from his single-pickup guitars. I consider it fortunate to have been out in the floor seats when they reached *way* back and pulled out a slow blues called "Just Got Back From Baby's"; it was a definitive tune that allows ZZ TOP to pay rightful homage to its blues roots, for what my opinion's worth.

There was one incident I observed while off Stage Right that I didn't immediately comprehend. Gibbons turned to face that side of the stage and began walking in our direction, and the crowd began to roar in approval. What the hell was going on? Then I realized that the guitarist wasn't going anywhere; he was walking in place! Craning my neck, I saw that Gibbons and Hill were on flush-mounted treadmills, going nowhere fast in opposite directions (Later on, Hill would walk over Gibbons' side of the stage during one song and ride the complete length of the treadmill behind the guitarist, who was busy singing. That would make a terrific concert video shot: Gibbons at his microphone while the bass player slowly glides from right to left behind him without missing a beat!).

Some audience members might have been expecting an appearance by the aforementioned trio of drop-dead models from ZZ TOP videos, but it didn't happen. Instead, the "glamour factor" was *doubled*, as a *half-dozen* female dancers made several appearances onstage during the performance; some of them had participated in the aforementioned shadow play during "Breakaway". One of their efforts had them decked out in full Vegas-showgirl regalia (natch, the tune was "Viva Las Vegas", which was heard during one of the encores).

One of the returns to the stage for an encore was a hoot: The band

Executive Rock

emerged once again from the elevated portion of the stage, but this time they were "encased" inside three more giant vacuum tubes similar to the other ones all over the set. Comparisons to a particular segment of *This Is Spinal Tap* are inevitable (and I think the band probably realizes such), but all three musicians exited their respective tubes in a smooth manner; sharp-eyed concert-goers may have noticed that the black leather jackets sported by Gibbons and Hill now appeared to be scorched and frayed....

After more than one encore, the final tune the band did was a riproaring version of "Tush". I was back at Stage Right as that song ended, and I noticed several of the tour staff with their hands over their ears. Something told me I might oughta assume the same position, and less than five seconds after I covered my own aural passages, a bomb went off onstage. I mean, that's the only way I know how to describe it. There'd been an earlier smoke bomb, but the concussion from that final detonation knocked my cowlick backwards (no small accomplishment, since I use Vitalis Super Hold hair spray). We were standing maybe fifteen or twenty feet from Ground Zero, and when I recovered sufficiently enough to converse with one of the aforementioned tour staff members, he said something like "You ought to see the one we use at *outdoor* concerts!" Uh, I'm not so sure about that....

I had been instructed to wait at the Production Office until I was summoned to see the band post-concert, and I didn't have to wait long. I must have had a dazed look on my countenance, on accounta Dusty Hill saw me walking down the hall towards the lounge area and chuckled: "You still alive?"

Whatever numbed appearance I might have been exhibiting had nothing to do with my proximity to any show finale pyrotechnics; I was simply in awe of having been allowed to witness a bona fide major production from a vantage point that most rock music fans will never be able to experience. Things slowly wound down after the show; workers in color-coordinated t-shirts quickly began disassembling the stage, the band went off to "meet and greet" certain folks, and I finally departed the venue when Rev. Gibbons boarded his tour bus in the wee hours of Saturday morning.

Weeks later, the imagery of that evening was still burned into my memory like a brand. ZZ TOP's concert conglomerate ran as smoothly as one would expect the Eliminator automobile to run, and if some other publication has a problem with such a professional effort, such a hang-up is something I can't understand.

"Tone, Taste, Tenacity". Ab-So-Loot-Lee.

Slog On, You Tarnished And/Or Out-Of-Hock Diamond

STARS AND BARS FOREVER

The October 1969 concert at the old Atlanta Civic Center featured The Chicago Transit Authority, Joe Cocker, and Santana for an admission charge of five dollars in advance, six dollars at the gate. At one point between acts, the M.C. announced an upcoming concert about six weeks hence, starring B.B. King and the Almond Brothers.

Curiously, the announcement that "the Almond Brothers" were on the bill got more applause from the audience than did the announcement that B.B. King was headlining.

Those concert-goers who applauded louder for the warm-up band slated for the upcoming show probably already knew that the correct surname was "Allman", not "Almond".

There might have been a smattering of Southern bands that made a dent somewhere on the national hit record charts sometime before the advent of the Macon-based Capricorn Records phenomenon (a One-Hit-Wonder group called the Hombres springs to mind, having clicked with the goofy "Let It All Hang Out", which for all intents and purposes had a spoken-word lead vocal). But the Southern Rock genre, with its blues/ boogie base, was really trailblazed by a band fronted by two brothers from Florida, who'd been in previous combos known as the Hourglass and the Allman Joys; all other "Southern" groups were merely pretenders to the throne.

Interplay was the key facet of the Allman Brothers Band's initial success; the amazing harmony leads of Duane Allman and Dickey Betts dumbfounded most aspiring guitar players back then, and the double drumming of Butch Trucks and Jaimoe probably had the same effect on fledgling percussionists. Anchored by Berry Oakley's imaginative bass and Gregg Allman's B-3 and world-weary vocals, the Allmans proffered an incredibly tight presentation that not only paid homage to the blues, but managed to cross over confidently into improvisational jazz territory as well.

As star-crossed as the Allman Brothers Band was, it's nevertheless survived umpteen personnel changes, the deaths of Duane Allman and Berry Oakley within about a year of each other in the early Seventies, and who knows what else to continuously resurrect itself over the last couple of decades.

Anyone who experienced an Allman Brothers concert prior to the death of Duane Allman should consider himself/herself lucky. They played the small cow college where I went to school about two weeks prior to recording the *Fillmore East* album, so for all intents and purposes we saw the same show, except "Mountain Jam" wasn't performed; a general stereotype of most of the students was that they were more into tunes by Bill Deal & the Rhondells instead of "In Memory of Elizabeth Reed", so the

Executive Rock

reception afforded the Allmans wasn't overwhelmingly adulatory.

Some music fans would cite the Charlie Daniels Band roster recitation of Southern bands, "The South's Gonna Do It Again", as an appropriate listing of the genre's participants (but citing ZZ TOP is off the mark, since as previously noted, Texas music is its own multifaceted genre). I'm unsure if some of the Allmans' erstwhile Capricorn labelmates such as Wet Willie are still active, and the last I heard from the Marshall Tucker Band it had two original members left and one of their videos was being played on CMT (which shouldn't be all that surprising, when ya think about it).

Lynyrd Skynyrd came barreling out of Florida with a grittier, multiple guitar format that rocked a bit more, and by the middle of the Seventies other Sunshine State bands began to be heard; there were Skynyrd clones like Molly Hatchet and the underrated Outlaws, plus the radio-ready .38 Special. Curiously, a lot of .38 Special's hits were written or co-written by the redoubtable Jim Peterik of Chicago(!); he's been with One-Hit-Wonders the Ides of March (he sang "Vehicle") as well as Survivor of "Eye of the Tiger" fame (plus other hits). By the way, there's a .38 Special concert (recorded at Long Island's Nassau Coliseum) on videotape that was never released as an album, and it's worth seeking out.

Ten years is a long time for band to be dormant (even if its members are involved with other projects), but Skynyrd cranked up again in the late Eighties, a decade after a horrifying plane crash had killed the lead singer (Ronnie Van Zandt), a recently-added guitarist (Steve Gaines) and a backup singer (Cassie Gaines, Steve's sister). What apparently started out in 1987 as a tribute ended up as an ongoing venture, but the rejuvenated Lynyrd Skynyrd also experienced personnel changes as Phase Two of the band's career progressed.

Another interesting phenomenon was the appearance of the Dixie Allstars, an aggregation composed primarily of former members of *other* Southern Rock bands like Molly Hatchet and Blackfoot (another Florida band whose best album was called *Blackfoot Strikes*).

Yet it was the standard bearers that surprised many listeners during the advent of the Nineties. To say that the Allman Brothers Band's career was revitalized is an understatement. Fortified with a hot new guitar slinger named Warren Haynes, the Allmans' *Seven Turns* was the best thing they'd done in years, and the follow-up album, *Shades of Two Worlds* (featuring a terrific extended workout called "Nobody Knows") was just as potent. Later on in the decade, the ABB took the unusual step of releasing two live albums about three years apart, with a studio album (*Where It All Begins*) sandwiched in between. The live albums were marketed as a "first set" and "second set"; the latter contained an *acoustic* version of "In Memory of Elizabeth Reed". The interplay (there's that word again) between Dickey Betts and Warren

Slog On, You Tarnished And/Or Out-Of-Hock Diamond

Haynes is every bit as laudable and listenable as was the interaction between Duane Allman and Betts. Some folks may consider such a statement to be heresy, but the music speaks for itself, and it's damn good these days.

Yet many of the bands in the Southern Rock genre are probably in what might be called journeyman status these days, which would most likely be okay with the majority of 'em, if they're stayin' busy. It remains to be seen what new musical aggregations will germinate in the South, but the Seventies heralded some remarkable music from that region, and some of it's still being heard.

And one last point: If a person were to attempt to assemble his/her own list of bands that should be assigned to the Southern Rock genre, the remarkable Dixie Dregs don't count.

"PHASE THREE" BANDS (AND BEYOND)

I know the title of this essay sounds like it might pertain to some kind of futuristic science program one might encounter on PBS (which reminds me of one of my all-time favorite gags in the late, lamented "Bloom County" comic strip, concerning a Carl Sagan doll that came with "an inflatable latex ego"), but what I'd actually like to address here is personnel changes in popular combos. Now please understand that I'm not considering bands that may have a revolving-door lineup but stick to the same format, music-wise (i.e., "Who's playin' in Whitesnake or Savoy Brown *this* week?"... "Who cares?"), nor would I cite bands with which there's been one major change that might have made for a slight shift sound-wise, but overall their style and popularity remain relatively unphased. Obviously, Sammy Hagar replacing Dave "The Human Whoopee Cushion" Roth in Van Halen is the definitive example of the latter circumstance.

Rather, there've been several examples of bands that might continue to use the same moniker for decades (and there might be one original member left to make things appear more legit), but there have been very distinct and abrupt changes in their styles, so much so that their record com-

205

Executive Rock

panies ought to classify each incarnation numerically anytime the combos shift creative gears. But since such a numbering system is a remote possibility, in the interest of consumer awareness yours truly has listed a few examples, *by the numbers:*

KING CRIMSON I: Considered by most folks to be the definitive British progressive rock band, their first few albums were mostly Mellotron-soaked adventures in weirdness, in spite of Pete Sinfield's grandiose-yet-hackneyed lyrics. Yet for every tune that was somewhat memorable ("Epitaph", for example), there was also sure to be a bunch of abstract jamming on the same album; such passages usually featured Robert Fripp's noodling guitar and Mel Collins' blatting saxophone, and usually ended up sounding artsy-fartsy, pretentious, and boring. There were some frantic moments as well, such as "21st Century Schizoid Man", the first album's first cut, so apparently the Crimsons meant to get the listener's attention right at the outset. Albums during this phase were (in chronological order): *In the Court of the Crimson King, In the Wake of Poseidon, Lizard*, and *Islands*, plus a badly produced live import that stunk.

KING CRIMSON II: In which Fripp goes even more abstract, so much so that some of the "music" is barely listenable. The core of this edition was comprised of Fripp, bassist John Wetton (awright!), and drummer Bill Bruford, who left Yes to join King Crimson because "I wanted to play wrong notes".... The name of the violinist who was on the studio stuff escapes me, and I think the weirdo percussionist's name was Jamie Muir; he's the one seen on one of those "Closet Classics"-type videos, bashing assorted noisemakers and furiously blowing a whistle. Albums from this lineup include *Larks' Tongues in Aspic, Starless and Bible Black, Red*, and the live *U.S.A*, on which Eddie Jobson played violin. Actually, the last two weren't bad, but the first two represent the lowest point of listenability in the Crimsons' saga.

KING CRIMSON III: *Fripp Sells Out!!!* This lineup wasn't even supposed to be called "King Crimson"; it was originally slated to be known as Discipline, which ended up as the title of this edition's first album, released in 1981. Once again, attention is *demanded* on the very first cut, "Elephant Talk", which is introduced by Tony Levin's phenomenal Electric Stick riffing. Bruford was on board for this phase as well, and the redoubtable Adrian Belew's other worldly bleeps and squawks wrenched from his guitar proved the perfect compliment to Fripp's hectic picking. Natch, Belew gets in a realistic elephant-like blare in the aforementioned first cut, and barely a Mellotron is heard. For that matter, listening to some of Belew's solo efforts such as *Twang Bar King* shows what a big influence he was here. Albums for this third incarnation after *Discipline* were *Beat* and *Three of a Perfect Pair* .

206

Slog On, You Tarnished And/Or Out-Of-Hock Diamond

KING CRIMSON (BEYOND): A decade after *Three of a Perfect Pair* was released, the foursome that made up King Crimson III reunited and added Stick player Trey Gunn and drummer Pat Mastelotto, so in essence the band became a "double trio" (two guitarists, two drummers, two bass/Electric Stick players). A late 1994 mini-album was dubbed a "calling card" by Fripp, and the 1995 full-length offering, the possibly-onomato-poeia-titled *THRAK*, was, as might have been expected, a "richer" and/or "denser" mix of the type of fare offered by the third incarnation. I'd been hearing somewhat similar music from players like Mike Keneally (the guitarist on Frank Zappa's final tour), but the Crimsons' chops on *THRAK* were a collective assertion that progressive rock/art-rock/whatever may still be a viable musical category.

FLEETWOOD MAC I: In the mid-Sixties, some former members of John Mayall's Bluesbreakers formed one of the rawest British blues units that ever existed. In addition to ongoing anchors Mick Fleetwood and John McVie, the first edition included the guitar triumvirate of Jeremy Spencer, Danny Kirwan and Peter Green. Albums from this era included *Fleetwood Mac*, *English Rose* (from which sprang an instrumental that garnered a bit of airplay, "Albatross"), *Then Play On* ("Oh Well", another minor hit, came from this one), and *Kiln House*. By the time the last album in this first phase came out, Green had departed, and it showed; *Kiln House* was considerably more mellow, and was a harbinger of things to come in Phase Two. *Then Play On* is nothing less than a *milestone* of blues/rock guitar music.

FLEETWOOD MAC II: A bit more of the "revolving-door" approach, but permanent additions in this lineup were Bob Welch and Christine McVie. The emphasis during this phase was more on songs and vocals rather than extended blues jams; airy, dreamy tunes such as "Woman of a Thousand Years" were the signature sound of the Macs in the early Seventies. *Future Games*, *Bare Trees*, *Penguin*, *Mystery to Me*, and *Heroes are Hard to Find* were releases during this era.

FLEETWOOD MAC III: Following Welch's departure for a solo career that went practically nowhere, the band added oh-so-serious thrush Stevie Nicks and sissy guitarist/vocalist Lindsey Buckingham and stormed into mega-platinum status, which is still confounding; while the songwriting, singing and musical chops are competent, Nicks' Gypsy Princess facade and Buckingham's quirkiness got tiresome very quickly, plus it was agitating to see Christine McVie relegated to second-string status. You already know the names of the albums; *Fleetwood Mac*, *Rumours*, *Tusk* (which some critics had the audacity to compare to the Beatles' White Album!), etc.

FLEETWOOD MAC IV: This incarnation could almost be lumped in with the Mac's Phase III variant, since it only lasted for one album. When

Executive Rock

Buckingham departed for a solo career, Billy Burnette was brought in as vocalist, and all-around good guy Rick Vito took up the guitar slot. The resulting album, *Behind the Mask*, was a bit more perky than some of the Phase III offerings.

FLEETWOOD MAC (BEYOND): The latest version of the mighty Mac consists of Mick Fleetwood, John McVie, Christine McVie (rumors had her departing when Stevie Nicks and Rick Vito left, but such wasn't the case), Billy Burnette, Dave Mason (of all people) on guitar and vocals, and Bekka Bramlett (who's Delaney and Bonnie's daughter) on vocals.

Mick Fleetwood's line in hyping this incarnation's initial offering, *Time* (released in the Fall of 1995) was that "the Mac is back", and I'll have to admit that the first listening to *Time* was a pleasurable experience, and the band probably couldn't have come up with a more suitable guitarist than Mason for the musical direction that they seem to be pursuing. Trouble is, in the photos of the band that are found inside the album, Mason and John McVie look like the same person...

What's more, Bekka Bramlett has an impressive set of pipes (she looks a lot like her mom). The main drawback on *Time* is the last track, a spoken-word-rumination-over-a-musical-background exercise in pretentiousness called "These Strange Times". While methinks that the first portion of Mick Fleetwood's commentary refers to Peter Green, nevertheless the initial listening to this effort reminds one of the Guess Who's morbid "Friends of Mine", from the Canadian band's late Sixties *Wheatfield Soul* album. But it'll be interesting to see how *Time* and this most recent Fleetwood Mac lineup fare compared to previous albums and incarnations, as the band trudges towards its thirtieth anniversary.

(SIDEBAR: This book's original manuscript was submitted in August of 1995, and I felt the need to jump back into this section and update things in late·October of the same year. Such are the advantages of being able to do revisions, eh?)

TANGERINE DREAM I: "What the hell are you doing putting a buncha Kraut techno-dweebs on a list like this?!?" demanded Malc. Well, they *have* been through a somewhat limited type of transition in their "style" (such as it is) from time to time; look for 'em in the "New Age" section of music stores. Phase One albums (pre-1974) by the Tangs are a bunch of incredibly boring psychedelic, quasi-electronic mumbo-jumbo; imagine another weirdo German group, Can, without a drumbeat and you sorta get the idea (and the idea is: LEAVE THIS MUNG ALONE!). Offending titles included *Atem*, *Alpha Centauri*, and others.

TANGERINE DREAM II: *Phaedra* was this group's, uh, "breakthrough" album, and I think the reason folks started taking notice was their expanded use of a VCS3 synth, which could be programmed with a

Slog On, You Tarnished And/Or Out-Of-Hock Diamond

repeating "riff" serving as a "beat" so they could layer other electronic programs on top in sort of an abstract kind of jam (NOTE: Perhaps the best known use of a VCS3 is found in "On The Run" on Pink Floyd's *Dark Side of the Moon* album). What's more, the sounds got more diverse as electronic music quickly advanced in the technological area; the group would segue from one "passage" or "movement" to another, using lightweight electronic noise as the bridge. This type of "music" represents Tangerine Dream at its most listenable, and the best of this lot include 1975's *Rubycon* and 1982's live *Logos*.

TANGERINE DREAM III: The secret's in the segue. Here's where things get a bit more complicated, because technically the Tangs are still doing some albums from Phase Two, but they've also occasionally put out albums that *don't* have any of the aforementioned lightweight electronic noise to segue from one passage or movement to another, so that makes for shorter, individual "songs", and the results stink, because it sounds like a bunch of abstract electronic gibberish that meanders around for a while then fades out ('cause that's exactly what it is, bubba). Every one of Tangerine Dream's movie soundtracks are like this (as might be expected), but some regular releases such as *Exit* or *Optical Race* suffer from the same tendency. A good rule of thumb might be to check and see how many titles are on the cover; the less there are the more listenable that particular Tangerine Dream album should be. What's more, live albums like *Livemiles* and *220 Volts* are usually a safe bet.

JEFFERSON AIRPLANE: I've saved perhaps the most bizarre odyssey for last, and in this case the various incarnations had different monikers, but big deal; this saga is strange: In the late Sixties and early Seventies, the Jefferson Airplane and Grateful Dead were generally acknowledged as the definitive examples of Frisco acid rock. Jorma Kaukonen's snarling leads, Paul Kantner's Rickenbacker 12-string rhythm guitar, and Jack Casady's pulsing bass were the anchors for two singers who could wail. Starting with *Jefferson Airplane Takes Off* (Signe Anderson was the female singer on this debut, replaced for the duration by Grace Slick) through *Bark*, this first-monikered band went through a few other personnel changes, including the more-or-less permanent addition of violinist Papa John Creach, and as Kaukonen and Casady got more and more into their Hot Tuna offshoot, they were eventually replaced as well.

JEFFERSON STARSHIP: Assorted personnel who were in the band by the time of the first name change included the likes of ex-Quicksilver bassist David Freiberg, Pete Sears, Craig Chaquico, blah, blah, blah. Beginning with the *Dragonfly* album, the band began a fateful pop-oriented turn, and singers Balin (who'd jumped off the Airplane but showed back up at this point for a short stint) and Slick were replaced by yelper Mickey

209

Executive Rock

Thomas (Slick was subsequently reinstated after drying out). Other albums from this incarnation included *Red Octopus, Spitfire, Earth, Freedom at Point Zero, Nuclear Furniture,* and perhaps a couple of others that mercifully I've been able to psych myself into forgetting.

STARSHIP: After Kantner departed, he apparently threatened legal action concerning the use of the name Jefferson Starship, so the group's name was shortened to simply Starship, with Slick as the sole remaining original member of Jefferson Airplane. Ultimately she left again, and listeners were left with a pop combo that technically had its beginnings forged in Frisco in the Sixties, yet with no real connection, personnel-wise. Kantner's first post-Starship venture, by the way, was an embarrassing retro-Sixties experiment called the KBC Band (which also included Balin and Casady) that *stunk.*

JEFFERSON AIRPLANE: Composed of all of the members from the band's finest hours, this is only slightly less embarrassing than the unlamented KBC Band, since it was also a calculated grab at nostalgia (I heard their tour was being cosponsored by VH-1!), not to mention the fact that their new release suffers from an Eighties techno-sound in spite of chops undiminished over the years. What's more, almost everyone I talked with who had heard the new album thought the lyrics are incredibly banal.

JEFFERSON AIRPLANE/STARSHIP/WHATCHAMACALLIT (BEYOND): Craig Chaquico was the only player who was on all of the albums recorded by Jefferson Starship and Starship, and as noted earlier he's now forging a commendable solo career as an instrumental guitarist. When interviewed in early 1994, Chaquico noted that "there's two bands that are using the Starship name; each band has one guy who was in the band, but neither person is me. Go figure ..." So who knows what's going on nowadays; it seems like one of the current bands has somebody's proper name in front of the band's name, and that ought to be a warning ("So-and-so & So-and so") not to expect a "classic" lineup...

Chaquico also stated that he thought the last Starship album charted higher than the Jefferson Airplane reunion album, which was released around the same time. Seems somewhat ironic, eh?

Such ongoing musical ventures (and controversies) could make one wonder to what extent a band should continue to exploit a certain moniker, but since when is ethics an integral part of the music business? In some cases, new incarnations of certain groups have been for the better, musically (it's like they should be labeled "NEW! IMPROVED!"), but in other situations I'd feel embarrassed for the participants, except for the probability that they're cashing in on old memories. They know who they are; I just wish the average listener did.

Slog On, You Tarnished And/Or Out-Of-Hock Diamond

SHORT VERSIONS

OL' RUBBER LIPS IS BACK: Ron Wood couldn't carry Mick Taylor's guitar strap. Didn'cha ebber notice that most of the albums cited by critics as all-time classics by the Rolling Stones are ones on which Taylor appeared? On the other hand, Keith Richards did have a legitimate rap about Taylor playing guitar leads *all the time* during a concert, yet it seems like even though the earlier Stones albums on which Brian Jones appeared may have had more songs that would be more likely to end up on a Classic Rock radio format, the tunes from the Taylor-as-lead -guitarist era probably had more *memorable musical riffs* for most aspiring rock guitarists (then *and* now).

As noted in the Pink Floyd commentary, any new Rolling Stones album release and tour that's occurred since the infamous 1969 tour that culminated in the horror of Altamont has been an *event* instead of simply an entertainment enterprise, and anytime the likes of Andy Warhol and Donald Trump have wanted to be involved, you know something's up.

I don't know to what extent the Stones have gotten to the point that they might appear to he parodying themselves, but 1994's *Voodoo Lounge* was hailed as the best thing they'd done in years.

Bill Wyman? Dirty old man. Good riddance.

And anybody who thinks rock and roll is such a laudable occupation needs to watch *Gimme Shelter.* The paradox of Jagger strutting and preening onstage at Altamont while bikers are beating up concert-goers at the same time is lurid and ludicrous (as is the slow-motion murder of one guy, who had apparently pulled a gun). So much for the Age of Aquarius.

About the only other thing that needs to be said is to note some stand-up comedian's observation that if there ever was an all-out nuclear war, a nuclear winter would ensue, and the only life forms that would survive would be cockroaches and Keith Richards.

KISS THIS: As was the case with the Dead, KISS's strong point is their live albums, although they've only put out three of 'em in a career that is now in its third decade. The drummer and lead guitar slots have revolved on more than one occasion, but affable picker Bruce Kulick has been in the latter position for over a decade now.

It's interesting that KISS managed to survive the disco craze in the late Seventies (even releasing a dance hit called "I Was Made For Loving You"). They *do* have a bit of common ground with the Stones in that a lotta their earlier material contained a lotta memorable riffs, but such songs weren't nearly as "classic"/"timeless" as those proffered by Jagger & company.

KISS's unique (and expensive) personal appearance tour in the summer of '95 elicited a bit of criticism, but seemed justified, and was probably

Executive Rock

worth it to their more rabid fans. I wonder how the attendance figures fared in certain cities.

And if I was Paul Stanley or Gene "Ol' Titan Tongue" Simmons, the older I got, the more I'd consider putting the kabuki makeup back on.

OL' FISH LIPS IS BACK: When Aerosmith came roaring out of Beantown in the mid-Seventies, music publications compared the visage of singer Steve Tyler and guitarist Joe Perry to Jagger and Richards, as had been the case with the New York Dolls' David Johansen and Johnny Thunders a couple of years earlier. The earliest Aerosmith albums were thunderous, riff-soaked adventures that still hold up, but I know one guy who's such a Crimson Tide fan that he bought a copy of *Toys in the Attic* simply because there's a toy elephant wearing a red jersey with a "A" on it on the cover illustration; he didn't give a **** about the music inside...

One might have thought that the usual demons that destroy many successful rock bands would have annihilated Aerosmith. The album that Tyler, Hamilton and Kramer did with two new guitarists wasn't half-bad; the video for "Lightning Strikes" (featuring Tyler as some gobbing hoodlum with ducktails) was somewhat memorable.

Once Perry and Whitford returned, the initial reunion offering (*Done With Mirrors*) wasn't so hot, but the next effort, *Permanent Vacation*, was loaded with riffs, and the video for "Dude (Looks Like a Lady)" was a hoot: Tyler was *all over* the soundstage (and the microphone never leaves his mike stand), and a guitar dealer in Ohio that specializes in Gretsch instruments reported that following the release of that video, he had umpteen calls from collectors regarding the mid-Fifties "Silver Jet" model that Joe Perry was brandishing. Such is the potency of "star power" in the vintage guitar phenomenon.

Ultimately, however, "Dude (Looks Like a Lady)" seems to have been the high point for the revitalized quintet. It seems like they've gotten into the dreaded "power ballad" area of popular music too much, and quite frankly, Tyler's ongoing impersonation of a fop has gotten a bit tiresome as well.

But I bet a lot of singers hope they've still got those kind of stage moves when they get to be his age.

Originally, this essay cited four bands instead of just three.

Jerry Garcia turned 53 on 1 AUG 95, and died a week later. The short rumination on the Grateful Dead was titled "UNCLE JERRY'S BAND", and noted how the band had for all intents and purposes developed, nurtured, and maintained a complete microcosm of what the so-called coun-

Slog On, You Tarnished And/Or Out-Of-Hock Diamond

terculture was supposed to be, considering the nomadic lifestyle of the band's (literal) followers. And the Summer '95 tour had its share of problems (a riot at one concert, a collapsed pavilion at another).

Now that segment's been eliminated, because Garcia's death occurred about three weeks before deadline, and at this point I'm not going to hold up anything to get an accurate handle on whether or not the Grateful Dead will be an ongoing musical entity.

I also went back and scratched Garcia's name off the list called "FAMOUS MUSICIANS AND SINGERS I THOUGHT WOULD BE DEAD BY NOW".

I wish the Who were still together, on accounta I thought of a sharp title for an essay or short commentary about 'em ("WHO NOSE AND WHO CARES?"). The title concerns Pete Townshend's ambivalence about the release of a live album from the Who's late Eighties "reunion" tour, which included a horn section, of all things. I *still* listen to their old albums more than I listen to Beatles, Stones or Kinks albums.

STILL IN THE GAME (IF NOT STILL THE SAME)

So when is it that a formerly super-successful rock band should be referred to as having assumed "journeyman" status? And how do you talk with some musician that might now be on such a lower plateau about his/her current status without sounding sardonic or condescending (I've been in such a situation as an interviewer on numerous occasions)?

There's nothing etched in stone about age limitations, success (if any) of recent recordings, etc., and granted, some of the more unenthusiastic individuals who are still performing may indeed deserve being catego-

Executive Rock

rized as has-beens and/or burnouts.

But refreshingly, most of the veterans that are over forty and are still playing loud, upbeat music for a living for smaller crowds than they may have entertained a couple of decades ago are aware of their respective situations, and they seem to be determined to continue to ply their trade in a professional manner... in fact, a lot of those veterans are more professional than a lot of younger (and more successful) bands.

Perhaps the number of original members left in a band might constitute one guideline, or perhaps the *size and locales* of the venues where such acts perform might be another indication of whether a specific act is past its pinnacle (and prime). Suffice to say that if a band is now part of a "package tour," it's doubtful that any of their recent albums have been on the *Billboard* charts.

Take the Band, for instance. Only three of the original members are left (Garth Hudson, Levon "Ridley" Helm, and Rick Danko), and they've been augmented with other musicians. It was a long, long time before any new product was released from the group, and they had a *considerable* task of coming up with good material, since erstwhile guitarist Robbie Robertson was one of the most gifted songwriters in the history of rock (Danko opined that every album after *Music From Big Pink* "was more like Robbie Robertson album" instead of a group effort).

But the mid-Nineties Band album *Jericho* was woefully ignored by most folks. It was humorous and whimsical, and when the group covered Springsteen's "Atlantic City" on "The Late Show", CBS Orchestra honcho Paul Shaffer was enthralled.

2/3 of the late Sixties horn triumvirate is apparently still active; Chicago looks tired anytime I see 'em on TV, and Blood, Sweat & Tears still plays (the last 1/3 of the triumvirate was the Butterfield Blues Band... is their live album available on CD?).

One fairly recent phenomenon for "journeyman" bands has been to release live albums (usually recorded at concert club venues), so a fan who might have heard such a gig could get an accurate representation of what the performance he/she attended was like. Among the combos or players who've issued such fare over the last several years are Al Kooper, The Robby Krieger Organization, the Outlaws, Spirit, and Wishbone Ash.

The Classic Rock All-Stars have opted for a slightly different (and novel) approach. Freely admitting and utilizing the "formerly with _____" marketing approach in their performances, this band's lineup consists of Mike Pinera (Blues Image, Iron Butterfly) on guitar, Spencer Davis (Spencer Davis Group, of course) on guitar, Pete Rivera (Rare Earth) on drums, and Jerry Corbetta (Sugarloaf) on keyboards, plus a bass player. Each of the personalities sings lead vocals on the hits made famous by his former band.

Slog On, You Tarnished And/Or Out-Of-Hock Diamond

While Davis is no Stevie Winwood, Rivera *was* the lead vocalist on songs like "Get Ready" and "I Just Want to Celebrate", so it's an interesting concept. From what I can determine, this aggregation plays the Vegas-Reno-Tahoe circuit a good bit, which seems appropriate. And they too have marketed a live album.

And when was the last time REO Speedwagon or Blue Oyster Cult were on the charts? They played a few double bills during the summer of '95, and at other times REO opened for Ringo Starr's All-Starr Band, a temporary equivalent of the Classic Rock All-Stars with perhaps more notable players; the 1995 incarnation included Randy Bachman (Guess Who, Bachman-Turner Overdrive) on guitar, Mark Farner (Grand Funk Railroad) on guitar, John Entwistle (Who) on bass, Felix Cavaliere (Young Rascals) on keyboards, plus Ringo and his son on drums.

There's a difference between the artists noted in this essay and bands or individuals who *are and have always been "journeyman" musicians,* which is another way of saying that some groups that are "cult favorites" may always remain in such a category. The definitive example for a lotta folks would be NRBQ. This eclectic ensemble has been around for about a quarter-century (their debut album opened with a cover of Eddie Cochran's "C'mon Everybody", followed by a Sun Ra tune, of all things). Critics and other musicians love 'em (Keith Richards hired their bass player, Joey Spampinato, to anchor the house band for the *Hail, Hail Rock and Roll!* documentary), yet to my knowledge the only time NRBQ ever experienced any action on a hit singles chart was when a novelty tune released during the gas crisis of the early Seventies clicked for this under-appreciated outfit.

Before a cynic tends to dismiss any of the musicians or bands cited in this entire section as "has-beens", it's important to remember that for the most part, dazed relics who are relying on a hit or two from who knows how long ago to still get bookings have pretty much been ignored herein, and that's probably the way it oughta be. To my way of thinking, such folks are the real has-beens of popular music, whereas bands ranging from the Pink Floyd to the Classic Rock All-Stars to NRBQ are, as of this writing, still striving to do what they do best, and most of 'em are being quite responsible about their occupations.

Hey, it's a living.... ain't it?

OUTRO

BLACK BIRDS, SILVER LINING

"Rock and Roll's got no future." — Roger Daltrey, in the 1979 documentary *The Kids Are Alright.*

I'd like to think I've been slowly but surely tapering down even more from my already-sublimated obsession with music, but some days I'm not so sure. These days I hardly ever buy a CD (particularly of new releases), and as noted early in this tome, I think I may have encountered all of the albums that are personal favorites on Compact Disc format that will ever be issued. The interesting aspect of putting a stop to building an audio collection in a new format will be to note how long the format lasts in the consumer market... which reminds me, whatever happened to DAT?

Parenthood hit the Missus and I quite late. It's my belief that the longer a couple delays having a child (and/or the longer it takes for Mother Nature to cooperate), the bigger "jerk" it's gonna be to a couple's lifestyle, because all of a sudden, here's this tiny, helpless, yowling individual that demands constant attention and/or nurturing, and that'll be the case until he/she leaves the nest permanently. These days it's an occasionally scary proposition, but that's been the case for every generation, even if the circumstances were different.

So hopefully this growing disinterest in popular music was facilitated by an occasionally awkward attempt at becoming a decent parent. Our VCR has Disney movies or Barney tapes playing much more often these days than any store-bought concert videotapes or even movies we'd taped off of HBO. Between familial and occupational obligations, I just don't have as much time to listen to music anyway, and I've let all of my subscriptions to music publications expire without renewing 'em.

Executive Rock

There's been the rare occasion where I'd channel-surf through the tuner on the VCR and discover something on MTV or VH-1 that merited checking out. The bottom line for music videos is to sell the artists' product, and a good example that stands out was the Mission UK's *Carved in Sand*, although the first track on the album is a morbid child abuse song called "Amelia" that grossed me out so badly I almost trashed the CD then and there (the video I'd seen on TV was for a song called "Deliverance"), but the balance of the album was pretty melodic.

There's also been the rare occasion where I'd pick up a copy of *USA Today* and happen to note some up-and-coming band and/or album in the "Life" section. And I think I remember seeing some band called Counting Crows being touted therein at one point.

Then in the early summer of that pivotal year of 1994, I was working out on the Nautilus machines at the local health club to which I belong, and what sounded like a very, very good Van Morrison song wafted out over the speakers in the exercise room; the volume was low enough so as not to be offensive, and I could discern the vocalist singing about somebody named Mr. Jones. A college kid who was working there for the summer advised me that the song was indeed called "Mr. Jones", and the group was Counting Crows (the summer employee was my then-minister's son, and was a walk-on place kicker for the Texas Christian University football team that Fall; he ended up earning a scholarship. Attaboy, Michael). That one listening was enough to convince me to purchase the cassette as a possible prelude to purchasing the CD.

And *August and Everything After* was the best album I'd heard in years.

Attempting to categorize Counting Crows is an exercise in futility. At times they sound like Van Morrison, other times like the Band, other times like U2 and God knows who else. The featured "instrument" on the album is the remarkable voice of one Adam Duritz, whose plaintive interpretations can give a listener chill bumps (there's only one lead guitar break on the entire album!).

And wouldn'cha just know T-Bone Burnett produced it.

August and Everything After had a cover that appeared to have been inspired by Ralph Steadman, and the cassette format didn't have any photographs inside, so it was interesting to speculate as to what someone who was as gifted as Duritz looked like.

Turns out he resembles Robert Downey, Jr. with dreadlocks, and the occasional snippets of Counting Crows videos I've seen indicate that his "video aesthetic" is smug and amateurish, yet somehow self-assured. That's yet another reason why I try to ignore videos; I *still* feel like the music ought to count for more than the image, but over five years after de-programming MTV, an occasional glance at it is all I need to show me that nothing's

218

Outro

changed (and Loder still has all of the on-camera charisma of a stale bagel).

What makes Counting Crows' album such a masterpiece is its simplicity and clarity. The lyrics lean towards banality at times ("Asleep in perfect blue buildings, beside the green apple sea"), but the sparse instrumentation and simple structure of the songs are incredibly refreshing, compared to what's been heard over the last several years.

Popular music is, by its very definition, always evolving; always changing, as are its participants. Just before this manuscript was shipped off to the *Vintage Guitar* home office, I had to revise and update portions of certain essays due to the death of Jerry Garcia, and an unexpected discovery of a new Alan Parsons album. That some of rock's veterans are still around after decades is a tribute not only to such players' tenacity, but to the music they purvey as well (even if a lot of it has a time warp feel to it by now).

But by the time this book is released, there's a statistical probability that some of the bands cited herein will have broken up, or that one or more of the musicians that have been noted will be dead (and the circumstances may be unfortunate and/or potentially controversial). If one opts to pay attention, it might be interesting to monitor what the future portends for rock music, its performers, and its listeners.

("AS-WE-GO-TO-PRESS" UPDATES: The Grateful Dead have indeed broken up, and Spencer Davis has departed from the Classic Rock All-Stars... y'see what I mean?)

I now own *August and Everything After* on Compact Disc, and I'm planning on purchasing the next Counting Crows album when it's released.

And the beat goes on. Maybe there's hope yet.

Vintage Guitar Publications

Vintage Guitar® Magazine
Issued monthly, this HUGE magazine has the most vintage information on the planet! There are articles to inform and entertain, save you money, and show you the secret repair tips of the experts. And each issue has thousands and thousands of vintage, classic, used and new guitars, amps, accessories, books, videos and more for sale or trade – you won't find more instruments in any other place!
Only $23.95 for a 12 month subscription (Priority, Foreign Airmail and Foreign Surface rates available; call, write, or fax for details).

Sell both in your store. Call for Details.

Vintage Guitar® Classics
Our quarterly, full-color Classics just won a national design award. You will see why when you flip through these pages of fantastic photos of the most collectible instruments on earth. Everything about Vintage Guitar Classics is first rate and each issue is destined to become a collectors item.
Only $18.95 for a four issue, one year subscription (contact us for foreign rates). Or get a single recent issue for $4.95 plus $2.50 shipping ($5 shipping outside the U.S.). Issue #2, #3 and #4 are still available.

TO ORDER CALL 1-800-844-1197*

Vintage Guitar Books

Guitar Stories, Vol. 1
By Michael Wright
320 pages.
Michael writes the hugely popular "Different Strummer" column in each month's Vintage Guitar and this incredible book continues his tradition of digging up the facts and his painstaking attention to detail. Guitar Stories, Vol. 1 has over 1100 photos, including over 100 in beautiful full color. $29.95 plus $3 shipping ($7.50 outside the U.S.).

The Official Vintage Guitar Magazine Instrument Price Guide
By Alan Greenwood
This is the one the dealers use. Thousands of values on hundreds of different models of guitars, basses, amp, effects, mandolins, banjos, ukuleles, steel guitars and more! Useful photos detail the pages of this ultimate guide to values. This book is indispensable when you are buying, selling or trading!
Only $19.95 plus $3.00 shipping ($7.50 outside the U.S.).
1995 edition pictured. Printed Annually.

Sell these books in your store. Call for Distributor details.

Stellas & Stratocasters
By Willie G. Moseley
Over four hundred photos highlight this 300 page book full of interviews and essays. Includes guitar factory tours and over 40 interviews with legends of the guitar — both players and builders. Highly informative. Only $19.95 plus $3 shipping ($7.50 shipping outside the U.S.).

VINTAGE GUITAR ON THE WORLD WIDE WEB. URL=http://WWW.VGUITAR.COM

To order Call or Write: Vintage Guitar • P.O. Box 7301 • Bismarck, ND 58507 • Phone: 1-800-844-1197* • Fax (701) 255-0250
e-mail: vguitar@vguitar.com * Outside U.S. & Canada (701) 255-1197.